United States
Department of
Agriculture

Forest Service

Southern
Research Station

General Technical
Report SRS–142

Western North Carolina Report Card on Forest Sustainability

The Authors:

Susan Fox, Bill Jackson, Sarah Jackson, Gary Kauffmann, Mary Carol Koester, Robert Mera, Terry Seyden, and **Charles Van Sickle**, USDA Forest Service, Asheville, NC 28804; **Sealy Chipley, Jim Fox, Jeff Hicks, Matt Hutchins, Karin Lichtenstein, Kelsie Nolan, Todd Pierce**, and **Beth Porter**, University of North Carolina, Asheville, Asheville, NC 28804.

In acknowledgment of the countless hours, contagious enthusiasm, and dedication to excellence that Mary Carol Koester provided to this project.

Cover Design
Front and back covers were designed and produced by Ian Johnson (ijohnson@unca.edu), student intern at the UNC Asheville's National Environmental Modeling and Analysis Center, University of North Carolina, Asheville, NC.

Cover Photo Descriptions and Credits
Front and back covers: rainy Blue Ridge Mountains – Ken Thomas, kenthomas.us.

Back cover, top box: Brevard white squirrel – R.K. Young, nativebackyard.com; Wilson Creek – Ken Thomas, kenthomas.us; black bear – Ken Thomas, kenthomas.us; great horned owl – Dave Herr, USFS; fall trees – SARCS Report Card, USFS.

Back cover, middle box: Appalachian tiger swallowtail – Ken Thomas, kenthomas.us; noonday globe snail – John Fridell, USFWS; wounded darter, SARCS Report Card, USFS; misty creek – SARCS Report Card, USFS; mountain fence – Susan Weatherford, NEMAC.

Back cover, bottom box: purple flowers – Susan Weatherford, NEMAC; American river otter – Ken Thomas, kenthomas.us; Laurel Creek Falls – Ken Thomas, kenthomas.us; northern raccoon – Steve Shirley, USFS; five-lined skink – Ken Thomas, kenthomas.us; pileated woodpecker, Ken Thomas, kenthomas.us; wild turkeys – Dave Herr, USFS.

September 2011

U.S. Department of Agriculture Forest Service
Southern Research Station
200 W.T. Weaver Blvd.
Asheville, NC 28804

Western North Carolina Report Card on Forest Sustainability

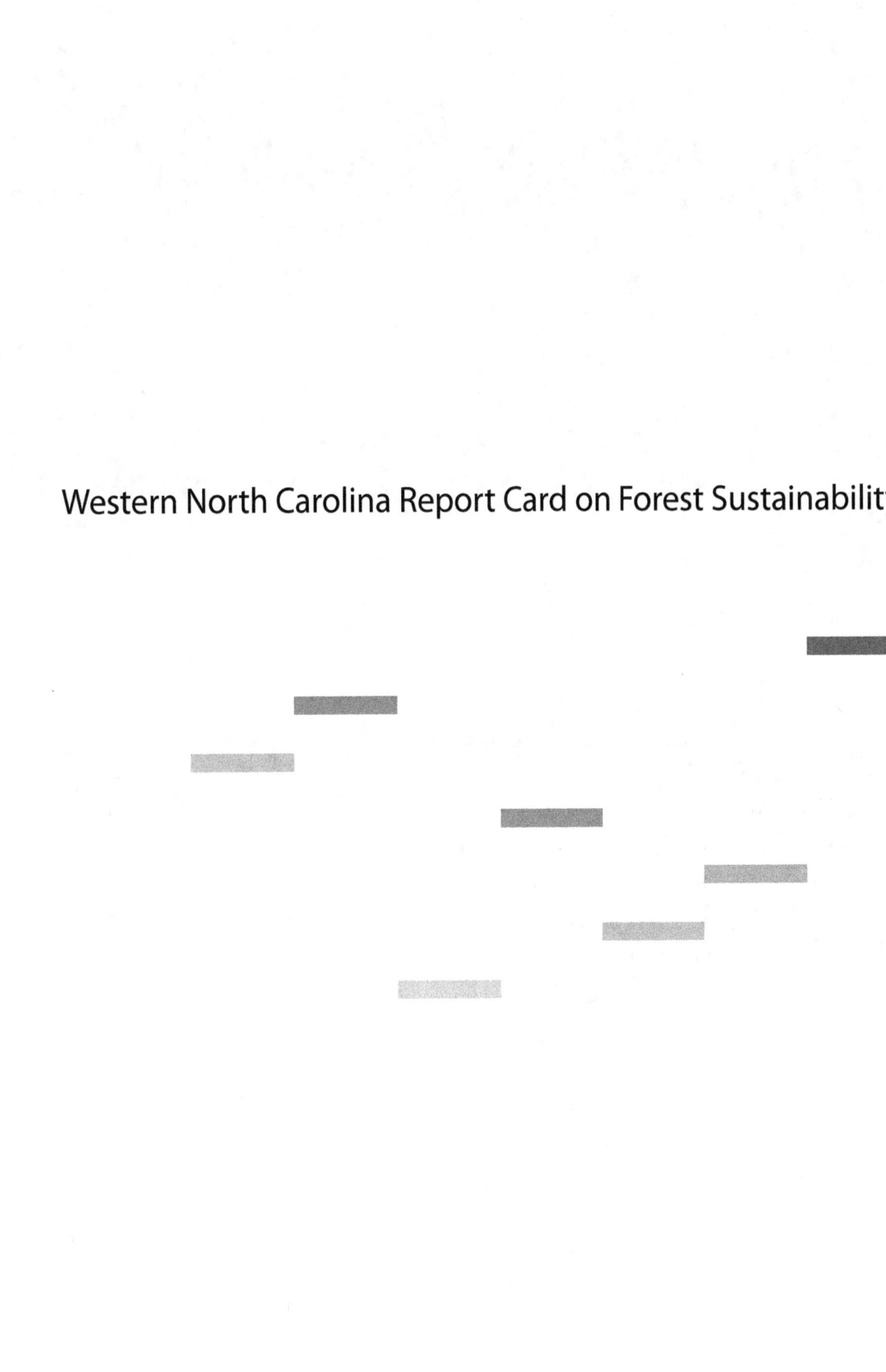

Authors—USDA Forest Service
Susan Fox, Bill Jackson, Sarah Jackson, Gary Kauffman, Mary Carol Koester, Robert Mera, Terry Seyden, and Charles Van Sickle

Authors—UNC Asheville
Sealy Chipley, Jim Fox, Jeff Hicks, Matt Hutchins, Karin Lichtenstein, Kelsie Nolan, Todd Pierce, and Beth Porter

Maps—UNC Asheville
Greg Dobson, Jeff Hicks, Kelsie Nolan, Todd Pierce, Beth Porter, and Leejah Ross

Graphics—UNC Asheville
Jeff Hicks, Josh Miller, Kelsie Nolan, Bridget O'Hara, and Beth Porter

Charts—UNC Asheville
Jeff Hicks, Kelsie Nolan, Bridget O'Hara, and Beth Porter

Layout—UNC Asheville
Nina Hall, Jeff Hicks, Josh Miller, Bridget O'Hara, and Susan Weatherford

Web Designers—UNC Asheville
Christina Papandrea, Amber Ramirez, and Marinus Tahu

We live at a fragile point in human history. We can choose to live as one of the last generations to witness and enjoy the majesty of this fertile and precious bioregion. Or we can become the generation that sets upon the path of true sustainability, the path that balances human, social, and economic activities with stewardship of a healthy and thriving ecology. With help from such tools as this report, we can study what is happening in the world around us and make the right decisions to ensure that the future is one we can be proud of. We can say, "We listened to what this earth was telling us, we learned from what we heard, and we became stewards of this land, so that you, our children's children, could enjoy this beautiful world too."

Robin Cape
Former Asheville City Council

Since the beginning of the 20th century, our researchers have worked to create the science and technology needed to sustain and enhance southern forest ecosystems and the benefits they provide. The Western North Carolina Report Card on Forest Sustainability provides a comprehensive description of this unique, diverse, and beautiful area in which we live. Let's join together to help decision makers sustain its many values.

Rob Doudrick
Director, Southern Research Station
USDA Forest Service

This report card on forest sustainability provides us with a quality document to aid consideration of how we, as a region, wish to move forward into the future. The 21st century presents challenges and opportunities, both old and new, that should be faced with new perspectives. Public and private leaders, organizations, and communities in our region are now steadily moving toward decision-making processes that take into account the economy, the environment, and our society as a whole. Knowledge-based decisions leading to actions must balance and serve all three of these elements. In order to make the best choices possible, complex and integrated information must be made available. It must be accurate and insightful. It must present a clear picture of where we are and where we may be headed in the near and long-term future based on current trends, growth patterns, policy, and more. This is not a small challenge, but it must be met if we are to optimize our quality of life today while preserving opportunities for future generations. This is why I am very pleased with this report card on forest sustainability. I sincerely hope everyone takes time to review this report and utilize its information when making decisions for both the public good and private gain.

Ron Townley
Director, Local Government Services
Land-of-Sky Regional Council

Table of Contents

Foreword
What Is Sustainability?

What is sustainability?

Sustainability means different things to different people. Whatever your definition of sustainability, we can all agree that forests are valuable to Western North Carolina. A sustainable forest is valuable and a goal that everyone in our region supports.

Forests add value to different groups in different ways, so it is important to understand our community's view of value. As a homeowner in Buncombe County, I value the trees on our lot for their shade that lowers our cooling bills in the summer. My wife, a gardener, asks which trees to plant to replace the ones that were blown over by the hurricanes in 2004. My son, an avid hiker, enjoys the walks from our yard into a neighboring 100-acre wood, where a conservation easement protects the forest land. Though these are personal examples, the breadth of how our forest adds value to my family is indicative of the range of values addressed in this report card.

So what makes a good report card?

• A trusted source of information is critical to a good report card. Our region needs a central repository of data that can be relied upon to be both accurate and current.

• Second, the data must be of a scale appropriate for use by both individual landowners and regional decision makers, such as county commissioners. For this kind of use on many scales, data should be presented in a map format.

• Third, our community needs a report card that can be used in a variety of decisions. The report card must organize the data in appropriate and scientific categories, while also presenting the data in a way that crosses technical and scientific "data silos." This relates to how the information can be accessed and applied. Many users find Web-enabled products to be useful; others rely on hard copy reports and posters.

• Fourth, data and information by itself is usually insufficient for our users. The data must be transformed into useful visualizations. These graphics must be tied together through storytelling to provide meaning and context. All of these steps can lead to successful group discussion and decision making.

We hope you enjoy using this report card as much as we have enjoyed creating it, in collaboration with the USDA Forest Service Southern Research Station and other community partners. Please let us know when the report card is helpful, and where it is lacking. Through access to information, we will have a better understanding of the value of our forests and make better regional decisions to sustain our forested land.

Jim Fox
Director, UNC Asheville
National Environmental Modeling and Analysis Center

Criterion 1—Biodiversity
Conservation of biological diversity—ecosystem, species, and genetic diversity; and forest fragmentation.

Criterion 2—Production
Maintenance of productive capacity of forest ecosystems—potential wood production, growth and removals, nontimber forest products, and forest biomass for energy.

Criterion 3—Ecosystem Health
Maintenance of forest ecosystem health and vitality—forest threats such as insects, disease, invasive species, fire, and climate change.

Criterion 4—Soil, Water, and Air
Conservation and maintenance of soil, water, and air resources—soil, water, and air resource conditions and preservation.

Criterion 5—Carbon Cycle
Maintenance of forest contribution to global carbon cycles—carbon pools and fluxes.

Criterion 6—Socioeconomic Benefits
Maintenance and enhancement of long-term multiple socioeconomic benefits to meet the needs of societies—value of forest products and forest services; employment in forest economy; recreational forest uses and tourism; importance of forests to people's spiritual, cultural, and social needs.

Criterion 7—Policy
Legal, policy, and institutional framework—forest planning and monitoring, laws, and public participation.

Forests provide clean water and habitat for wildlife. They protect and enrich soil, filter the air, and provide settings for recreation and renewal. Following severe exploitation of the forests of Western North Carolina a century ago, we now find ourselves in a substantially renewed forest ecosystem. Over the next century, it is our collective responsibility to ensure that our forests continue to be restored and are managed and protected for current and future generations.

Several issues threaten Western North Carolina's forest ecosystems. These include, but are not limited to: loss of native species and natural communities; spread of invasive species; fire, insects, and disease; water pollution; erosion; and loss of contiguous forest land. As our dependence on and demands for natural ecosystems increase, we need to ensure that our forests are healthy and viable.

In Western North Carolina, the USDA Forest Service's Southern Research Station is evaluating the sustainability of the area's forests. The Western North Carolina Report Card on Forest Sustainability is the product of a collaborative partnership between the USDA Forest Service and the University of North Carolina at Asheville's National Environmental Modeling and Analysis Center. This report card provides a current picture of economic, ecological, biological, and social information relevant to the region. By evaluating how forests are impacted by natural and human-caused change, the report card can have a positive impact on decision-making processes and policies.

Forests are important all over the globe. The report card is organized around the Montreal Process Criteria and Indicators, recognized internationally as the standard for measuring forest sustainability. These criteria include indicators describing sustainable management of temperate and boreal forests (see http://www.rinya.maff.go.jp/mpci for more details). For each criterion, a series of maps provides current data on the 18-county focus area.

For the purpose of the report card, the definition of sustainability is that put forth in Executive Order 13423—Strengthening Federal Environmental, Energy, and Transportation Management, January 26, 2007: "Sustainable" means to create and maintain conditions, under which humans and nature can exist in productive harmony, that permit fulfilling the social, economic, and other requirements of present and future generations of Americans.

Executive Summary
Report Card

Biodiversity

Indicator: Sustaining natural diversity and species diversity

Natural communities at risk	Worsening	There are currently 47 natural communities in Western North Carolina, of which 13 are imperiled and 5 critically imperiled. Based on observation over the last 5 years, regional experts believe communities are declining at a faster rate than seen in previous years—primarily due to impacts by invasive plants and pests.
Species at risk	Worsening	There are 35 vascular plant and 31 vertebrate species at risk in Western North Carolina. Seven plants and two vertebrates are critically imperiled; the rest are imperiled or vulnerable. While some species are increasing, many are in decline. Based on field observation coupled with insufficient monitoring over the last 5 years, regional experts believe even more species are in decline.

Indicator: Sustaining ecosystem diversity

Lands managed for conservation	Improving	In the last 6 years, 60,000 acres of prime ecological and cultural natural areas have been put in some form of conservation.
Land conversion	Worsening	As the region's population grows (a 22.7-percent increase is projected from 2010 to 2030), the amount of forest land converted to urban use will increase.
Forest fragmentation	Worsening	With the exception of public lands, forest fragmentation increases with urban encroachment and produces a decrease in forest interior, thus limiting the habitat for many species and making the forest interior more susceptible to nonnative invasive species.

Productivity

Indicator	Status	Description
Indicator: Ownership of timberland	**Stable**	While some land conveyances have occurred in the past 22 years, timberland ownership has essentially remained the same.
Indicator: Timber volume, growth, and removals	Improving	Average annual removals drained less than 1 percent of the total inventory of growing stock trees, while average annual net growth contributed 3.9 percent.
Indicator: Composition and age	**Stable**	Sawtimber size trees dominate the landscape while the loss of early successional stands is of concern.
Indicator: Harvest of nontimber forest products	Uncertain	The harvest level of nontimber forest products is largely undocumented. Fluctuation in the harvest of nontimber forest products is primarily due to fluctuating wholesale prices. On public lands, ginseng and Galax are the most heavily harvested products.
Indicator: Potential for biomass production	Uncertain	Although the supply of harvest residue is abundant, a stable market for wood-based energy production does not currently exist in Western North Carolina.

Executive Summary
Report Card

Indicator: Insect and disease occurrence

Dynamic

Ecosystems are dynamic. Although some tree species, such as eastern hemlock, Carolina hemlock, and flowering dogwood, are currently in decline, the overall health of the forest is stable.

Indicator: Spread of invasive species

Worsening

Very few resources are available to curtail the spread of invasive species throughout the region.

Indicator: Fire, drought, storms

Uncertain

Recent events suggest fire, drought, and severe storms could play a greater role in the future condition of the region's forests.

Indicator: Changes in climate

Uncertain

Climate change is of global concern, and impacts to regions such as Western North Carolina will be highly variable. By looking at the range of possibilities, we can begin to plan for the future of our forests and maximize sustainability of our forest land.

Soil, Water, and Air

Indicator: Soil resource

Stable/
At Risk

The region's forest soils are in stable condition, with erosion occurring naturally at sustainable levels. However, increased erosion from steep slope and stream bank disturbance present a need for improved protection of the soil resource, thereby ensuring ecosystem health and the prevention of injury, damage, and disruption to communities. Recovery of nutrient losses from sensitive soils will probably take centuries unless mitigation measures are implemented.

Indicator: Water resource

Improving

Water quality has improved in many rivers and streams that were historically polluted; however, habitat degradation continues to threaten aquatic communities. Increased development and urbanization, poorly managed crop and animal agriculture, and mining impact aquatic systems with point and nonpoint source inputs. Dams and impoundments on rivers and tributaries alter the hydrologic regime of waterways and result in fish population isolation and habitat alteration.

Indicator: Air resource

Improving

Much effort has been put forth over the last four decades to improve air quality. Reduction in emissions of sulfates and nitrogen oxides, fine particulates, and organic compounds has reduced ozone levels and improved ambient air quality. High-elevation sites, however, continue to experience significant pollution exposure. Visibility conditions are expected to continue to improve over the next 50 years.

Executive Summary
Report Card

Carbon Cycle

Indicator: Carbon storage — **Stable**

The forests of Western North Carolina currently represent a significant carbon pool, but in the future carbon losses will almost certainly outpace carbon gains.

Indicator: Carbon market — Uncertain

An "avoided deforestation" carbon offset market in Western North Carolina may not be competitive with offsets that offer higher carbon sequestration capability; however, conservation of its existing carbon pool will have significant public benefits.

Socioeconomic Benefits

Indicator: Economic condition — Improving

Western North Carolina's economy has been growing over the past four decades. Economic conditions vary considerably between the region and the State and within the region. Growth sectors include recreation and tourism, retirement and second homes, arts and craft, vehicle parts assembly, metalworking, and chemicals and plastics.

Indicator: Recreation resource — **Stable/** At Risk

The recreation resource in the region is recognized as outstanding, with activities such as bicycling and whitewater boating ranked world-class. With projected demand increasing, public agencies, which manage many of the highest use areas, are struggling to protect, maintain, and restore sites.

Socioeconomic Benefits (continued)

Indicator: Forest output — **Stable**

Annual variation in roundwood production closely mirrors national economic trends. The region has seen a variable trend in output and value over the last 15 years; however, a downward trend has dominated since 2003. Because the region's forests are reaching maturity, an increase in the available volume of high-value sawtimber and veneer logs is expected for the next several decades.

Indicator: Cultural/spiritual values — Improving

The contribution of arts and craft to the regional economy is significant and is considered an industry with a demonstrated competitive advantage relative to the rest of the State and the Nation. With over 100 spiritual retreats, the region continues to offer the opportunity to experience the mysteries of the natural world.

Policy

Indicator: Planning and monitoring — Improving

With some exceptions, Federal, State, and local planning and monitoring programs are enabling the region to assess information and prepare for change.

Indicator: Legal protection — **Stable**

Current statutes help limit environmental degradation and provide guidance on best management practices; however, erosion on steep slopes, septic system failures, and air and water quality remain issues of concern.

Indicator: Public participation — Improving

Western North Carolinians benefit from a high level of local, State, and national commitment to sustaining the unique resource values found here.

Introduction
Cultural and Ecological Timeline of the Southern Appalachians

Cultural

Since humans entered the mountains over 12,000 years ago, they have experienced periods of cultural isolation and exchange. The intensity of human impact on the landscape has varied over time.

Paleo-Indians arrived in the Southern Appalachians. Distinguished by their flute-pointed tools and cooperative hunting methods, they are believed to have migrated originally from Asia and are known to have been expert big-game hunters.

After the Paleo-Indians, North American Indians appeared. They may have used the mountains only as hunting territory and relied on plant gathering as an important source of food, largely collecting such seeds and nuts as acorns and hickory nuts.

American Indian settlements became permanent. Hunting, fishing, gathering, and farming made up their livelihood. Basketry and textiles appeared. There was a progression from hunting to crop production, such as maize.

Semi-permanent settlements began. Native plant crops were cultivated, such as gourds, squash, and sunflowers.

490 mya | 251 mya | 65 mya | 10,000 BCE | 5,000 BCE | CE | 700 CE

Ecological

The Appalachian Mountains have been called a "Microcosm of the Earth" because they hold evidence of nearly every geological event the Earth has gone through. As a result, the area contains an exceptionally diverse natural system.

Ordovician Period
A micro-continent collides with the east coast of America, resulting in the creation of a mountain range.

Mesozoic Era
During tectonic, climatic, and evolutionary activity, the continents gradually shifted from a state of connectedness into their present configuration.

mya – million years ago
BCE – before the Common Era
CE – Common Era

Cenozoic Era
The climate cooled and the region again uplifted, creating what we now call the Appalachian Mountains.

Boreal forests of spruce and pine with open parklands dominated the landscape. By the end of the period, mixed oak-hickory forests became predominant, with spruce remaining only at the highest elevations.

Plant collecting added to human impact on the land through increased seed dispersal. People carried plant foods away from parent plants, sometimes into new habitats, while their camps provided small areas of disturbed soil that encouraged the growth of weedy species. The result was an increase in range for plants that provided food for humans.

American Indians cleared the land by girdling trees and burning the understory vegetation, both to clear the ground for crops and to provide fertilizing ash. As yields declined in old fields, this practice allowed for repopulating of trees and for clearing of new fields. When enough time had passed to restore the fertility of the soil, these areas were cleared anew. The land was no longer an unpopulated wilderness.

Disease epidemics such as typhoid were introduced by European settlers to the Southeastern United States and are estimated to have killed at least 75 percent of the original native population.

In 1685, about 32,000 Cherokees lived in the Southern Appalachians. In North Carolina, the Cherokee population persisted, but in the French Broad River Valley disease and displacement dramatically diminished their settlements.

Settlers of European descent populated the Southern Appalachian Mountains. The European inhabitants took over trade from the now displaced American Indians. Mountain inhabitants turned their animals out onto open range in forests and old fields.

In 1868, the U.S. Congress recognized the Eastern Band of Cherokee Indians as a distinct tribe.

During the American Civil War, secession separated Appalachia from the rest of the South. The absence and loss of men during the war created labor shortages on farms.

The Southern Appalachians were viewed as a distinct region, separated from the rest of the country by rough terrain and strange, backward customs.

The industrial development of the Southern Appalachians gravely affected the health and well-being of inhabitants of the mountains. In 1914, a new mining method—strip mining—began a long history of environmental disruption and also severely impacted the health of workers. Due to worsening erosion and soil exhaustion, the productivity of mountain farms declined. Tenancy and part-time farming combined with wage labor became prevalent.

In 1964, with per capita income 23 percent lower than the U.S. average, President Johnson created the Appalachian Regional Commission to help mountaineers through work corps, road building, and economic diversification.

| 1540 CE | 1700s CE | 1800s CE | 1900s CE |

Spanish Conquistadors brought not only social disruption and change to established Indian towns, but also environmental disruption. Non-native plants and animals entered the landscape.

Trade routes were permanently established in the mountains. As wars and disease took their toll on Indian settlements, secondary forests began to overtake open fields and prairies. Places maintained as hunting territory were kept open with fire.

Extinction and restriction of wildlife ranges, coupled with the introduction of exotic plants and livestock, caused widespread change in native ecosystems.

The last bison were killed before 1800; the last elk were killed by the 1850s.

The population of Asheville, NC, grew from 2,600 to about 10,000 between 1880 and 1890.

During the American Civil War, environmental damage increased. Forests were clear cut for the war effort and farms were abandoned. Crops were destroyed and mountaineers were forced to rely more heavily on game animals. Erosion ensued.

In 1901, it was estimated that 75 percent of Southern Appalachia was still forested and 10 percent was still in virgin growth. Over the next 20 years, timber cutting reduced the forest cover substantially, leaving eroding cropland and pasture and heavily logged forests in which little of value was left.

Mount Mitchell was cut over, and much of it was burned—logging did not end until 1922.

1915 Mt. Mitchell designated a State park
1916 Pisgah National Forest established
1921 Appalachian Forest Experiment Station
1934 Coweeta Experimental Forest established
1934 Great Smoky Mountains National Park
1937 Appalachian Trail created
1968 National Wild and Scenic Rivers System
1969 National Environmental Policy Act
1973 Endangered Species Act
1975 Eastern Wilderness Act

Western North Carolina
Today

The 18 counties in this report cover 7,480 square miles or 4.8 million acres and are divided into three Councils of Government: Region A (Southwestern Commission), Region B (Land-of-Sky), and Region D (High Country). The area closely corresponds to the Blue Ridge Mountain Section ecoregion (as mapped in the Ecoregion Extent section on page 19).

Located east of the Tennessee State line and west of the Piedmont plateau, Western North Carolina contains few major urban centers. It is nestled in the Southern Appalachian Mountains between Atlanta, GA; Greenville, SC; Charlotte, NC; and Knoxville, TN. The 18 counties had a population of 743,885 in 2005. Population centers include Asheville (68,889), Boone (13,472), Hendersonville (10,420), Waynesville (9,232), and Black Mountain (7,511). The area is connected to other regions by two interstate highways: I-40, which runs from Tennessee southeast toward the Piedmont, and I-26, which runs north/south through the most populated counties in the region. Largely a rural area, most of the region is connected by State highways and county roads.

Western North Carolina has several colleges and universities, most notably Appalachian State University in Boone, the University of North Carolina at Asheville, Western Carolina University in Cullowhee, Warren Wilson College in Swannanoa, and Brevard College in Brevard.

Western North Carolina is home to many third- and fourth-generation residents, many of European descent. The region is currently experiencing an influx of retired residents and second-home owners, both groups citing the natural beauty and cultural opportunities of the area as major reasons for their move. The Eastern Cherokee Indian Reservation is located in Western North Carolina, just south of Great Smoky Mountains National Park. The main part of the reservation lies in eastern Swain County and northern Jackson County, but there are many smaller noncontiguous sections to the southwest in Cherokee County and Graham County. The 2000 U.S. Census cites the Eastern Cherokee Indian Reservation (the Qualla Boundary) as having a resident population of 8,092.

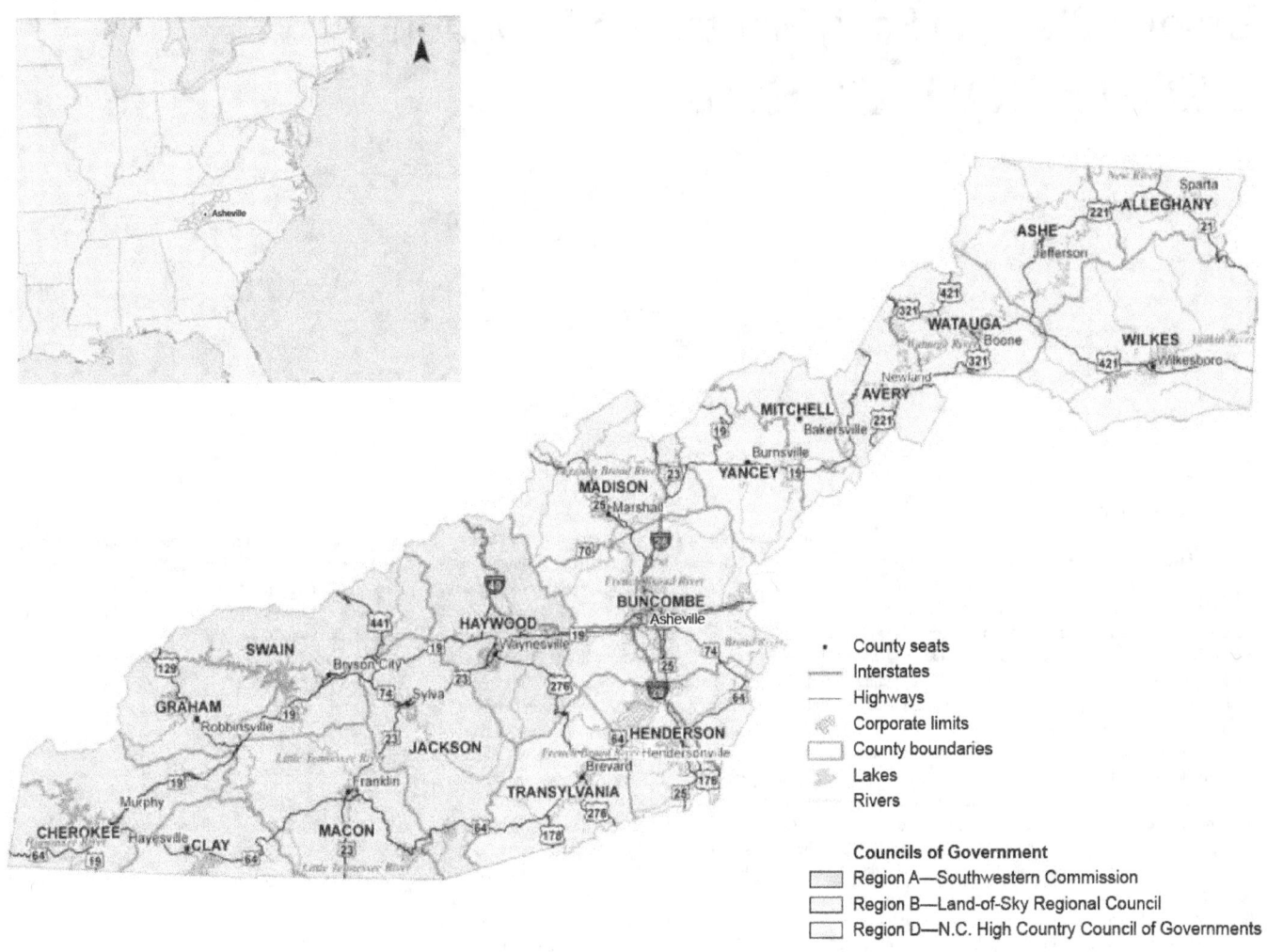

Asheville

* County seats
— Interstates
— Highways
🐾 Corporate limits
☐ County boundaries
🗾 Lakes
— Rivers

Councils of Government
☐ Region A—Southwestern Commission
☐ Region B—Land-of-Sky Regional Council
☐ Region D—N.C. High Country Council of Governments

Unique Blend of Soils, Plants, and Elevation
Ecoregion Extent

What is an ecoregion?

Typically, an ecoregion covers large areas of land and water and is broadly mapped using specific climate, vegetation, and physical characteristics. An ecoregion is divided into subregions, or "sections." These sections are defined by similar physical (slope and aspect) and biological (vegetative types) components and have a unique combination of ecological characteristics (including geology, soils, vegetation, weather, climate, and biological diversity) that distinguish it from its neighbors.

The ecoregion of Western North Carolina lies in what is called the Blue Ridge Mountain Section (see p. 21). The distinctive characteristics of this section follow the backbone of the Appalachian Mountains from northern Georgia to southern Pennsylvania.

The formation of the highly weathered mountain range began during the Precambrian era to the Cambrian period (between 4.5 billion and 542 million years ago). The range now consists of gneiss and schist bedrock formed from the re-crystallization of sedimentary, volcanic, and igneous material. Over time, the geology of the region has become a dissected landscape of rounded peaks and wide concave valleys defined on the east by a steep escarpment rising 1,800 feet over the neighboring section. The ranges consist of low (<2,300 feet), moderate (2,300–4,000 feet), and high peaks (4,000–6,560 feet). The range has 82 peaks greater than 5,000 feet, and 43 peaks greater than 6,000 feet. Mid-elevation soils are deep, well-drained, and acidic and are classified as "infertile sandy" or "gravelly loams," while high-elevation soils typically have high organic content.

The landscape is covered predominantly by forest communities consisting of montane oak-hickory and mixed oak-pine types. Above 5,500 feet, the forests become dominated by spruce-fir forests.

Rainfall can be highly variable, ranging from over 78 inches to less than 47 inches per year. More rain falls in areas along the escarpment that are influenced by mountain elevations (called an orographic effect), particularly near the neighboring section in South Carolina. Less rain falls in the nearby Asheville basin, located in a rain shadow.

The climate of the Blue Ridge Mountain Section is cooler and wetter than that of adjoining sections, especially in the high-elevation forests where several species exist on the edge of their natural range. These mountaintop islands provide habitat for the Carolina northern flying squirrel, Magnolia Warbler, and spruce-fir moss spider. The region also contains Southern Appalachian brook trout, which are associated with the cold water of high energy streams, and is home to more species of salamanders than are found anywhere else on earth.

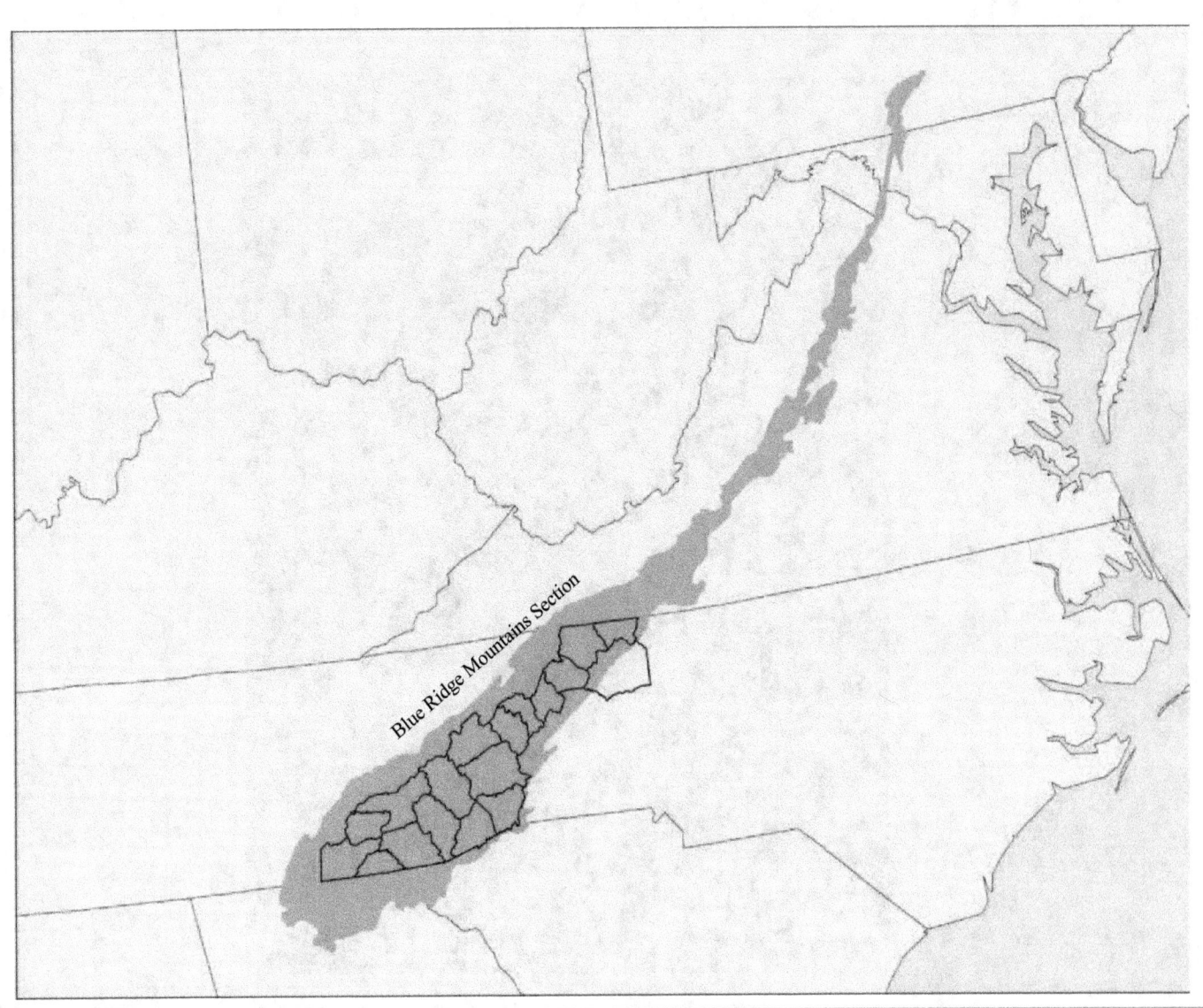

Blue Ridge Mountains Section

Swamp Pink

Biodiversity
Southern Appalachian Treasures

What is biodiversity?

Biological diversity, or biodiversity, describes the variety and abundance of all life forms in a given place—plants, animals, and other living organisms such as fungi, lichens, and mosses. Biological diversity also describes the processes, functions, and structures that sustain that variety and allow it to adapt to changing circumstances. Moreover, it encompasses the complexity of gene pools, species, communities, and ecosystems at spatial scales from local to regional to global.

Is biodiversity important in Western North Carolina?

The temperate ecosystems of the Blue Ridge Mountains are exceptionally diverse. Ancient geological events followed by climatic reversals and weathering formed the mountains that today feature the highest peaks in the eastern United States. In the moist, deep-soiled, densely forested valleys, the daily range of temperature, wind, and humidity remains relatively constant. On the thin-soiled and exposed ridges, balds, and mountain tops, the daily range of climate conditions is much wider. This variability in elevation, aspect, climate, geology, and soils accounts for the occurrence of hundreds of plants and animals that exist at the edge of their natural range.

The geographic isolation of high-altitude species in the Blue Ridge Mountains has allowed some to evolve into unique species of their own, adding further to the biological diversity of these mountains. Examples are the Blue Ridge goldenrod and the spreading avens.

Why should we be concerned?

The Southern Appalachian Ecoregion (which encompasses the Blue Ridge Mountain Section) contains an estimated 80 species of amphibians and reptiles, 175 species of terrestrial birds, 65 species of mammals, 2,250 species of vascular plants, and possibly as many as 25,000 species of invertebrates. These organisms live in low- and high-elevation forests, caves, bogs, waterfalls, wetlands, grassy balds, rock outcrops, cliffs, and seeps.

The Blue Ridge Mountains contain the highest number of federally listed and proposed threatened and endangered terrestrial species in the Southern Appalachian chain. Most occurrences of federally listed species are associated with rare community groups, such as spruce-fir, grassy bald, high-elevation rocky summit, southern Appalachian bog, montane alluvial, and spray cliff.

Extinction is a natural process that has been occurring since long before the appearance of humans on the planet. Normally, new species develop through a process known as speciation at about the same rate that other species become extinct. However, because of air and water pollution, forest clearing, loss of wetlands, and other human-induced environmental changes, extinctions are now occurring at a rate that far exceeds the speciation rate. Since 1620, more than 500 species, subspecies, and varieties of our Nation's plants and animals have become extinct. By contrast, during the 3,000 years of the Pleistocene Ice Age, all of North America lost only about 90 species.

How can we sustain biological diversity?

All species and natural communities are important for the region's biological diversity. The maintenance of large scale habitats and micro-niches will require a range of activities from prescribed burning (since wildfire is largely controlled) and vegetation manipulation to protection from human use and development.

Since habitat is found on mixed ownership, it is critical that landscape scale planning is adopted and implemented. We must work together to adopt policy and cooperative decision frameworks that encourage biodiversity. To reach private landowners, we need educational tools that offer adaptive management strategies based on the best available knowledge about how to provide a sustainable balance among biological diversity, economic uses, and cultural values.

Community Types Across the Mountain Landscape
Classifying Communities

Natural communities generally occur in continuously varying patterns. Most of the environmental factors that determine communities vary over continuous gradients. We can best decipher the tremendous complexity of natural communities by categorizing them according to their ecology.

Natural communities are valuable elements of natural diversity for a variety of reasons. They are generally regarded as "coarse filters" for diversity of organisms. By protecting examples of all the natural community types, the majority of species can be protected without laborious individual attention. Like species, communities have an intrinsic value as natural systems, as well as an aesthetic value to human beings. These thirteen communities represent some of the most common communities as well as those considered of high visual interest across the landscape.

Spruce-Fir
Generally found above 5,500 feet (though locally lower in suitable sites) and extending to the tops of all but the highest peaks.

Beech Gap
High elevations, within the range of spruce-fir forests. Primarily in south-facing gaps, but may occur on exposed ridgetops in areas lacking spruce and fir or adjacent to grassy balds.

Grassy Bald
Slopes, ridgetops, and domes of high mountains, usually on gentle slopes.

Heath Bald
Extremely exposed high-elevation sites: peaks, sharp ridges, and steep slopes.

Northern Hardwood
Medium to fairly high-elevation coves, flats, and slopes, particularly on north-facing slopes.

High Elevation Red Oak
Found on dry to moderately moist slopes and ridgetops at mid to high elevations (around 3,500–5,500 feet).

Pine-Oak/Heath
Exposed sharp ridges, knobs, low-elevation peaks, and steep south slopes.

Oak-Hickory
Dry to moderately moist slopes and partly sheltered ridgetops at moderate to fairly high elevations (about 2,500–5,000 feet).

Hemlock
Slightly less moisture than cove forest sites, including open valley flats, slopes above cove forests, sheltered low ridges, narrow ravines, and open north-facing slopes at fairly high elevations.

Acidic Cove
Sheltered low- and moderate-elevation sites, primarily narrow, rocky gorges, steep ravines, and low gentle ridges within coves.

Rich Cove
Sheltered, moderately moist, low- to moderate-elevation sites, primarily broad coves and lower slopes.

Short Leaf Pine-Oak
Found at low elevations, generally below 2,300 feet.

Low Montane Alluvial
Stream and river floodplains at low elevations, generally below 2,300 feet.

Natural Communities and Threatened Species
Community and Species Inventory

County occurrences by natural community

Acidic Cove Forest
Basic Oak-Hickory Forest
Boulderfield Forest
Canada Hemlock Forest
Carolina Hemlock Bluff
Chestnut Oak Forest
Dry Oak-Hickory Forest
Dry Rocky Slope
Dry-Mesic Oak-Hickory Forest
Floodplain Pool
Fraser Fir Forest
Grassy Bald
Heath Bald
High Elevation Granitic Dome
High Elevation Mafic Glade
High Elevation Red Oak Forest
High Elevation Rocky Summit
High Elevation Seep
Low Elevation Granitic Dome
Low Elevation Rocky Summit
Low Elevation Seep
Mesic Mixed Hardwood Forest (Piedmont Subtype)
Montane Acidic Cliff
Montane Alluvial Forest
Montane Calcareous Cliff
Montane Mafic Cliff
Montane Oak-Hickory Forest
Montane Red Cedar-Hardwood Woodland
Montane White Oak Forest
Northern Hardwood Forest (Beech Gap Subtype)
Northern Hardwood Forest (Typic Subtype)
Piedmont/Low Mountain Alluvial Forest
Piedmont/Mountain Semipermanent Impoundment
Piedmont/Mountain Swamp Forest
Pine-Oak/Heath
Red Spruce-Fraser Fir Forest
Rich Cove Forest
Rocky Bar and Shore
Southern Appalachian Bog (Northern Subtype)
Southern Appalachian Bog (Southern Subtype)
Southern Appalachian Fen
Spray Cliff
Swamp Forest-Bog Complex (Spruce Subtype)
Swamp Forest-Bog Complex (Typic Subtype)
Ultramafic Outcrop Barren
White Pine Forest

- Presence verified
- Presence not verified
- Possible presence

County occurrences by federally listed vertebrate animal

Allegheny Woodrat
Appalachian Bewick's Wren
Blotchside Logperch
Bog Turtle
Carolina Northern Flying Squirrel
Crevice Salamander
Eastern Hellbender
Eastern Small-Footed Myotis
Gray Myotis
Green Salamander
Hellbender
Indiana Myotis
Junaluska Salamander
Kanawha Minnow
Ohio Lamprey
Olive Darter
Pygmy Salamander
Rafinesque's Big-Eared Bat
Santeetlah Dusky Salamander
Seepage Salamander
Sharphead Darter
Sicklefin Redhorse
Smoky Dace
Southeastern Myotis
Southern Rock Vole
Southern Water Shrew
Spotfin Chub
Tellico Salamander
Virginia Big-Eared Bat
Weller's Salamander
Wounded Darter

County occurrences by federally listed invertebrate animal

Appalachian Checkered-Skipper
Appalachian Elktoe
Clingman Covert
Cumberland Bean
Fragile Glyph
French Broad River Crayfish
Gammon's Stenelmis Riffle Beetle
Green Floater
Hiwassee Headwaters Crayfish
Littlewing Pearly Mussel
Lost Nantahala Cave Spider
Mountain River Cruiser
Noonday Globe
Pygmy Snaketail
Regal Fritillary
Roan Supercoil
Sculpted Supercoil
Spruce-fir Moss Spider
Tawny Crescent
Tennessee Clubshell
Tennessee Heelsplitter
Yancey Sideswimmer

■ Federally listed vertebrate
▪ Federally listed invertebrate

Natural Communities and Threatened Species
Community and Species Inventory

County occurrences by vascular plants

Alabama Least Trillium
Alexander's Rock Aster
Appalachian Oak Fern
Bent Avens
Blue Ridge Goldenrod
Bog Bluegrass
Bog Oatgrass
Bunched Arrowhead
Cain's Reed Grass
Carolina Saxifrage
Cuthbert's Turtlehead
Divided-Leaf Ragwort
Fen Sedge
Fort Mountain Sedge
Fraser's Loosestrife
French Broad Heartleaf
Glade Spurge
Gorge Filmy Fern
Granite Dome Goldenrod
Gray's Lily
Green Pitcher Plant
Heller's Blazing-Star
Large-Flowered Barbara's Buttons
Large-Leaved Grass-of-Parnassus
Lobed Barren Strawberry
Mountain Bittercress
Mountain Catchfly
Mountain Heartleaf
Mountain Sweet Pitcher Plant
Mountain Thaspium
New Jersey Rush
Piratebush
Radford's Sedge
Rhiannon's Aster
Roan Mountain Bluet
Rugel's Ragwort
Small Whorled Pogonia
Small-Leaved Meadowrue
Smoky Mountain Mannagrass
Southern Shortia
Spreading Avens
Swamp Pink
Sweet Pinesap
Tall Larkspur
Torrey's Mountain Mint
Virginia Spiraea
West Indian Dwarf Polypody
White Fringeless Orchid
White Irisette

County occurrences by nonvascular plants

Anderson's Melon-Moss
Bluff Mountain Reindeer Lichen
Gorge Moss
Hornwort
Liverwort (*Plagiochila sharpii*)
Liverwort (*Plagiochila sullivanti*)
Liverwort (*Plagiochila virginica*)
Liverwort (*Porella wataugensis*)
Liverwort (*Sphenolobopsis pearsonii*)
Rock Gnome Lichen
Worthy Shield Lichen

■ Federally listed vascular plant
▫ Federally listed nonvascular plant

Natural community occurrences by county

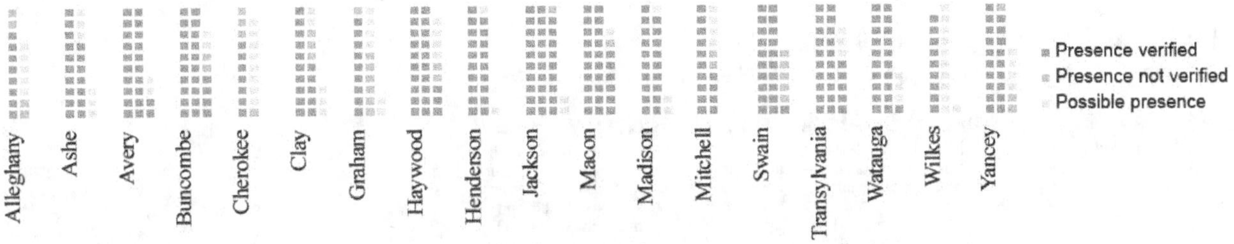

Presence verified
Presence not verified
Possible presence

Alleghany · Ashe · Avery · Buncombe · Cherokee · Clay · Graham · Haywood · Henderson · Jackson · Macon · Madison · Mitchell · Swain · Transylvania · Watauga · Wilkes · Yancey

Federally listed vertebrate and invertebrate animal occurrences by county

Federally listed vertebrate animal
Federally listed invertebrate animal

Alleghany · Ashe · Avery · Buncombe · Cherokee · Clay · Graham · Haywood · Henderson · Jackson · Macon · Madison · Mitchell · Swain · Transylvania · Watauga · Wilkes · Yancey

Federally listed vascular and nonvascular plant occurrences by county

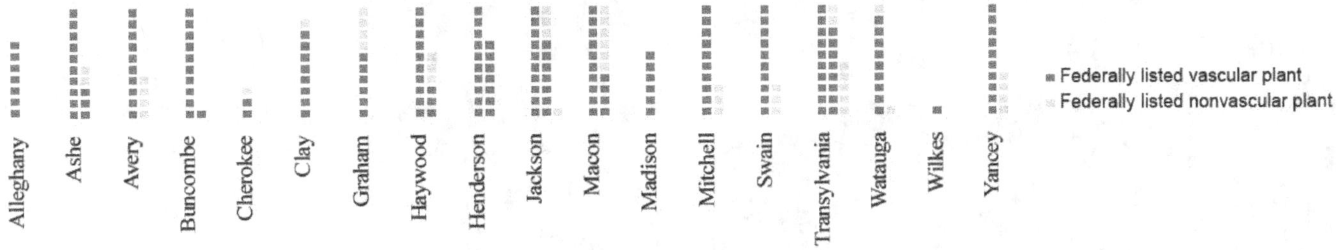

Federally listed vascular plant
Federally listed nonvascular plant

Alleghany · Ashe · Avery · Buncombe · Cherokee · Clay · Graham · Haywood · Henderson · Jackson · Macon · Madison · Mitchell · Swain · Transylvania · Watauga · Wilkes · Yancey

Natural Communities and Species That Depend on Them
Community Examples

Secure Habitats, Threatened Species
Many natural communities are secure but often provide habitat for rare or imperiled species.

Acidic Cove Forest
Red maples, tulip poplars, rhododendron, sweet birch, and eastern hemlock are the dominant species in this forest. The presence of thick rhododendron and hemlock indicates that the soil is acidic. Fewer types of plants and trees can tolerate this acidic soil.
Example: White Water River Gorge

G5

Montane Oak–Hickory Forest
This forest receives less rainfall even though it is at a moderate elevation. The dryer soil supports white oak, red oak, chestnut oak, pignut hickory, and mockernut hickory, plus a variety of small trees such as dogwood and sourwood. A diverse understory of shrubs and herbs is present, but not as diverse as in a Rich Cove forest.
Example: The Black Mountains

G5

Rich Cove Forest
The rich, moist soils of the Rich Cove Forest support a wide range of trees and plants. Sugar maple, sweet buckeye, basswood, and Carolina silverbell are only a few of the types of trees growing in this forest. Spring wildflowers are well known in the lush, diverse herb layer present in the type. Mosses and rotting logs make the damp forest floor suitable for salamanders.
Example: Joyce Kilmer Memorial Forest

G4

Small Whorled Pogonia — G2
Shortia — G2
Fraser's Loosestrife — G1
Indiana Bat — G2
Pale Yellow Trillium — G4
Santeetlah Dusky Salamander — G3

Gone

GX = Believed to be extinct

GH = Of historical occurrence throughout its range, may be rediscovered

G1 = Critically imperiled globally because of extreme rarity (five or fewer occurrences or less than 1,000 individuals) or because of extreme vulnerability to extinction due to some natural or man-made factor.

G2 = Imperiled globally because of rarity (6 to 20 occurrences or less than 3,000 individuals) or because of vulnerability to extinction due to some natural or man-made factor

G3 = Either very rare and local throughout its range (21 to 100 occurrences or less than 10,000 individuals) or found locally in a restricted range or vulnerable to extinction from other factors

G4 = Apparently secure globally (may be rare in parts of range)

G5 = Demonstrably secure globally

Abundant

There are threatened communities that are rare or imperiled in their own right and that also provide habitat for threatened species.

Presence Verified
This forest type has been recorded in this county.

Presence Not Verified
This forest type has been reported in this county.

Possible Presence
This forest type could exist in this county.

No Information
This forest type does not likely exist in this county.

Red Spruce–Fraser Fir Forest

This rare and extremely endangered community type only exists above 5,500 feet. More than a mile above sea level, the high rainfall, fog, and low temperatures make the climate similar to Maine and Canada. Logging and fires in the 1910s and 1920s radically changed these communities, with some sites no longer supporting spruce-fir forests.
Threats: Balsam woolly adelgid, air pollution
Example: Mt. Mitchell

G2

Grassy Bald

The origin of these treeless mountain tops is unknown. Grassy Balds are gentle slopes, ridgetops, and domes of high mountains where grasses, sedges, and herbs dominate with patches of shrubs and some small trees.
Threats: Woody plant invasion
Example: Roan Mountain

G2

Montane Alluvial Forest

Sycamore, tulip poplar, sweet birch, and hemlock are found at low to mid elevation. Subject to occasional flooding, water scrubs away perennials and leaves behind many seeds from annuals. For this reason, fewer large trees survive and more dense shrubs and small plants are found here.
Threats: Development
Example: French Broad River

G2*

Spruce-Fir Moss Spider — G1

Carolina Northern Flying Squirrel — G5T1
This subspecies is imperiled due to...

Gray's Lily — G3

Appalachian Bewick's Wren — G3

Virginia Spiraea — G2

✳ The Montane Alluvial Forest designation is technically "G2?" The "?" denotes uncertainty or inexactness.

Protecting our Natural and Cultural Heritage
Lands Managed for Conservation

In 1901, it was estimated that 75 percent of Southern Appalachia was still forested and 10 percent was still in virgin growth. By 1920, heavy cutting had reduced this forest substantially, resulting in rapidly eroding cropland and pasture and heavily logged forests where little of value was left.

A fledgling conservation community worked to create national forests to protect the headwaters of major rivers, the Blue Ridge Parkway stretching almost 500 miles along the crest of the Blue Ridge Mountains, the Great Smoky Mountains National Park, and the Appalachian Trail, among other significant areas.

Most of the conservation issues raised in the early 1900s remain today. Although many large blocks of public land are now guided by sustainable management plans, the vast amount of forest land in the region is privately owned. The long-term goal of Western North Carolina's conservation community is to protect and conserve places of important wildlife habitat, water quality, cultural and economic significance, and scenic value. This is accomplished on public lands as well as through

the careful combination of private land acquisitions from willing sellers and conservation easements by individual property owners.

Since 2005, the acres of land managed for conservation in the 18-county area has increased by 5 percent, or about 60,000 acres. The majority of these new acres are found on private lands and are acquired through purchase or gift or are guided by a conservation agreement with the property owner.

Many people feel that the Southern Blue Ridge Mountains are at a pivotal point for species, habitat, natural beauty, and even mountain culture. The conservation community, the legislature, and the public are making strides in reducing the risk of irreparable losses. The addition of lands managed for conservation during the past decade, along with a stated goal to continue putting land into a protected status, is one of many strategies in place to sustain biodiversity in Western North Carolina.

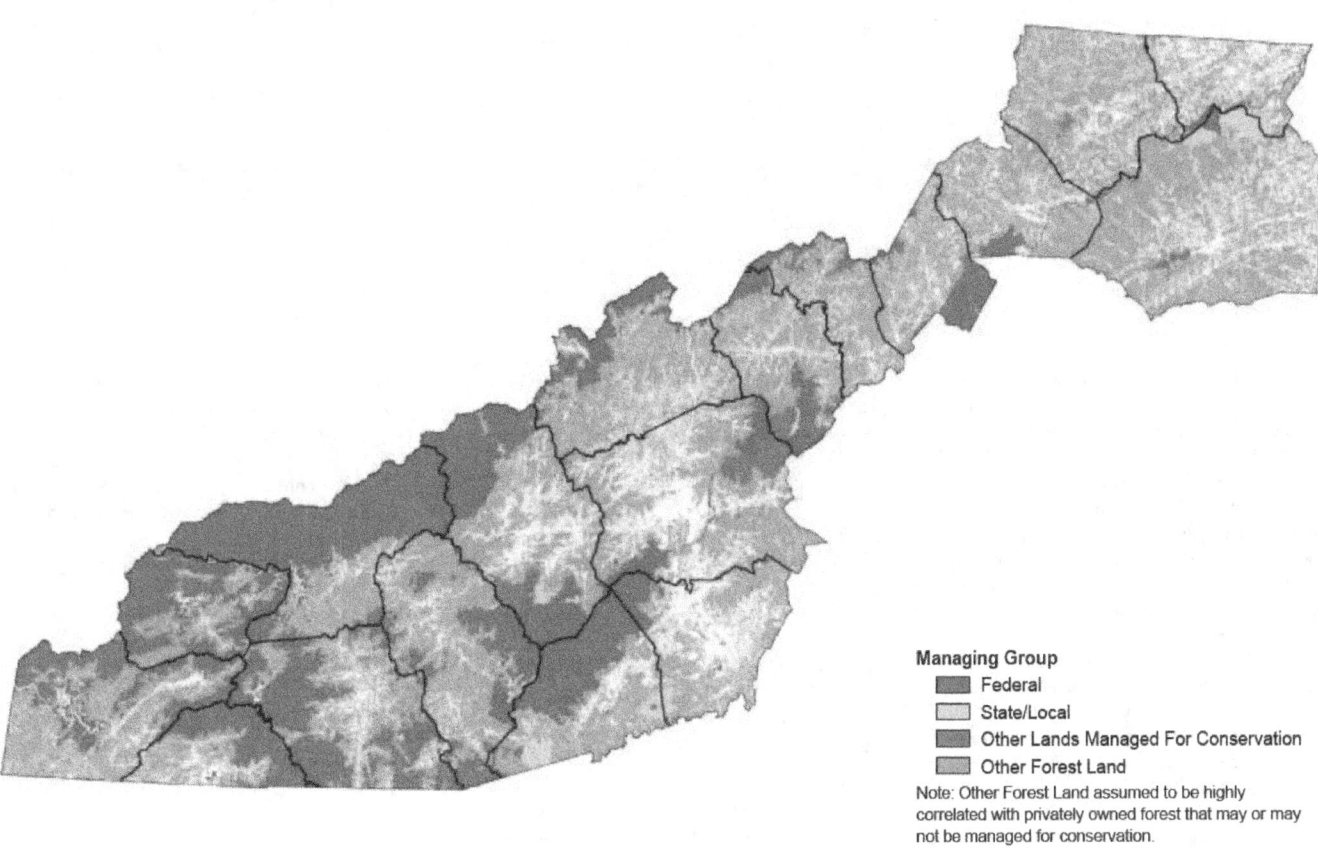

In the last six years, 60,000 acres of prime ecological and cultural natural areas have been put in some form of conservation.

Managing Group

- Federal
- State/Local
- Other Lands Managed For Conservation
- Other Forest Land

Note: Other Forest Land assumed to be highly correlated with privately owned forest that may or may not be managed for conservation.

Protected Treasures
Significant Natural Heritage Areas

The natural heritage of Western North Carolina includes all the region's native plants and animals, as well as the places they live and grow. North Carolina is home to thousands of native plants and animals, and Western North Carolina supports a large part of the State's biodiversity. Significant Natural Heritage Areas, identified by biologists in the North Carolina Natural Heritage Program, contain the land and water needed to support and help preserve biodiversity in North Carolina. These areas often are the best examples of natural communities and usually include rare and endangered species.

Over 2,400 such areas have been identified on both public and private land in North Carolina. Focusing on these areas helps planners prioritize conservation efforts and send financial resources where they have maximum ecological benefits. The North Carolina Natural Heritage Program is not a State regulatory program, so Significant Natural Heritage Areas have no protected status. Once an area has been named a Significant Natural Heritage Area, however, the owner can register the property with the North Carolina Natural Heritage Program to show their commitment to keep the land in its natural state. The land can also be permanently protected through purchase and dedication as a State Nature Preserve.

Each area is assigned a significance rating indicating how important it is. The four levels are:

National
The site contains one of the best occurrences of a rare or high-quality plant, animal, or natural community known to exist anywhere in its range.

State
The site contains one of the best occurrences within North Carolina of a rare or high-quality plant, animal, or natural community that is not already considered of national significance.

Regional
The site contains one of the best occurrences within a priority region of a rare or high-quality plant, animal, or natural community that is not already considered of national or State significance.

County
The site is a biological resource within the county but not of regional significance.

Western North Carolina has about 500 of the statewide Significant Natural Heritage Areas. Of the acreage of these areas (622,530 acres):
- **68.5 percent is of national significance**
- **17.9 percent is of State significance**
- **9.8 percent is of regional significance**
- **3.8 percent is of local significance**

Long Hope Valley/Elk Knob/The Peak
Significance: National
Topography: A high-elevation "hanging" valley, surrounded by peaks up to 5,500 feet high
Key Communities: Northern Hardwood, Spruce Swamp
Biodiversity: Major concentration of rare plant and animal species, including spreading avens, Northern flying squirrel, stalked holly, holy grass, and Canada yew.
Ownership: In part by the North Carolina Department of Parks and Recreation and The Nature Conservancy; the remainder is privately owned.

Stone Mountain State Park

Roan Mountain Massif
Significance: National
Topography: Sheer cliffs and a 6,267 foot mountain
Key Community: Grassy Bald
Biodiversity: Seventy-six rare plant and animal species, including the Roan Mountain bluet, the Northern flying squirrel, and the Southern Appalachian Northern Saw-Whet Owl.
Ownership: USDA Forest Service, Pisgah National Forest

Nolichucky River Gorge

Grandfather Mountain

Great Smoky Mountains National Park

Cane River Upper Watershed

Hierarchy of Significance
- National
- State
- Regional
- County

Joyce Kilmer–Slickrock Wilderness Area

North Fork Watershed

Shining Rock Wilderness Area
Significance: State
Topography: High rugged mountains
Key Communities: Spruce–Fir, Northern Hardwoods Forest, and Boulderfield Forest
Biodiversity: Several Federal Species of Concern, including the Appalachian Cottontail, Southern Rock Vole, eastern woodrat, Northern Saw-Whet Owl, and Appalachian Yellow-Bellied Sapsucker.
Ownership: USDA Forest Service National Wilderness System

Green River Headwaters

Toxaway River Gorge

Fires Creek Watershed

Panthertown Valley

Horsepasture River Gorge

Historical Perspective
Land Use Change

Since humans arrived in this region, they have disturbed the land—sometimes lightly, other times severely. Human impacts have included the utilization of natural resources, the introduction of exotic plants and disease, extirpation/extinction of species, and urban development. These impacts raise concern because their long-term consequences are often unknown. Also, the human process of disturbance is often much greater in magnitude than typical natural disturbances.

Land conversion is a significant threat to biodiversity in Western North Carolina. As the landscape becomes more developed, areas that were once forest or other natural systems are cleared for houses and infrastructure. With habitats removed and natural systems fundamentally altered, many native plants and animals cannot survive. These plant and animal species must move to other suitable areas—which may or may not exist nearby.

Land use patterns have changed dramatically over the past few decades. The map on the facing page, constructed from satellite imagery collected in 1976, shows four primary land use categories: developed, undeveloped, water, and protected. Developed land is defined as land that has large amounts of paved (impervious) surfaces. This includes major roads, subdivisions, towns, and shopping areas. Undeveloped land includes forests and farms with minor roads and farm buildings. Protected land is owned or managed by entities that strive to limit the amount of land use conversion, such as national and State forests and parks and land conservancies.

By comparing past and present land use, assumptions can be made about future land use trends. If these trends are inconsistent with our desired future condition, we can attempt to identify and implement alternate outcomes that sustain natural systems while still providing services for a growing population.

The land use in 1976 did not vary greatly from land use for the preceding 50 years. There are a few urban centers, connected by interstates, and large regions of connected green space. The map shows initial pressure from development along secondary roads, but only 0.7 percent of the land is truly developed. Per capita land consumption, which can be thought of as a "human footprint," stood at only 0.06 acres per person. Following 1976, land use patterns show a very different picture.

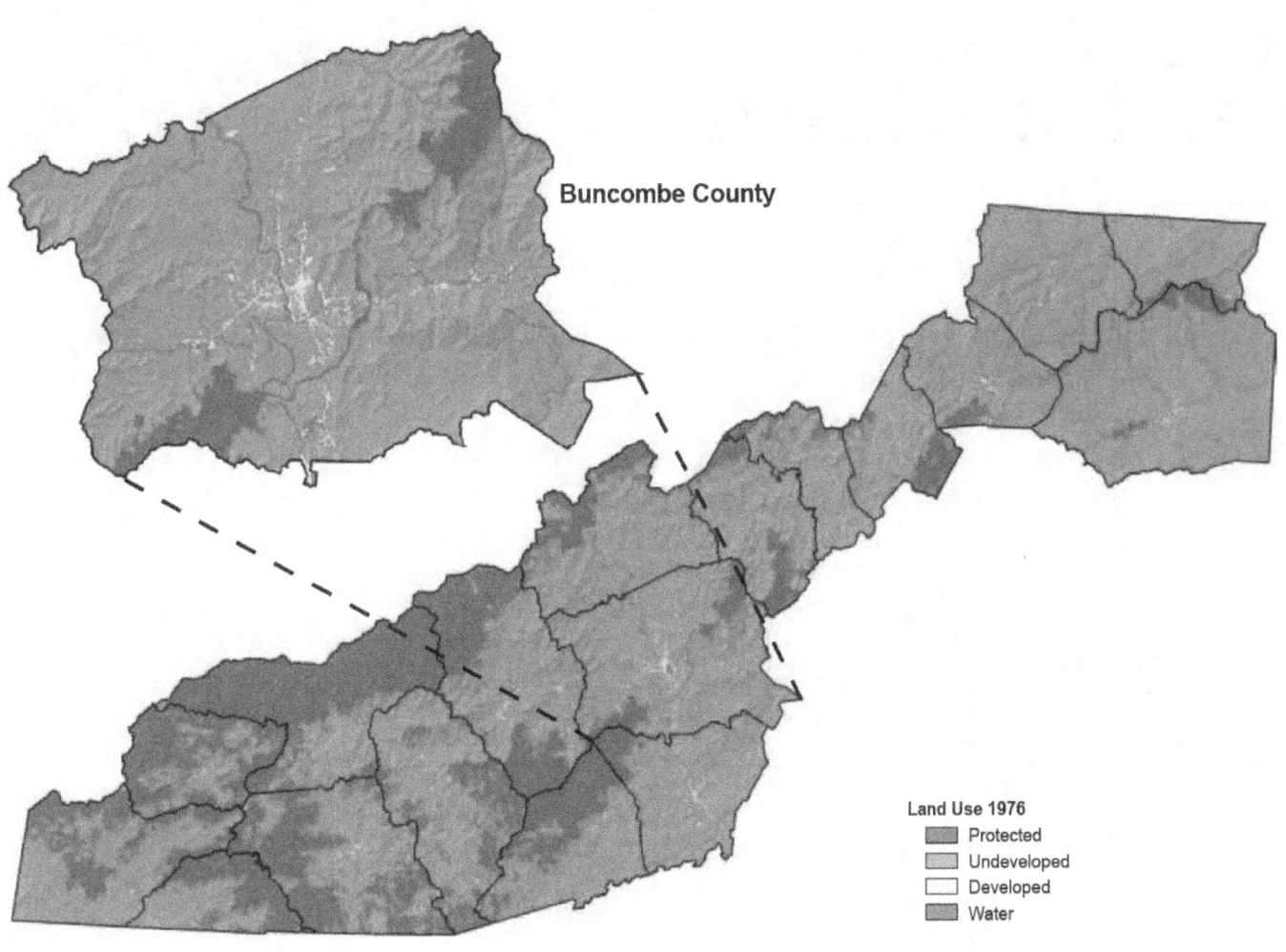

Buncombe County

Land Use 1976
- Protected
- Undeveloped
- Developed
- Water

Current Picture
Land Use Change

In the late 1970s, Western North Carolina experienced change in land use patterns. The completion of Interstate 40 through the region, a strong domestic economy, and a desire to travel reopened Western North Carolina to tourism and to seasonal home markets. In addition, low energy costs allowed residents to commute long distances to work, making it easy to live in rural areas and work in urban centers. Land values in most of Western North Carolina were inexpensive compared to the rest of the country. These factors, coupled with an ideal mountain climate compared to the surrounding Southeastern United States, gained the attention of a national audience.

The 2006 land use map for the 18 counties of Western North Carolina shows some astonishing changes over the previous 30 years. Not only was there a rapid conversion of land from rural to developed, but now each individual occupied more land. Per capita land consumption, the "human footprint," increased from 0.06 acres per person in 1976 to 0.30 acres per person in 2006. While only 0.7 percent of the land was developed in 1976, 4.8 percent of the land was developed by 2006. This is a land use conversion rate of almost 17.4 acres per day.

Few natural systems can withstand this rapid rate of change, and Western North Carolina is no different. While many new residents to the region settled on old farms and in valleys, there has also been a move "up the mountain." In the pursuit of better views and perceived quality of life, many new homes are built on land that had been forested for generations. This trend displaces wildlife and exposes the forest to a wide range of threats. Fortunately, many forward-looking individuals and groups recognize the need to protect important natural systems. In the period 1976–2006, the 4.1 percent increase in the amount of developed land in these 18 counties was matched by a 4.7 percent increase in the amount of protected lands.

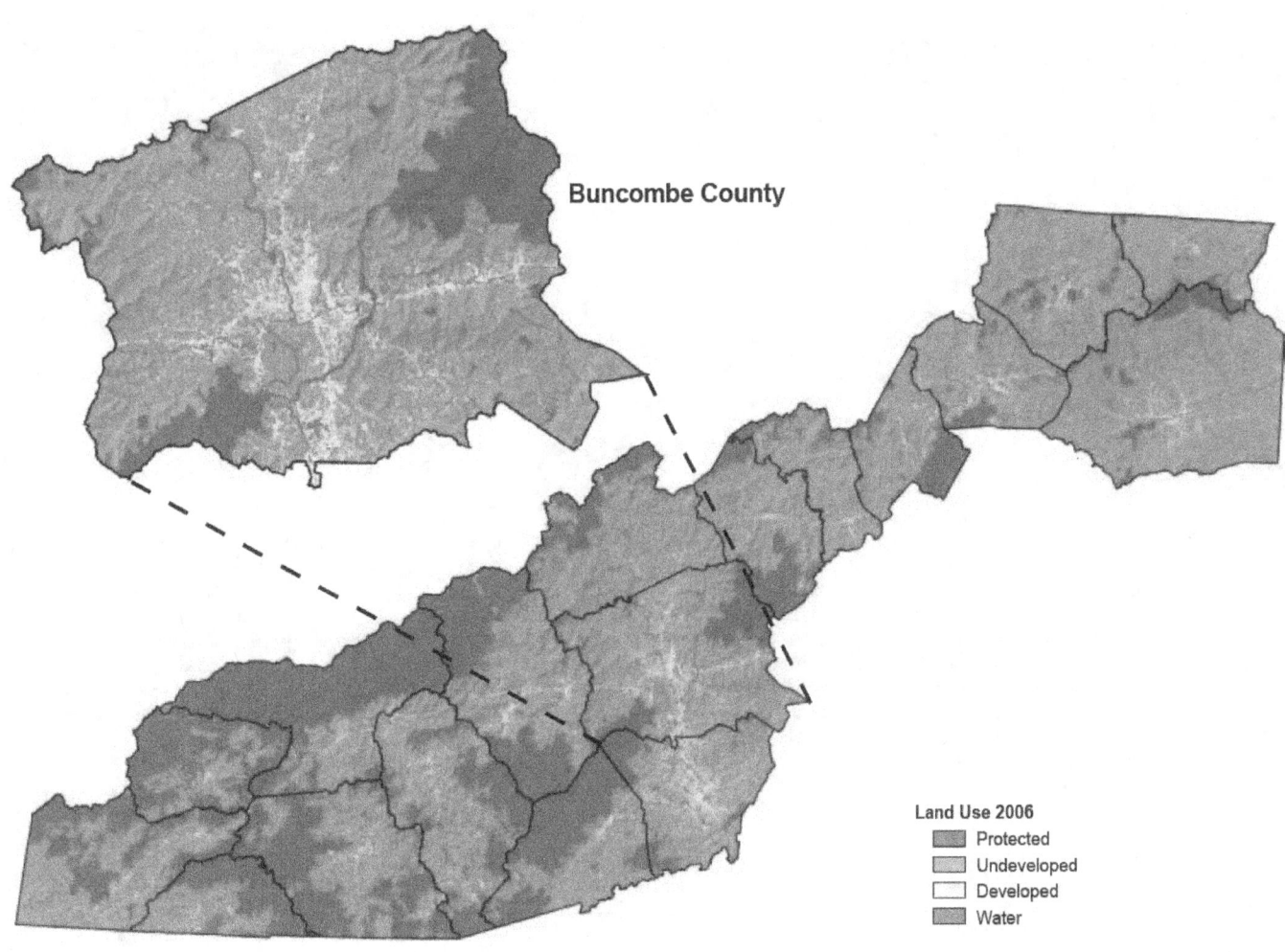

Buncombe County

Land Use 2006
- Protected
- Undeveloped
- Developed
- Water

One Possible Future
Land Use Change

As the region's population grows (a 22.7-percent increase is projected from 2010–2030), the rate at which rural land is converted to urban use will increase. The map on p. 41 projects land use change by 2030 for eighteen counties. The projection is based on a statistical model that incorporates factors such as distance to roads, attraction of employment centers, percent slope, and "pressure" exerted by previously developed areas. A separate factor is the millions of acres of national and State forest and park lands that annually attract well over 10 million visitors to the region. It is likely some small percentage of these visitors will relocate to the area. It is hard to know whether the high rate of development that occurred during the previous 30 years will continue; however, this map shows one possible future scenario. Based on this model, by 2030 an additional 144,818 acres will be developed in the eighteen counties at a conversion rate of almost 16.5 acres per day. This increase is equivalent to about 4.9 percent of the region's private, undeveloped land in 2006. The human footprint will increase from 0.30 acres per person in 2006 to 0.39 acres per person in 2030.

Continued development leads to several challenges, including the amount municipal governments must spend to provide services to residents, increasing erosion of steep slopes, more frequent flooding, and more fires (studies show that 96 percent of all fires are caused by human activity). In addition, as demand for recreation grows, use patterns will creep toward the center of the mountain ranges, disturbing vulnerable habitat.

Although land conversion is one of the biggest threats to Western North Carolina's forests, it is also one over which humans have direct control.

There are effective ways to mitigate the negative impacts of land conversion, including:
*   the preservation and restoration of critical habitat so that species may adapt and survive,
*   the control of invasive species through chemical and mechanical treatment,
*   the management of lands around water bodies (which are among the most sensitive areas likely to experience environmental stress with increased human activity), and
*   reduction of the risk of wildfire by creating residential landscapes that, by design, reduce the spread of fire.

As land is converted from "undeveloped" to developed, the economics, politics, infrastructure, and quality of life of the region also change. New partnerships and constituencies are needed to help communities, developers, and property owners make informed decisions. Mechanisms that enable and encourage cooperative and cross-boundary management are also necessary.

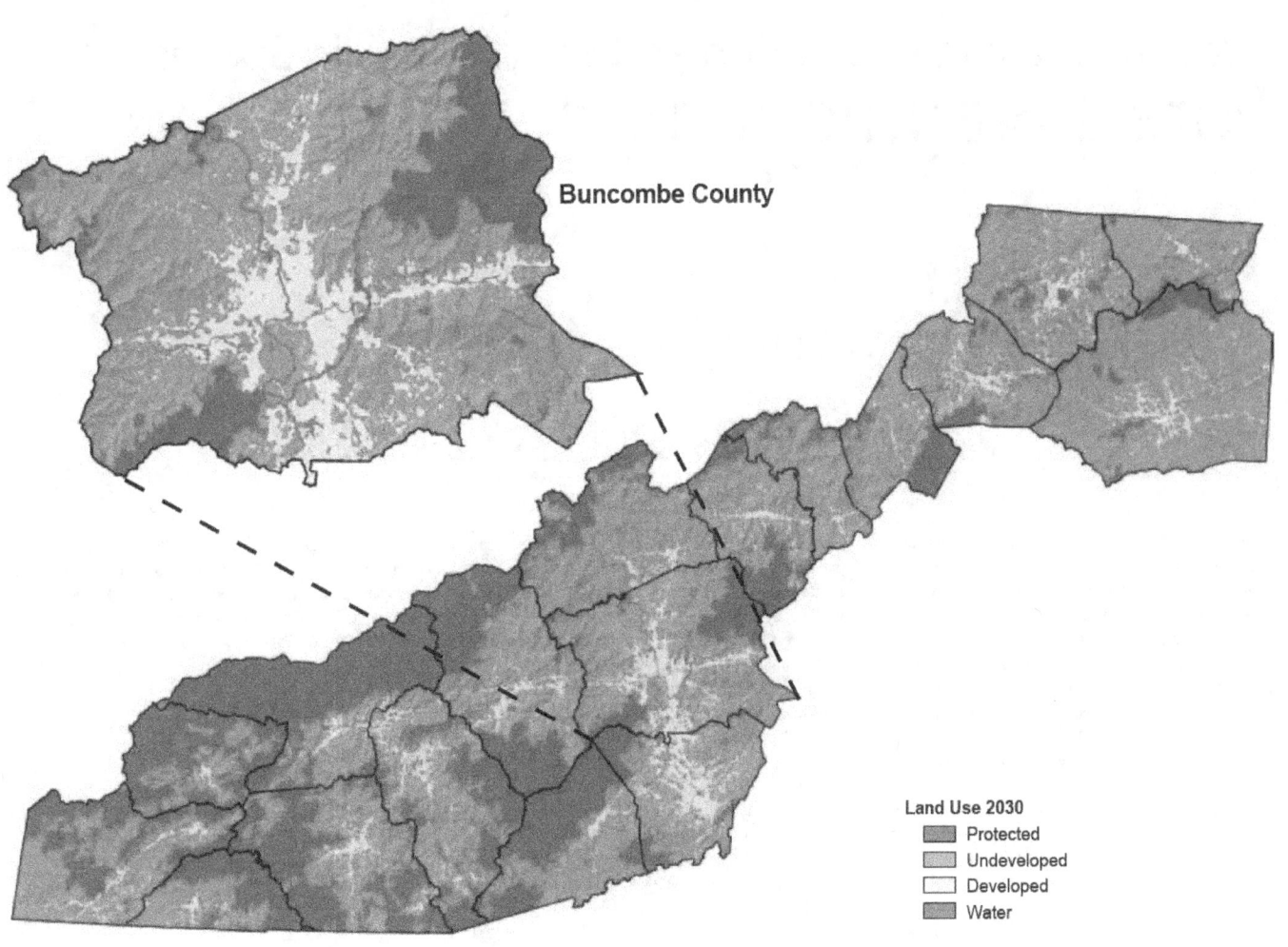

Buncombe County

Land Use 2030
Protected
Undeveloped
Developed
Water

Growing Human Population and Shrinking Wild Spaces
Forest Fragmentation

Forest fragmentation occurs when agriculture, urbanization, roads, or other human development breaks up large, contiguous blocks of forest into smaller isolated patches. Fragmentation can create negative impacts on contiguous forest ecosystems in Western North Carolina.

Forest fragmentation produces a decrease in the forest interior, thus limiting the habitat for many species, including songbirds. The decrease in interior habitat leaves these animals more susceptible to predators and nest robbers. As land becomes more fragmented and habitat is lost or degraded, wildlife is forced to adapt to survive. They may suffer high levels of mortality or displacement from increased traffic on existing and new road systems. Noise and light from development may also drive them from their habitats.

In addition to a loss of wildlife habitat, there is a loss of plant habitat. Much like animals, plants have a unique habitat that is often threatened by fragmentation. When certain sections of the forest are cut and not reforested, the species that make up that forest often do not survive. Fragmentation also leaves the forest interior more susceptible to nonnative invasive species. Invasive plants compete with and replace native plants, reduce plant diversity, and cause other disruptions of ecosystem function. Disease and insects can also be introduced into wildland by nursery plants used in nearby landscaping.

Forest fragmentation also can impair water and air quality. Impervious surfaces of roads, parking lots, homes, and businesses replace woodland plants, trees, and soils that previously stored carbon dioxide, produced oxygen, absorbed pollutants, and protected against erosion. Increased runoff and the introduction of nonpoint source pollutants diminish the function and change the character of forest wetlands.

Finally, forest fragmentation has an economic impact. When forests are broken into small parcels, the economy of scale for forest management is lost. Increased costs coupled with fewer opportunities for long-term management and protection lead to mismanagement and underutilization of forests. Some of the more populated counties in the region are projected to have no privately owned parcels larger than 10 acres by 2070.

The population of Western North Carolina is expected to increase by 22.7 percent from 2010 to 2030. To mitigate potential problems associated with increased forest fragmentation, adaptive forest management activities are needed in the wildland-urban interface. New strategies for managing forests across multiple ownerships and on much smaller scales are required.

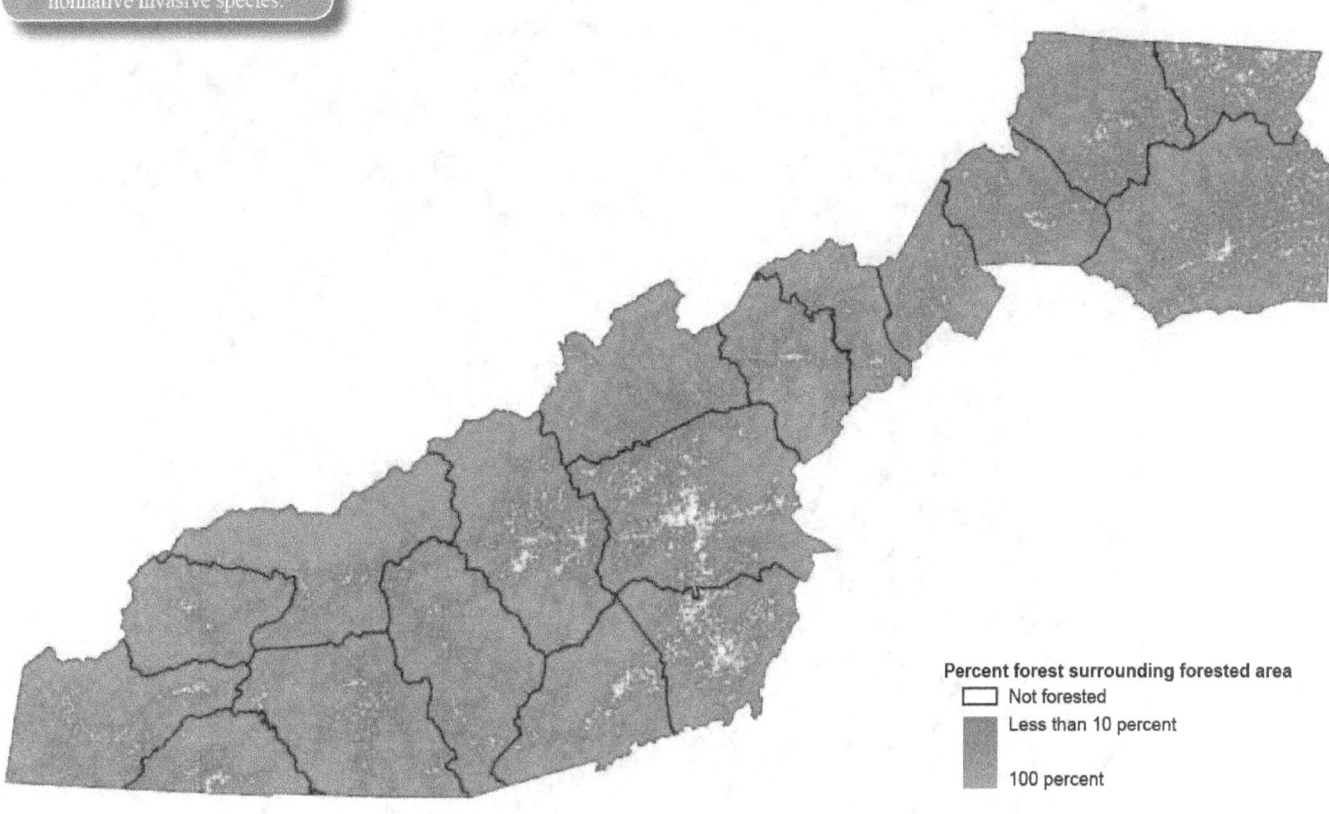

Forest fragmentation increases with urban encroachment. As a result, the habitat for many species becomes limited, and the forest interior is more susceptible to nonnative invasive species.

Percent forest surrounding forested area

☐ Not forested

■ Less than 10 percent

■ 100 percent

Production
Ownership, Volume, and Products

Knowledge of the availability and capability of forest land to provide goods and services is important to end users. Many factors influence the availability of timber. These include the type of ownership, product supply and demand, access, and other environmental constraints. An analysis of growing stock of the various species that make up the forest and how growing stock changes over time is central to determining whether or not a sustainable wood supply and the sustained health of the forest ecosystems providing that timber is achieved. While indicators of the timber resource are an important part of evaluating this region, it is also important to recognize the forests of Western North Carolina as unique for their rich biological diversity, scenic quality, cultural heritage, and relatively high proportion of public ownership, especially in the Eastern United States.

Forestland Available for Timber Production
Timberland Ownership

The majority of timberland in Western North Carolina is in private ownership. No apparent region-wide loss of timberland acreage is occurring. While some lands are being converted from forest to nonforest use, abandoned farmland is reverting to forest, resulting in a relatively stable timberland base. This criterion, however, does not reflect increases or decreases in forest fragmentation.

Forests have strongly shaped the landscape of Western North Carolina. Wood has been vital for subsistence and commerce for many generations. Practically all of the region's forests have been harvested at least once since the mid-1800s, and a timber industry exists here today.

Western North Carolina has 3.2 million acres of timberland, which is defined as forest land capable of producing 20 cubic feet of industrial wood per acre per year and not withdrawn from timber utilization. Approximately 2.4 million acres (74 percent of timberland) is owned by industrial and nonindustrial private landowners. The remaining 862,628 acres (26 percent of timberland) is in public ownership. The public ownership is primarily national forest land with small parcels of other Federal, State, county, and municipal lands.[1]

While some land conveyances have occurred in the past 22 years, notably acquisitions of 6,400 acres in the Pisgah National Forest and 9,300 acres in the Nantahala National Forest, as well as over 3,000 acres in the Rendezvous State Forest and 10,400 acres in the Dupont State Forest, the percentages of private and publicly owned timberland has essentially remained the same. The Pisgah and Nantahala National Forests represent the region's majority of publicly owned timberland. In fact, national forest timberland is found in all but two of the counties in Western North Carolina. Moreover, approximately 60 percent of Clay, Graham, and Macon Counties are designated national forest timberlands.

Forest productivity depends on many factors, including natural conditions (such as climate, soils, elevation, aspect, and latitude) and timber management, which influence timber stocking levels, forest health, and species mix. While the effects of natural conditions are seen across all ownerships, land management strategies tend to be applied differently on public and private lands.

---

[1]Excluded from timberland data are Blue Ridge Parkway and Great Smoky Mountains National Park lands

Timberland Ownership in Western North Carolina (1984–2006)

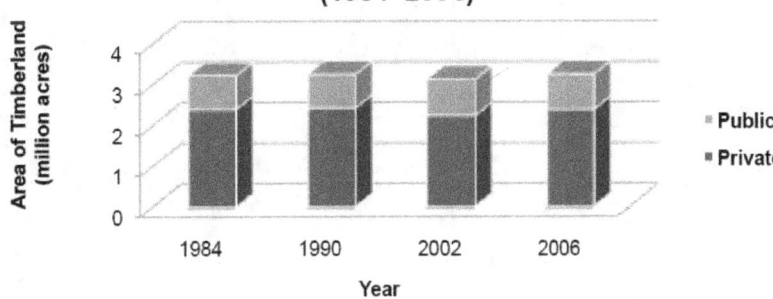

Timberland Ownership in Western North Carolina Councils of Government, 2006

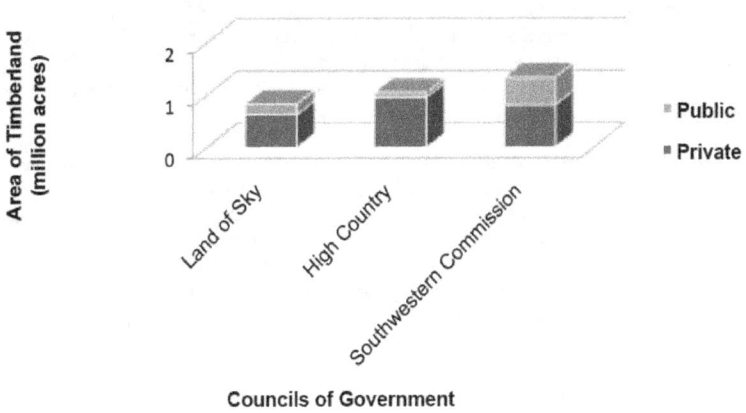

Ownership Influences Land Management
Timberland Ownership

How does ownership influence land management?
National forest management differs significantly from private land management, resulting in different forests and patterns of timber production. In national forests, the terrain is usually more rugged and there are fewer roads, making these lands more expensive to harvest. A mandate to manage for nontimber values, such as protection of biodiversity, restoration of degraded systems (e.g., reintroducing fire to fire-dependent communities or restoring viable native plant communities by controlling invasive species), and public access also represents a significant difference.

While all forests are environmental and economic assets for the region, clearly privately owned forests contribute a significant proportion of these assets in terms of providing clean and abundant water, clean air, employment and economic opportunities, habitat for plants and animals, and carbon sequestration. Although access to privately owned timberland is often restricted, these lands provide all citizens with environmental benefits and services; for example, private timberlands still sustain

wildlife and provide scenic vistas even though the public may not be permitted to hunt on the land or use it for recreational purposes.

Nonindustrial private landowners across the State retain their timberland for a number of reasons. In addition to investment and income generation potential, the value of family inheritance, pride of ownership, wildlife-watching, hunting, and recreation are also important. There seems to be a strong relationship among all of these factors rather than an ordered priority.

Forests take a long time to grow, and today's decisions have long-term impacts and benefits. A management plan allows a forest landowner to identify goals for timber production as well as protection of other forest attributes and to determine what the best course of action would be to achieve their goals.

Timber and nontimber goals can be planned at the same time. Owners can protect soil and water, wildlife habitat, natural beauty, or other important resources with little expense if planned before harvest. Timber stand

improvements can address sites that are seriously damaged and in need of a salvage operation, over-mature stands, or stands deficient in stocking. Timber harvests create open areas and road access that can also improve wildlife habitat, provide recreation, and enhance natural beauty. Careful planning of management activities can also help assure a periodic cash flow.

When asked about future intentions regarding ownership, the majority of nonindustrial timberland owners plan only minimal or no activity. When an activity is cited, it is typically harvesting timber and firewood, deeding land to heirs, or investing in more timberland.

THE GRANDIN FARM
A NORTH CAROLINA TREE FARM

WOOD
WATER
TREE FARM
RECREATION
WILDLIFE

Stewardship
FOREST

JETT'S INVESTMENTS, LLC
INVESTING IN THE FUTURE OF
AMERICA'S FORESTS

AMERICAN TREE
FARM SYSTEM

NCFA
NORTH CAROLINA
FORESTRY ASSOC.

CERTIFIED 1958

Amount of Standing Timber
Volume of Timber

In Western North Carolina, timber volume continues to expand steadily. The volume of growing stock increased 38 percent from 1984 to 2006.

Volume of Timber

Growing stock is a common term used to describe timber volume. The volume of growing stock trees is a subset of all live trees in a forest or stand. Growing stock includes sawtimber, pole timber, saplings, and seedlings; but excludes rough, rotten, and cull trees. It is a fundamental element in determining the productive capacity of an area identified as forest available for timber production. Knowledge of growing stock of the various species that make up the forest and how growing stock changes over time is central to considerations of a sustainable supply of wood for products and the sustainability of the ecosystems that provide them.

Between 1984 and 2006, the total volume of growing stock on timberland increased from 6.1 billion cubic feet to 8.4 billion cubic feet, an increase of 38 percent. The volume of growing stock increased by 39 percent on private lands and 35 percent on public lands. Positive trends in growth on timberland are attributable to maturation of forests cut in the early 1900s, investments in fire protection, land owner education, and silviculture.

Volume of Growth and Removals

Net growth on timberlands is defined as gross growth minus mortality. Removals include trees removed from the inventory by harvesting, cultural operations such as timber-stand improvement, land clearing, or changes in land use. While comparing net growth to removals conveys no information about quality, biodiversity, other attributes of ecology, or management objectives, it does allow us to look at implications of forestry operations over time.

From 1984 to 2006, average annual net growth almost doubled, increasing from 174.3 million cubic feet to 324.3 million cubic feet. In this same period, total average annual removals doubled from 38.8 million cubic feet to 76.7 million cubic feet. To put this in perspective, just 24 percent of growth was removed annually on average. Moreover, average annual removals drained less than 1 percent of the total inventory of growing stock trees, while average annual net growth contributed 3.9 percent to the total growing stock inventory. From a timber supply standpoint, therefore, the region's forests are managed sustainably.

There has been a net increase in growth and removals for hardwoods and softwoods over the study period. The decrease in hardwood average annual net growth from 1984 to 1990 is almost certainly due to the effects of the longest and most severe drought in the last century (see Precipitation Patterns, p. 76). Many large trees, particularly oaks, died from a scarcity of water, while other drought-stressed trees succumbed to various diseases and wind damage. The sharp decline in softwood growth from 1990–2002 reflects the devastating effects of the southern pine beetle on yellow pines, especially in the southwestern counties.

For uses of this data, the statistics are generated from 80 percent of inventory samples, the percent of measured points available at time of publication. This should provide reliable statistics for key totals at the 18-county level. However, users should note that sampling error increases as the area or volume decreases.

Total Volume of Growing Stock on Timberland (1984–2006)

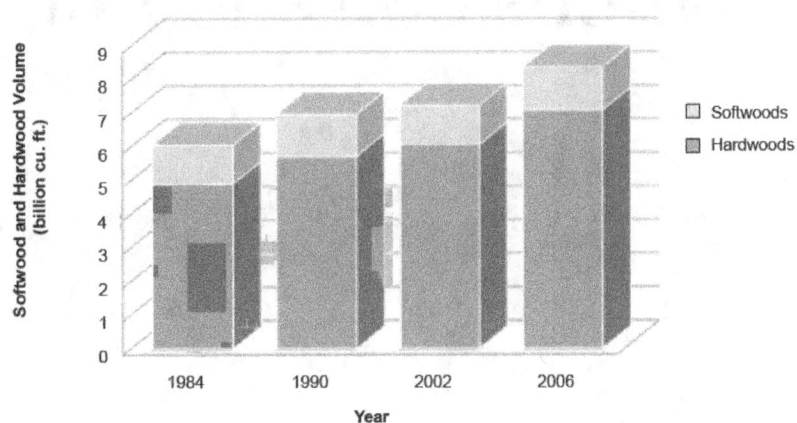

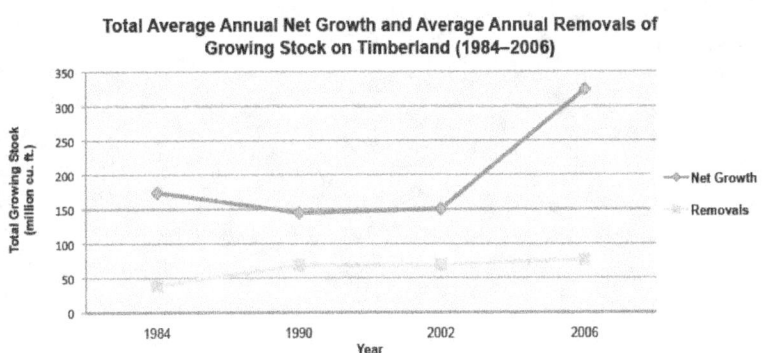

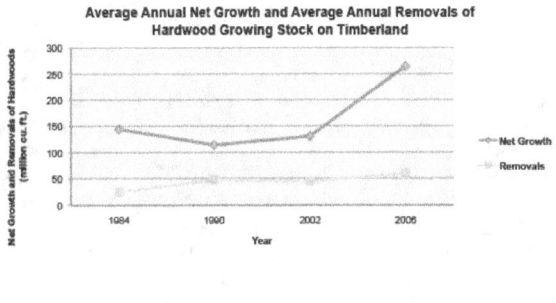

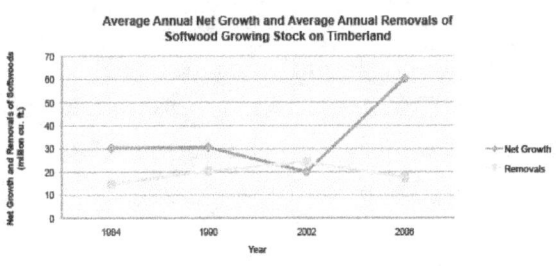

Western North Carolina Forests Are Maturing
Timber Composition and Age

Forest structure is the distribution of trees by species and size (diameter class). Structure is the result of several factors: the growth habit of tree species, especially the degree of shade tolerance; ecological conditions; and the history of disturbance and management. The forests of Western North Carolina have over 100 tree species. Species such as oak, ash, poplar, hickory, and some pines do not tolerate shade well and are normally found in the overstory. Other species, such as beech, maple, dogwood, red bud, and black gum, survive well in shade and make up the understory of the forest canopy. Ecological conditions are highly correlated with elevation and forest types change dramatically with increases in elevation. Harvesting practices in Western North Carolina, particularly in the early 1900s, have led to a predominately even-aged forest that is reaching maturity.

Various size classes within a forest are important because they provide different goods, services, and values. In Western North Carolina, volume of growing stock is accumulating in all diameter classes 10 inches and larger. In 16-inch and larger classes, volume rises exponentially and more than doubles beyond 20 inches. The volume of 6–8 inch classes has declined; however, the decline is by less than 10 percent.

Sawtimber-size trees dominate the mountain landscape. The supply of high-quality saw logs is increasing; however, the wood products sector is currently experiencing a decline in production.

Volume of Growing Stock Trees by Diameter Class (1984–2006)

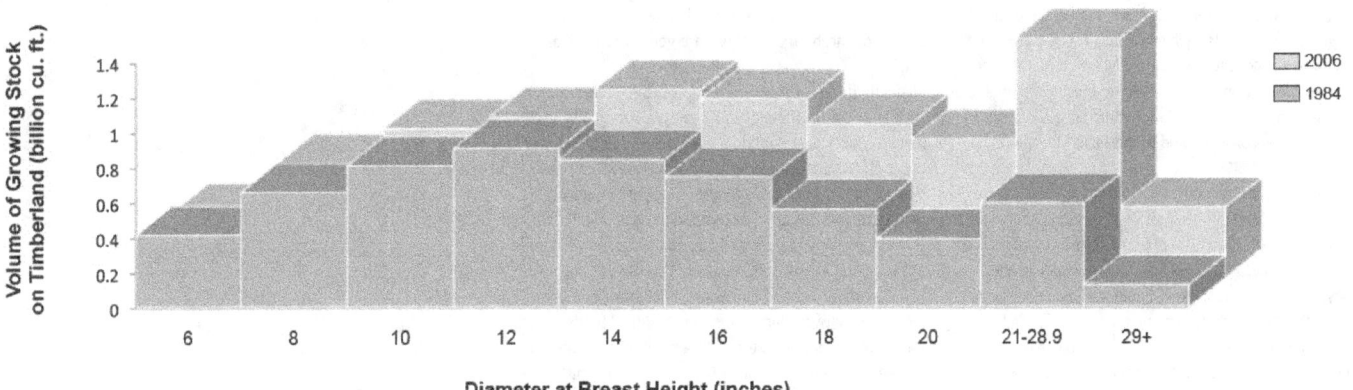

Volume of Growing Stock on Timberland (billion cu. ft.)

Diameter at Breast Height (inches)

2006
1984

Different Aged Forests Provide Different Habitats
Timber Composition and Age

What are the implications of size class distribution?
Presently, volume is accumulating in trees of a size suitable for high-value products such as veneer, barrel staves, and the better grades of factory lumber. Much of the behavior of lumber production can be related to changes in lumber prices. With a currently depressed housing market, consumption has dropped and numerous mills have cut production.

Regionally, indigenous wildlife populations depend on early-, mid-, and late-successional forests. Succession is the natural replacement of plant or plant communities in an area over time. The larger size classes (mid- to late-successional vegetation) provide habitat for turkey, bear, squirrel, fox, and bobcat, to name a few. Small den trees might house chickadees, woodpeckers, screech owls, or flying squirrels. Large den trees are used by squirrels, raccoons, wood ducks, and, occasionally, even a bear. Older, mast-producing trees produce fruits and nuts used by wildlife for food. Hickory, oak, beech, persimmon, serviceberry, black gum, holly, hawthorn, dogwood, grapevine, and many other species found in mid- to late-successional forests are valuable to wildlife.

Early successional forests, characterized by dense growth of shrubs and saplings, are very different from that of mid- to late-successional forests, and provide distinctly different habitats. Some wildlife (breeding birds such as certain warblers, ruffed grouse, cottontails, wild turkey, American woodcock, and white-tailed deer) are either closely associated with younger forests or tend to have higher populations in them. Without an increase in management activities that create openings in a mature forest, it is likely there will be decline from current levels and potential loss of species associated with young stands.

As private timberlands account for most of the region's patchwork landscape of abandoned fields, young forest, and small, older forest fragments, private lands may become the locus of most early successional habitat. The maintenance and restoration of older, late-successional habitat are provided on public land, where there is potential for maintaining and creating large tracts of unfragmented forest.

A paucity of early stage successional stands could lead to a decline from current levels, or loss of, wildlife species associated with young forests.

Other Forest Resources
Nontimber Forest Products

The forests of Western North Carolina provide many nontimber products. They include plants, parts of plants, and other biological material as well as fungi, mosses, lichens, herbs, vines, shrubs, and trees. Many different parts of plants are harvested, including roots, tubers, leaves, bark, twigs and branches, fruit, sap and resin, as well as wood. The most important edible forest product in Western North Carolina is ramps, a mainstay of many festivals. The collection of ramps in early spring generates significant revenue for local civic groups. Other culinary products include mushrooms, fiddlehead ferns, black walnuts, blueberries, raspberries, persimmons, and acorns. Floral and horticultural products include grapevines, Galax, azaleas, log mosses, other annual and perennial plants, cones, shrubs, and trees. Medicinal products include American ginseng, false unicorn, black cohosh, bloodroot, and many others.

People harvest nontimber forest products for both market and non-market reasons. Before the European settlers entered the mountains, Native Americans traded these products among themselves. Early European settlers gathered the products for subsistence as well as income.

Over time, ecological knowledge, built through generations of gathering, tending, using, and trading, has been preserved and shared.

As demand for these products increases, it is important to monitor their removal and the impact that harvest has on their long-term viability. Recognizing the need to monitor the consumption of nontimber forest products, the USDA Forest Service has developed a permitting process that sets a unit price for each product and provides guidelines for gatherers, ensuring a sustainable harvest.

The USDA Forest Service has tracked the total value of nontimber forest products sold in the Pisgah and Nantahala National Forests since 2005. The total annual value varies, averaging about $73,000 per year, with the highest income producers being Galax, ginseng, rhododendron and laurel, and firewood. Using "value sold" to express nontimber forest products may indicate trends, but the actual dollar amount can be a misleading measure of real value and could trivialize the social benefits of these products. The quantity and value of nontimber forest products collected on private lands is not currently monitored.

Nontimber Forest Products Sold in Pisgah and Nantahala National Forests, 2009

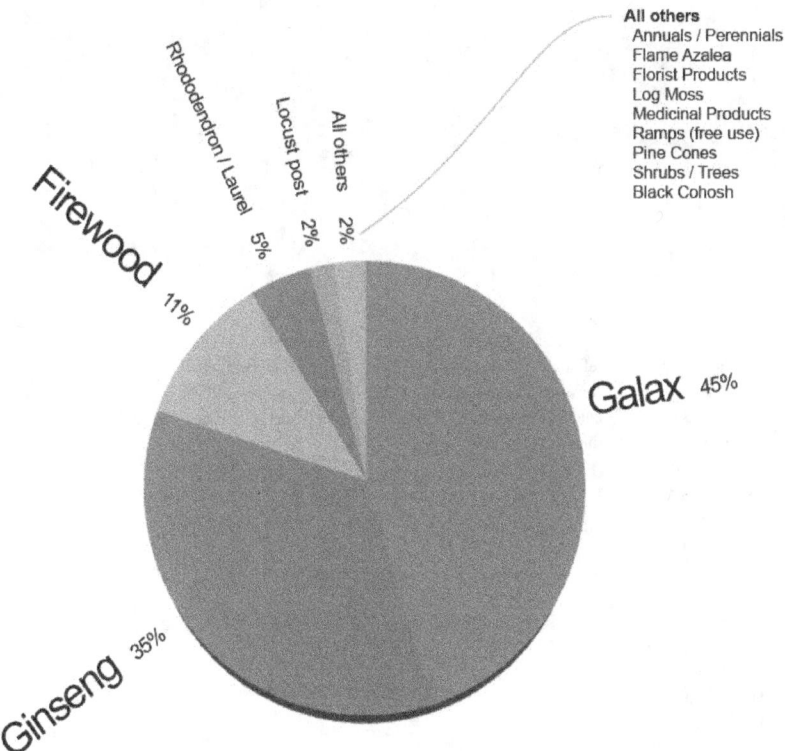

Firewood 11%

Rhododendron / Laurel 5%

Locust post 2%

All others 2%

All others
Annuals / Perennials
Flame Azalea
Florist Products
Log Moss
Medicinal Products
Ramps (free use)
Pine Cones
Shrubs / Trees
Black Cohosh

Galax 45%

Ginseng 35%

Renewable Energy
Biomass Production Potential

Wood, used for heat, was the main source of U.S. energy until the early part of the 20th century. In recent decades, concerns with energy security, energy costs, rural economies, and environmental matters have increased interest in the use of forest biomass for energy. Forest biomass can be obtained directly from the forest in the form of trees or portions of trees. It can also be obtained from forest product manufacturing facilities in the form of by-products, such as bark, sawdust, shavings, and other residues.

Probably the greatest barrier to bioenergy lies in the logistics and costs of cutting, handling, and transporting small-diameter wood. Early studies indicate that damage to the ecosystem may not be an issue; however, the economics of harvesting biomass are not encouraging. The cost of labor, equipment, and transport is more than the price paid for the wood chips sold for energy. Renewable energy sources such as wood provide an advantage over finite fossil fuels only when the benefits of reducing pollution and emissions of greenhouse gases, improving forest health, and decreasing the risk of wildfire are added in.

Although there was almost 1.2 million tons of residue left in the woods following traditional logging operations in Western North Carolina in 2007, there is, to date, little evidence of a viable infrastructure to facilitate the use of this wood for bioenergy.

Renewable energy sources such as wood provide an advantage over finite fossil fuels only when the benefits of reducing pollution and emissions of greenhouse gases, improving forest health, and decreasing the risk of wildfire are added in.

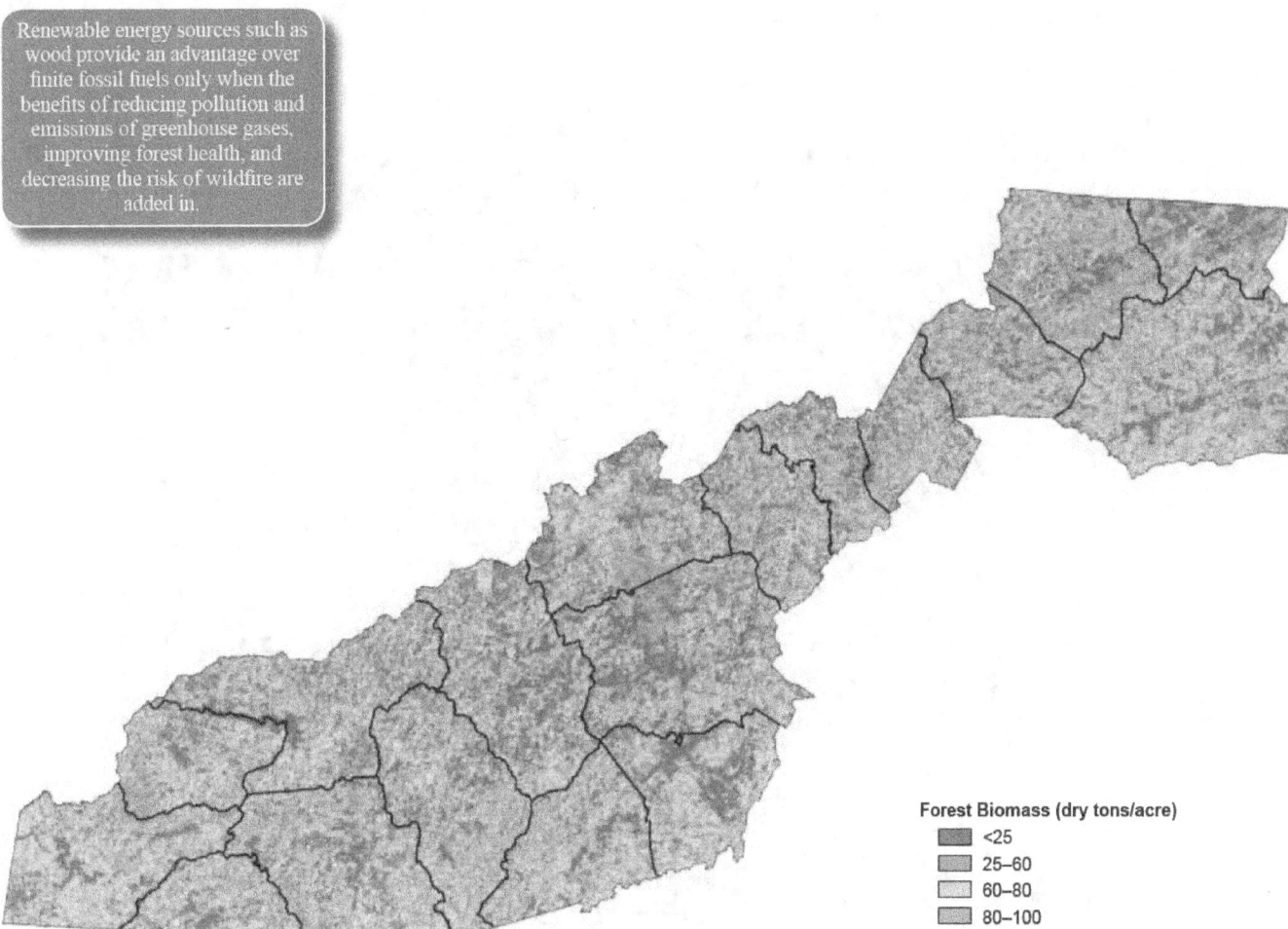

Forest Biomass (dry tons/acre)

■ <25
■ 25–60
□ 60–80
■ 80–100
■ 100–250+

Ecosystem Health
Mitigating Environmental Threats

The forests of Western North Carolina are threatened by a wide variety of environmental stressors and disturbances such as insects, disease, invasive species, drought, fire, hurricanes, tornadoes, and ice storms. A stressor is any kind of event or action which, at certain levels, causes stress to organisms; for example, a period of drought. A disturbance is a relatively discrete event in time that disrupts ecosystem, community, or population structure and changes resources, substrate availability, or the physical environment; for example, a wildfire. Organisms may adapt to a level of disturbance, but when another threshold is exceeded, degradation occurs. Degradation is the destruction of complex natural environments.

When one ecosystem is under attack as a result of natural or man-made events, it is extremely difficult to calculate the ripple effects throughout the natural system. Sometimes stress, disturbance, and degradation occur individually, but more often they come in combination. The resulting effects can be severe and cause significant, lasting impact on ecological and socioeconomic values.

To effectively sustain the forests of North Carolina, there is a need to integrate how we deal with interacting, multiple threats so that land managers may anticipate disturbances and act to prevent or lessen the effects, or restore either the structure or the function of affected ecosystems.

Ecosystem Threat
Insects and Diseases

Insects and pathogens are a natural part of ecosystems and are essential to ecological balance in natural forests. Population dynamics of insects and pathogens are influenced by climate, management activities, natural tree defenses, and natural enemies. Trees can be weakened by a disease or an insect, and that weakened tree is then more vulnerable to insects, disease, and changes in temperature and precipitation. The effect on forested landscapes can be tree mortality and/or reduced tree vigor. Examining trends of individual insect and pathogen populations is useful in understanding their dynamic nature.

Over the last century, several forest types in the region have experienced significant declines due to infestations of insects and diseases.

In the last century the American chestnut, once one of the most abundant species in the region, was all but lost to disease. More recently, the southern pine beetle has led to significant mortality of yellow pines. Presently, eastern and Carolina hemlocks and spruce-fir forests are threatened by an infestation of adelgids.

Southern Pine Beetle

In the period 1984 to 2006, the volume of southern yellow pine trees decreased 57 percent in Western North Carolina. Eastern white pine was also attacked and killed. Southern pine beetle, an insect native to southern forests, attacks loblolly, shortleaf, Virginia, pitch, and table mountain pine. The insect periodically increases to epidemic proportions, causing severe mortality. Devastating outbreaks have been reported across the South since the early 1800s. The most recent outbreak peaked in 2002. In the aftermath of large infestations, dead and downed trees provide abundant fuel for wildfires and pose additional threats to transportation corridors and public safety. The number of years of outbreak of southern pine beetle in Western North Carolina is shown from 1960 to 2005. Due to the preponderance of mixed pine forests in the southwestern part of the region, Graham, Cherokee, Swain, Macon, Jackson, and Buncombe Counties had the highest occurrence.

Southern pine beetle
number of outbreak
years 1960–2005

■ 2
■ 3–5
□ 6–8
■ 9–12
■ 13–14

Balsam Woolly Adelgid

Fraser fir stands, which grow in association with red spruce on scattered mountain tops such as Mount Mitchell in Yancey County, have declined significantly due to an infestation of the insect balsam woolly adelgid and air pollution. The adelgid, which appeared in North Carolina in the 1950s, is a tiny, sucking insect that robs the tree of nutrients, leading to its decline and eventual death. The foliage in a dying tree turns yellow, then deep red, then falls to the ground. In our region, significant mortality of Fraser fir has occurred, followed by scattered regeneration. Although the species is still present in the ecosystem, red spruce is the dominant species in the spruce-fir forest type.

Hemlock Woolly Adelgid

Although decreases in the volume are not yet reflected in the data, eastern and Carolina hemlocks are dying rapidly due to an infestation of hemlock woolly adelgid. The hemlock woolly adelgid is similar in biology to its relative, the balsam woolly adelgid. The insect feeds in fall, winter, and spring, depleting the tree of nutrients, leading to mortality in less than five years. The tiny adelgid is dispersed by wind, birds, and mammals.

The loss of eastern hemlock in coves and Carolina hemlock on steep south- or west-facing slopes across Western North Carolina will affect other biological values. Hemlock forests are used by many species of wildlife as a food source, a nesting site, a roosting site, and seasonal shelter. Hemlocks provide shade near creeks and streams and their disappearance is likely to increase water temperature, negatively impacting aquatic species.

Eradication of the hemlock woolly adelgid is not feasible; therefore, many regional groups, both public and private, are working together to protect highly valued stands of hemlock. Treatments include insecticides and the introduction of several beetle species that feed only on the hemlock woolly adelgid. These controls are the best long-term hope to save the hemlocks.

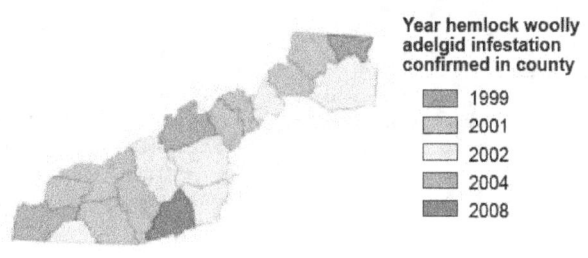

Year hemlock woolly adelgid infestation confirmed in county

- 1999
- 2001
- 2002
- 2004
- 2008

Gypsy Moth

The gypsy moth was introduced into the United States in the mid-1800s. The insect, now permanently established in 17 States, defoliates trees, making them vulnerable to other killing agents. Gypsy moths feed on a wide variety of trees, shrubs, and vines but prefer all oak species, apple, beech, birch, basswood, and willow. Although gypsy moth is not yet permanently established in our counties, there have been numerous instances of human-mediated introductions of this pest over the past 10–15 years. A few of these introductions developed into small, isolated pockets of infestation that were subsequently eradicated. Additionally, the USDA Forest Service is implementing a program to slow the spread, which will delay the establishment of gypsy moth in Western North Carolina. The most effective strategy is continued efforts to delay permanent infestation combined with active forest management before the gypsy moth arrives. Pre-outbreak treatments focus on reducing the vulnerability of stands by removing the trees most likely to die and regenerating stands that are close to maturity or understocked.

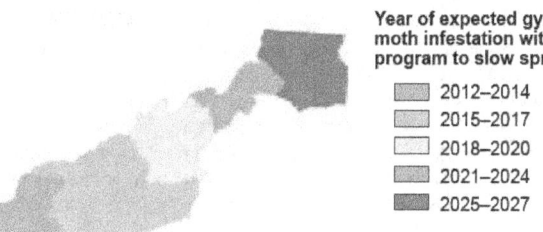

Year of expected gypsy moth infestation without program to slow spread

- 2012–2014
- 2015–2017
- 2018–2020
- 2021–2024
- 2025–2027

Ecosystem Threat
Insects and Diseases

Oak Decline

A high incidence of oak decline has been observed in Western North Carolina. When mature and over-mature oaks experience adverse climatic and site conditions, combined with stress from disease or insects, they are susceptible to decline and death. Losses are heaviest during extended periods of drought, on dry, south-facing slopes, and on shallow soils and rocky outcrops. Oak decline will probably increase as oak forests continue to age.

Dogwood Anthracnose

In the period 1984 to 2006, the volume of flowering dogwood declined by 48 percent. The increase in mortality is due, in large part, to anthracnose, a fungus introduced into Western North Carolina in the 1980s. Dogwood anthracnose is expected to intensify in the future, and losses will be heaviest at higher elevations and on shaded, north-facing slopes. Eventually, trees in the forest setting will be largely eliminated above 3,000 feet. Trees in full sun exposure below 3,000 feet are expected to sustain little damage. Besides being admired for their beautiful spring flowers, dogwood trees are an important source of soft mast for many species of wildlife. Rabbits, deer, squirrels, and a remarkable variety of game birds and song birds rely on dogwood to build up energy reserves to survive the winter. There is not a ready substitute with fruit of equal value to make up this loss.

Beech Bark Disease

Beech bark disease occurs when the bark of the beech tree is attacked and altered by an insect, the beech scale, and then invaded and killed by fungi. The first sign of the disease is isolated dots of white "wool" on the bole of the tree. As the insect population increases, the entire bole of the tree may be covered by the waxy secretion. The disease in forest stands cannot be controlled at a reasonable cost, and maintenance of apparently resistant trees is the best way to reduce disease losses. Virtually all high-elevation beech stands and beech gaps in Western North Carolina are already seriously impacted by beech bark disease.

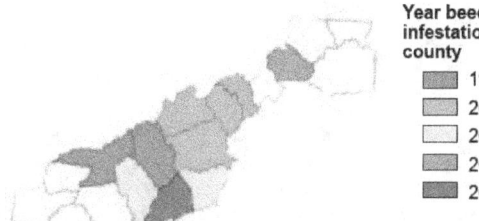

Year beech bark disease infestation confirmed in county
- 1993
- 2003
- 2004
- 2005
- 2009

Chestnut Blight

A century ago, the dominant tree in the canopy of Western North Carolina forests was the American chestnut. In some areas, the species grew in almost pure stands. During the early 1900s, the species was decimated by a fungal disease that destroys the bark tissue and kills the tree.

Early in the century and continuing to this day, groups of private and public cooperators have worked to find a way to save the chestnut. Following years of research, a disease-resistant American chestnut has now been reintroduced into eastern woodlands. New efforts to hybridize surviving American chestnuts with blight-resistant Chinese chestnuts resulted in a species that is about 94 percent American chestnut with the protection found in the Chinese species. In the next decade, the success or failure of the hybridized trees should be apparent.

Ecosystem Threat
Invasive Species

> Invasive species multiply rapidly and, once established, can be difficult to remove.

Invasive plants are introduced accidently into a natural system or brought into an area for ornamental use, food or medicinal use, living fences, or livestock forage. They multiply rapidly because they are not kept in check by insects and diseases that evolved with them in their native setting. Extensive landscape disturbances over the past century have allowed invasive plants to impede the functions of native systems.

The first invasive species undoubtedly arrived with European settlement 400 years ago. Many species have become so familiar that the public no longer recognizes their exotic and invasive behavior; for example, Japanese honeysuckle and starlings. More recently, the tempo of new introductions has increased with global trade, often accidentally through shipments of other cargo. Western North Carolina, with its variety of climates and growing conditions, provides fertile ground for these plants.

With their rapid early growth and dense infestations, invasive plants alter the ecology of forests, affecting water and soil quality and causing declines in both the numbers and diversity of native species. Non-native imported species literally overrun native plants, creating unique

new habitats amenable to yet more invasive plants. Shrubs can actually retard or stop hardwood regeneration and prevent forests from forming. Vines climbing over native vegetation block sunlight and break small trees. Grasses form dense impenetrable mats. Herbs can release chemicals to exclude other species.

Due to the harmful impacts of invasive species to existing ecosystems, Federal agencies have identified them as the second most important threat to the natural environment in the United States, behind only habitat destruction. Invasive plants are a major threat to parks and forests, greenways, and gardens, as well as endangered species. It is important to note that not all nonnative plants are considered harmful or invasive. Over 15 percent of the flora found in the Southern Appalachian Mountains is not native to the region. However, only a few of these plants are considered invasive. The majority of the nonnative plants have naturalized and are not considered harmful to natural ecosystems. Criteria suggested for classifying a plant as an invasive species include plants that alter ecosystem functions (e.g., increase fire likelihood or alter hydrologic flows), become established in undisturbed

natural communities, outcompete native species after a natural disturbance, and prevent or depress the regeneration of native species.

Invasive species are opportunists. They cross all ownerships and therefore require a cooperative approach to treatment, control, and eradication. Preventing introductions, choosing which species to battle, mitigating impacts, restoring native ecosystems, and managing new ecosystems are all issues that need to be addressed.

The National Forests in North Carolina have adopted a strategy to annually treat up to 1,100 acres of nonnative invasive plants using manual and chemical treatments. Sites prioritized for treatment include legally designated rare species, rare plant communities, and/or areas including unique habitats.

Mimosa

There are several invasive trees, shrubs, and herbs impacting the forests of Western North Carolina. Invasive trees include princess tree (*Paulownia tomentosa*), tree of heaven (*Ailanthus altissima*), and mimosa (*Albizia julibrissin*). Common around old homes, on roadsides, riparian areas, and forest margins, these trees seed prolifically and spread rapidly by wind and water. They invade after disturbances and form colonies in a wide range of soil conditions. Mimosa is seldom found in forests with full canopy cover or at elevations above 3,000 feet. It can, however, become a serious problem along riparian areas. Princess tree, in contrast, can occur from low to mid elevations and are found along open riparian areas and particularly in dry sites with recent intense fires.

Multiflora rose

Oriental bittersweet

Crimson fountaingrass

Many invasive shrubs were introduced in the late 1800s as ornamentals, living fence rows, or to control erosion. They continue to invade a variety of habitats including fields, forests, stream banks, and many disturbed areas. Once established, they form dense stands that displace native vegetation and close open areas. These plants include multiflora rose (*Rosa multiflora*), Japanese spiraea (*Spiraea japonica*), autumn olive (*Elaeagnus umbellata*), Chinese (*Ligustrum vulgare*) and European privet (*Ligustrum vulgare*), and Japanese knotweed (*Fallopia japonica* var. *japonica*). Other less widespread shrubs, although still damaging in select locations, include Japanese barberry (*Berberis thunbergii*), butterfly bush (*Buddleja davidii*), and winged burning bush (*Euonymus alatus*).

Invasive vines severely damage and can ultimately kill vegetation by climbing over native shrubs and trees and shading them out, constricting and girdling stems, forming dense thickets, and consuming their habitat. Invasive vines in Western North Carolina include Chinese yam (*Dioscorea polystachya*), Oriental bittersweet (*Celastrus orbiculatus*), kudzu (*Pueraria montana*), Japanese honeysuckle (*Lonicera japonica*), and porcelain-berry (*Ampelopsis brevipedunculata*). Less damaging but still of concern are periwinkle (*Vinca minor*) and English ivy (*Hedera helix*).

Invasive grasses include Japanese stiltgrass (*Microstegium vimineum*) and Chinese silvergrass (*Miscanthus sinensis*). These tufted grasses multiply to form extensive patches, displacing native species that are not able to compete with them. Japanese stiltgrass is found in damp areas such as Southern Appalachian bogs. Chinese silvergrass is more typical of drier sites and can present a fire hazard as it is highly flammable. Invasive herbs originally cultivated for food, medicinal, or horticultural use include garlic mustard (*Alliaria petiolata*), coltsfoot (*Tussilago farfara*), and spotted knapweed (*Centaurea stoebe* spp. *micrauthos*).

Ecosystem Threat
Forest Fire

Recent events suggest fire could play a greater role in the future condition of the region's forests. Historically, fire was caused by lightning, but now most forest fires are caused by humans.

Historically, fire was caused by lightning, but now most forest fires are caused by humans. Careless or accidental use of fire or a heat source and the deliberate setting of a fire represent a constant threat to forest ecosystems. Fire patterns from 1970–2007 tended to follow major population clusters and corridors.

Forest fire and its exclusion in the last century have been key elements in the development of Western North Carolina's forests. Following heavy cutting beginning in the 1890s and lasting through the 1920s, laws were enacted to suppress forest fires. It was not until the 1930s that scientists began to challenge the practice of eliminating fire from natural ecosystems. After much debate, the practice of intentionally igniting wildland fires and permitting naturally occurring fires to burn was adopted.

As a natural component of the forest environment, periodic fire contributes to the diversity of plant communities, the natural succession of pine-hardwood communities to hardwood stands, and reduction of fuel loads. Many native forest communities are fire-dependent or fire-influenced, including chestnut-oak, dry oak-hickory, dry-mesic oak-hickory, high elevation red oak, montane oak-hickory, and pine-oak heath.

Wildland fires burn in a mosaic pattern due to variability in wind direction, temperature, moisture, and type of vegetation. Fire can be managed to increase benefits and decrease damage to forest ecosystems. By controlling the intensity of a fire, soils become richer in nutrients rather than more erosive. Wildlife populations benefit from new nutrient-rich plant growth, the creation of open areas, and lowered risk of catastrophic fire. In this region, prescribed fire is necessary to enhance habitat for some threatened and endangered species and to initiate recovery in areas impacted by insect infestations. While a few invasive plants are controlled by fire; conversely, fire can dramatically increase some invasive plants, including princess tree, tree-of-heaven, Chinese silvergrass, and spotted knapweed.

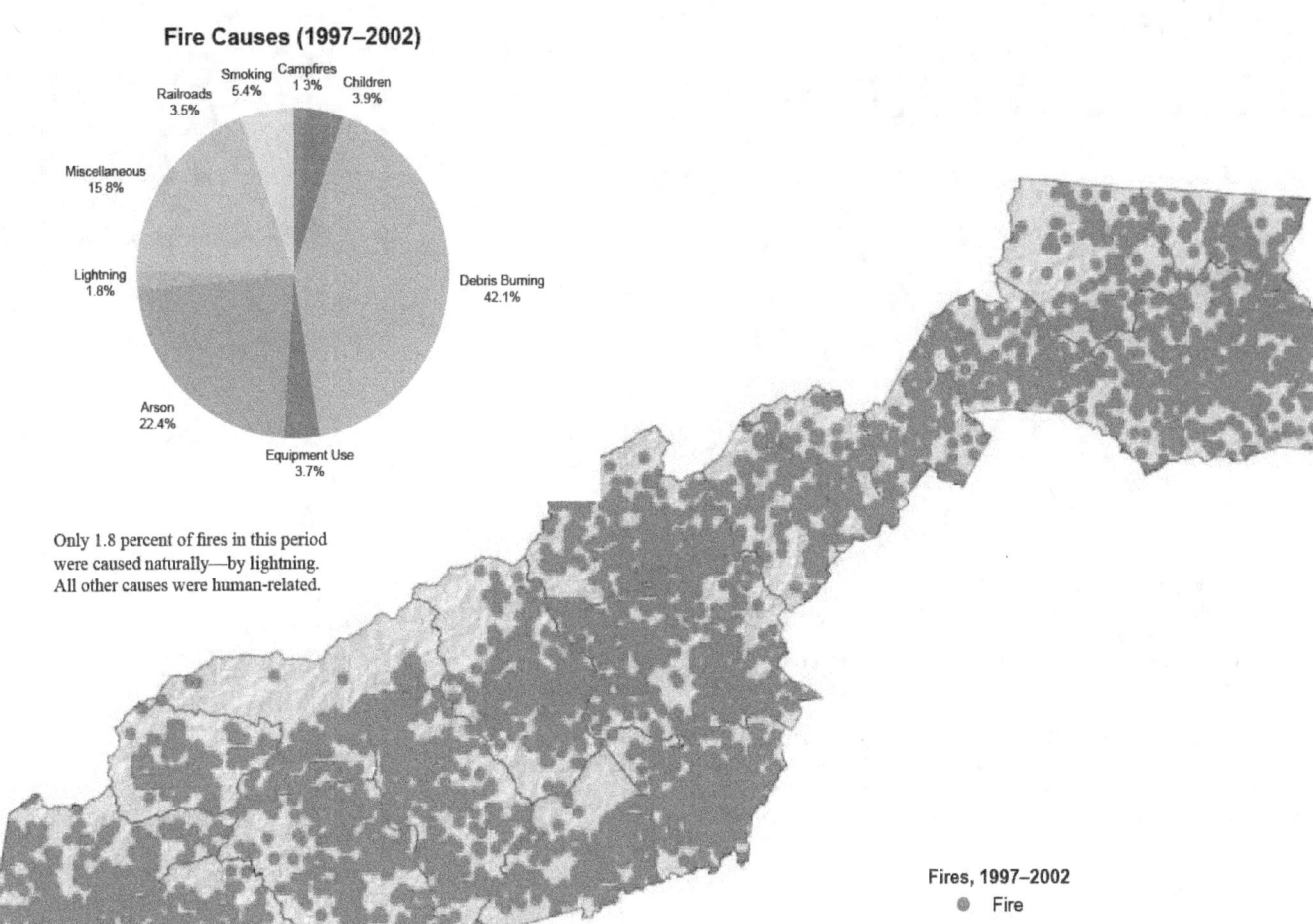

Fire Causes (1997–2002)

- Smoking 5.4%
- Campfires 1.3%
- Railroads 3.5%
- Children 3.9%
- Miscellaneous 15.8%
- Debris Burning 42.1%
- Lightning 1.8%
- Arson 22.4%
- Equipment Use 3.7%

Only 1.8 percent of fires in this period were caused naturally—by lightning. All other causes were human-related.

Fires, 1997–2002
● Fire

Ecosystem Threat
Severe Weather

Recent events suggest severe storms could play a greater role in the future condition of the region's forests. At least six tropical systems have passed over Western North Carolina since 1985, causing wind and water damage.

Drought and flooding, both naturally occurring stressors to forest communities, are a function of the amount of rain, snow, ice, and fog present in addition to soil characteristics. Growing periods with little water can lead to decreased growth, poor resistance to other stresses, and impaired physiological functions in trees. For example, extreme drought predisposes oaks to the oak decline disease complex involving root disease (Armillaria) and insect infestation. Resulting reductions in hard mast (acorns and beech nuts) production negatively affect wildlife populations, such as mice, voles, chipmunks, deer, bears, turkeys, and even wood ducks and blue jays. The two longest dry periods over the last century in Western North Carolina have occurred since the early 1980s (see Precipitation Patterns p. 76).

The major impacts of flooding on tree and site resources are poor aeration, alteration of soil structure, anaerobic soils which are much more inefficient at decomposition, and reduced chemical activity.

Hurricanes, although uncommon in the region, have recently left wide-ranging devastation. In 2004, rainfall from the remnants of Hurricanes Frances and Ivan caused flooding and triggered numerous landslides in Western North Carolina. Sixteen Western North Carolina counties were designated a Federal disaster area. The National Weather Service reported that Mount Mitchell received 46.6 inches of rain. The previous record, set in 1916 at Linville Gorge, was 37.4 inches.

The impacts of severe weather events may play a greater role in the widespread shaping of forests of the Southern United States than has been previously accepted. This threat is more thoroughly addressed in the next indicator, climate change.

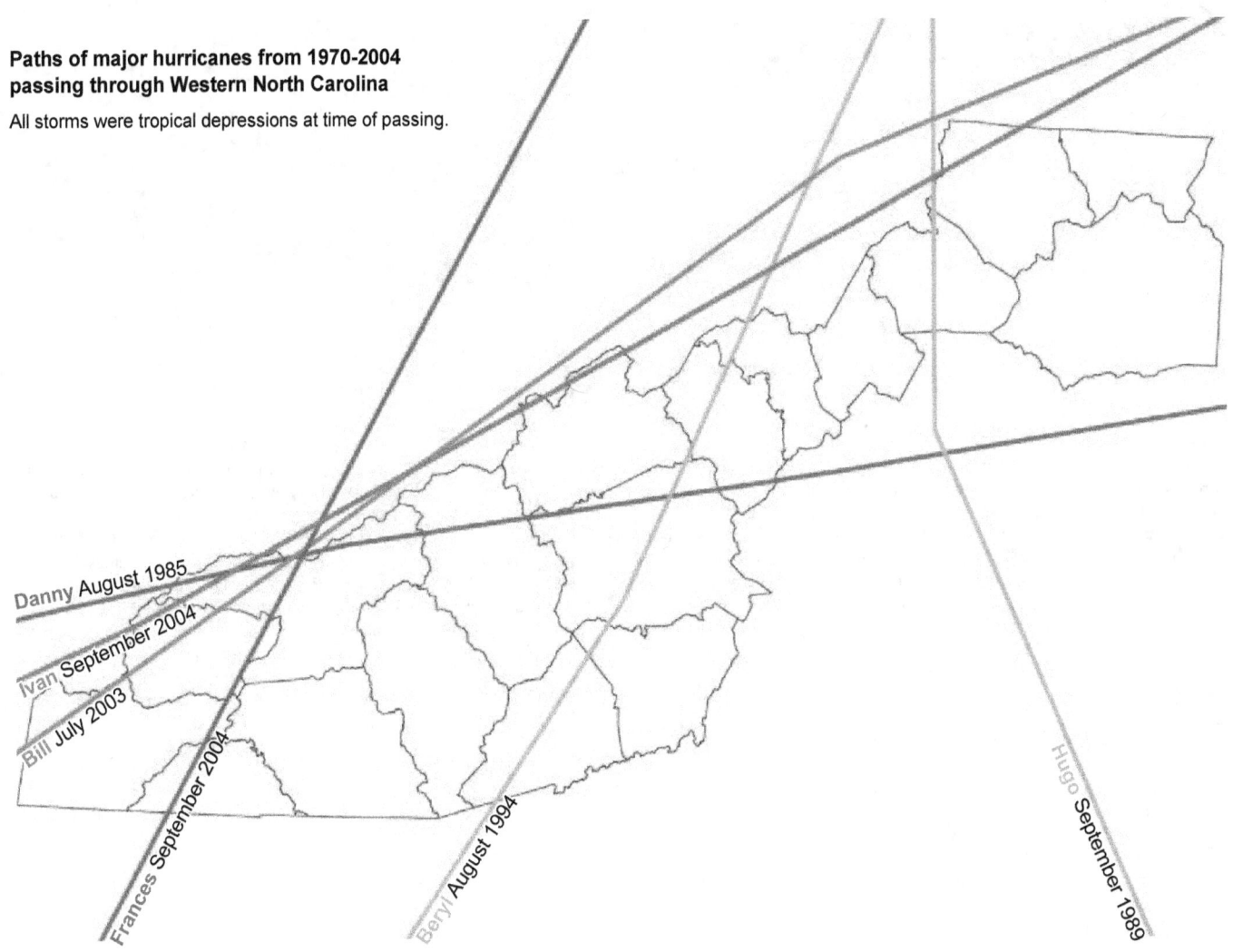

**Paths of major hurricanes from 1970-2004
passing through Western North Carolina**

All storms were tropical depressions at time of passing.

Danny August 1985

Ivan September 2004

Bill July 2003

Frances September 2004

Beryl August 1994

Hugo September 1989

Ecosystem Threat
Climate Change

What is climate change?

Climate is the average weather in a location over a long period of time. As some climate scientists like to say, "Climate is what you expect, weather is what you get." Climate is not only the measure of average conditions but also the characteristic range of variability from those conditions. Therefore, climate change refers to shifts in the average state of the climate and in its variability. For example, climate change may be evident in changes to expected temperature or precipitation, but also to the occurrence of variable weather events such as heat waves, floods, or drought. Changes in the frequency and severity of climate variability (weather events) often cause more damage and are more difficult to adapt to than gradual change.

Globally, changes in climate are already impacting forests through higher average temperatures, altered precipitation patterns, and more extreme weather events. Changes in temperature and precipitation can influence the occurrence and intensity of forest disturbances such as wildfire, introduced species, and pathogen (disease) outbreaks. Forests will play a crucial role in adapting to a changing climate because they will continue to serve as natural reservoirs for high-quality water and as refuges for biodiversity. Therefore, it is important to have healthy and resilient forests that rebound after disturbance.

By looking at historical climate data and prevalent climate trends, we can assess what changes Western North Carolina might expect, and begin to understand how to prepare for possible changes.

What is the climate in Western North Carolina?

The climate in Western North Carolina is largely defined by the region's topographical features. The elevation gradients of the Southern Appalachian Mountains range from around 1,500 feet along the eastern boundary to 6,684 feet at the summit of Mount Mitchell (the highest point east of the Mississippi River). Some of the valleys in the Southern Appalachians drop to 1,000 feet above sea level, while some 82 peaks exceed 5,000 feet and 43 tower above 6,000 feet. These elevation gradients result in varying average temperature and precipitation, creating a unique range of microclimates, each of which supports unique forest types and globally rare species. Due to the different climates in the region, the effects of climate change will vary and impact the forests in different ways.

Climate change is of global concern, and impacts to regions such as Western North Carolina will be highly variable. By looking at the range of possibilities, we can begin to plan for the future of our forests and maximize sustainability of our forest land.

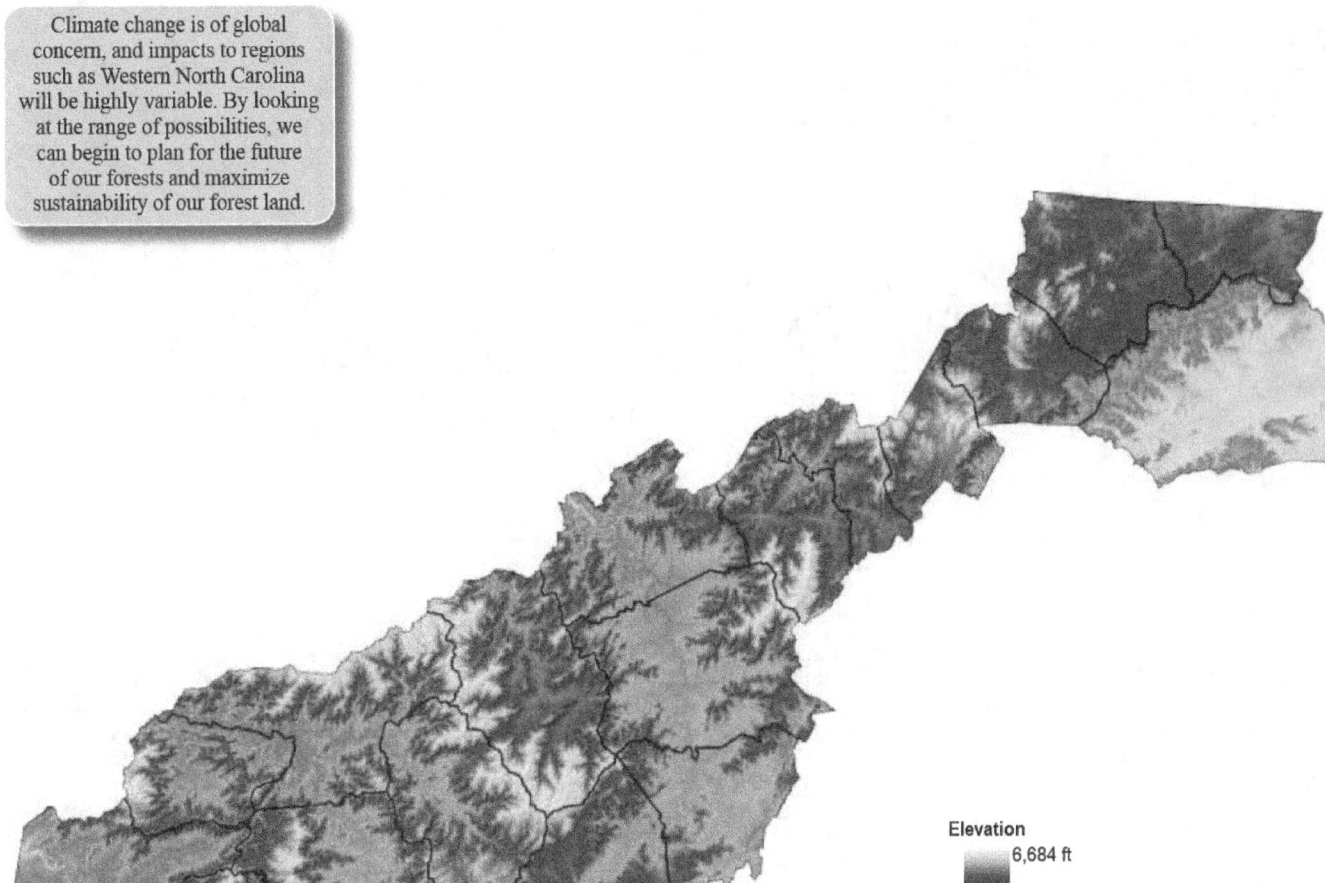

Elevation

6,684 ft

900 ft

Historical Temperature
Climate Change

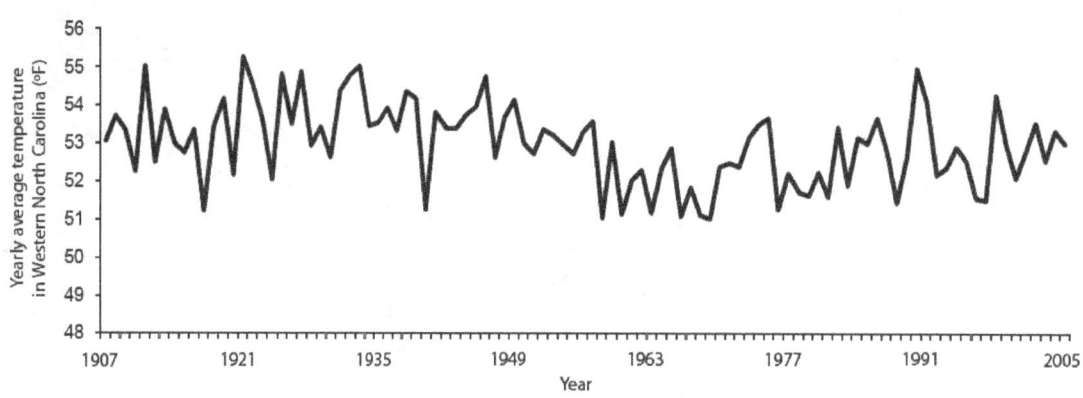

Why is temperature important?

Temperature and forest types are closely related. This relationship shows the great extent of acclimation of forests to the temperature zones in which they are found. Temperature directly affects biotic processes and water requirements, thus organisms, species, and forest types respond to changes in temperature. Temperature, along with sunlight, is a driving force behind photosynthesis, and temperatures regulate the demand plants have for water. Forests depend on certain soil moisture levels for growth and respiration, and air temperature affects soil moisture through evaporation as well.

Temperature in Western North Carolina

The terrain of the Southern Appalachians creates a range of average temperatures in Western North Carolina. Average temperatures generally decrease with an increase in elevation. On any day, from mountain top to valley floor, the difference in temperature across the region may be as much as 20 °F.

The cold average temperatures in the highest elevations of the Southern Appalachians serve as refuges for several forest types, ecological communities, and many species. Changes to these temperatures will have devastating impacts to high-elevation forests types. Forest types, such as the spruce-fir and northern hardwoods, are currently at the limit of their suitable habitat range. The unique temperatures and acclimated forest types at high elevations (>5,500 feet) in Western North Carolina are isolated in the southeast—where the climate resembles that of southern Canada and the most northeastern United States.

Maximum temperature

Maximum temperatures decrease with increasing elevation. Average maximum temperatures also tend to be higher on south-facing slopes, due to sun exposure. Trees and forest types have specific maximum temperature tolerances, and the relatively low maximum temperatures in high-elevation areas account for the unique forest types and species. Maximum temperatures regulate important factors, such as soil moisture through evaporation. Forests depend on soil moisture levels for uptake and to establish fire regimes—drier soil moisture results in higher fire risk.

Minimum temperature

Minimum temperatures generally decrease with increasing elevation. But unlike average maximum temperatures, average minimum temperatures are not as closely related to aspect or cardinal direction. Minimum temperatures are important to forests because they limit biological activity of pests, such as invasive insects. Like maximum temperature, minimum temperature is important to natural disturbance regimes and overall health of the forest.

The mountainous terrain creates a range of temperatures to which forests are accustomed and also accounts for the great biodiversity of the region.

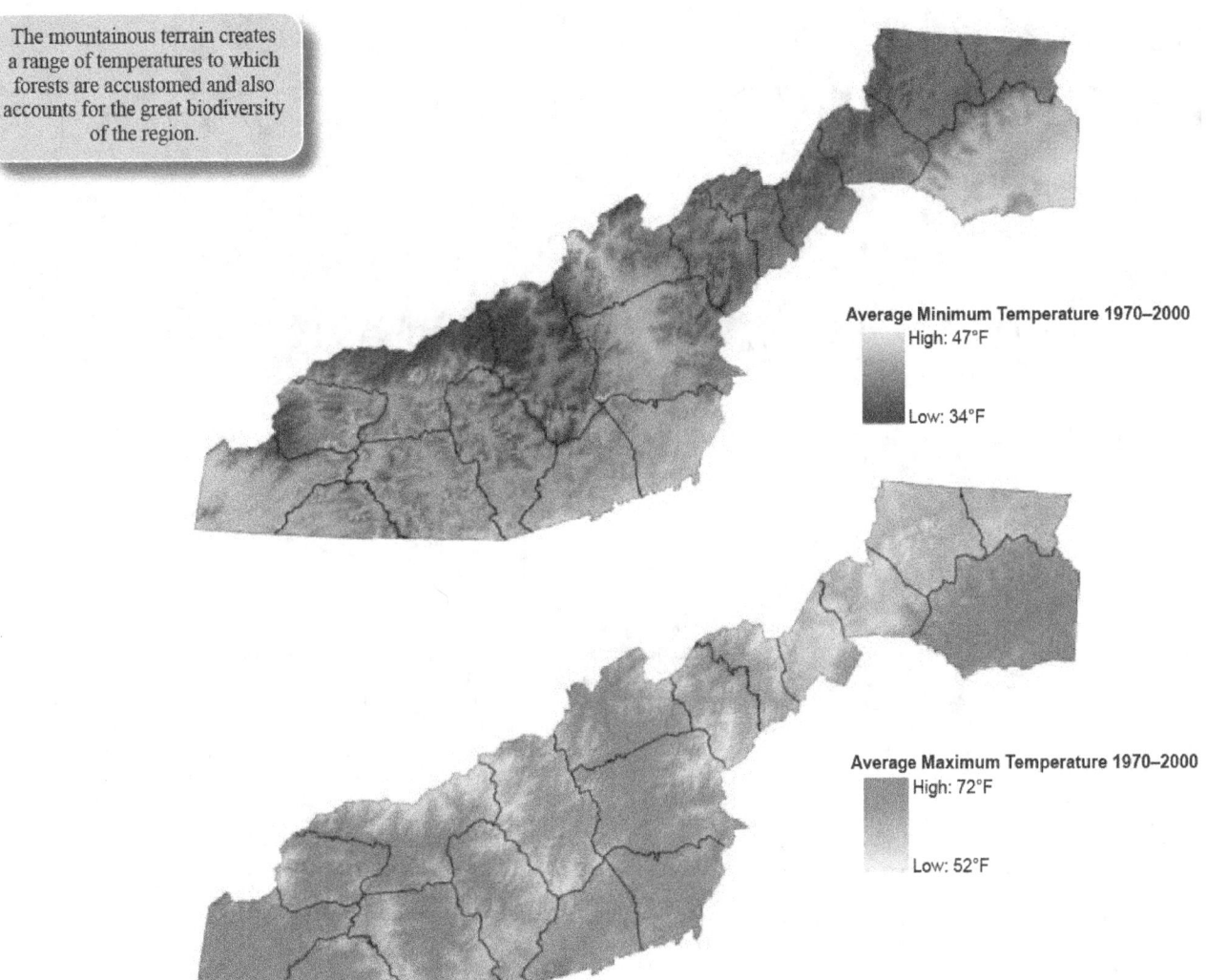

Average Minimum Temperature 1970–2000

High: 47°F

Low: 34°F

Average Maximum Temperature 1970–2000

High: 72°F

Low: 52°F

Historical Precipitation
Climate Change

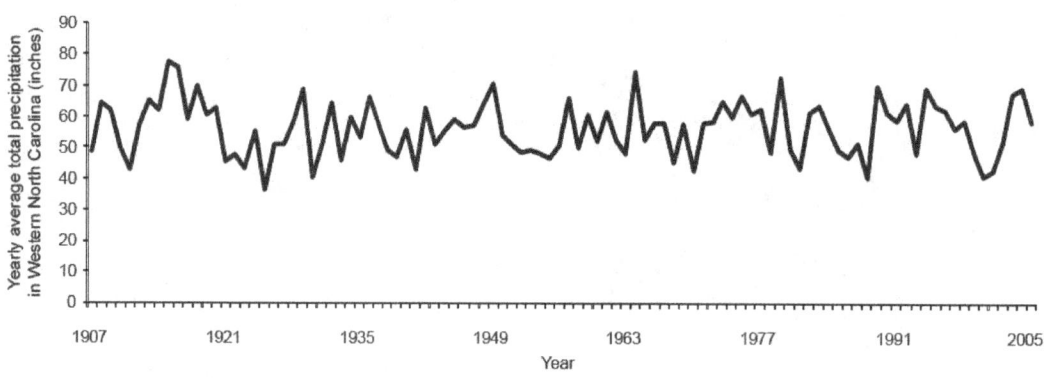

Why is precipitation important?

Precipitation is essential to ecosystem processes and to water supplies for municipalities. Precipitation is any form of water—rain, snow, or hail—that falls from the atmosphere and reaches the ground. Upon reaching the ground, precipitation enters the hydrologic cycle. This cycle involves water traveling from the land to the ocean, during which water molecules evaporate back into the atmosphere. A portion of precipitation soaks into the ground and moves downward through small openings in the soil and rock. This water that soaks into the ground becomes groundwater or is available to be taken up by vegetation; thus, the amount of precipitation is essential to forest growth. The water that does not soak into the ground runs off into the streams and rivers.

Precipitation in Western North Carolina

Western North Carolina has some of the most variable average precipitation in the Southeastern United States. In fact, the wettest and driest points in Western North Carolina are separated by only 45 miles. Elevation gradients of the mountains contribute to the differences in precipitation. Consider average rainfall in two towns, Highlands and Marshall. Highlands sits at the southern edge of the Blue Ridge Escarpment, so moist air lifted over the mountains drops heavy amounts of rain on this high-elevation town. Nearby areas are wet enough to be considered rain forests, and waterfalls abound. The town of Marshall, however, sits at the north end of the French Broad River basin. Shielded from the prevailing moist winds from the south and west by the Balsam and Smoky Mountains (where most of the rainfall is squeezed out), this area is the driest in the entire State of North Carolina.

Elevation gradients also contribute to the variable forms of precipitation the region receives. Lower elevations receive most precipitation as rainfall. On the other hand, the tallest mountain peaks receive up to 50 inches of snowfall each year. The range of precipitation zones create suitable conditions for the diversity of forest types and species found in the region.

Precipitation in Western North Carolina is highly variable due to the mountainous terrain— the wettest and driest points in Western North Carolina are separated by only 45 miles. Due to the different climate conditions, climate change will impact the region in different ways.

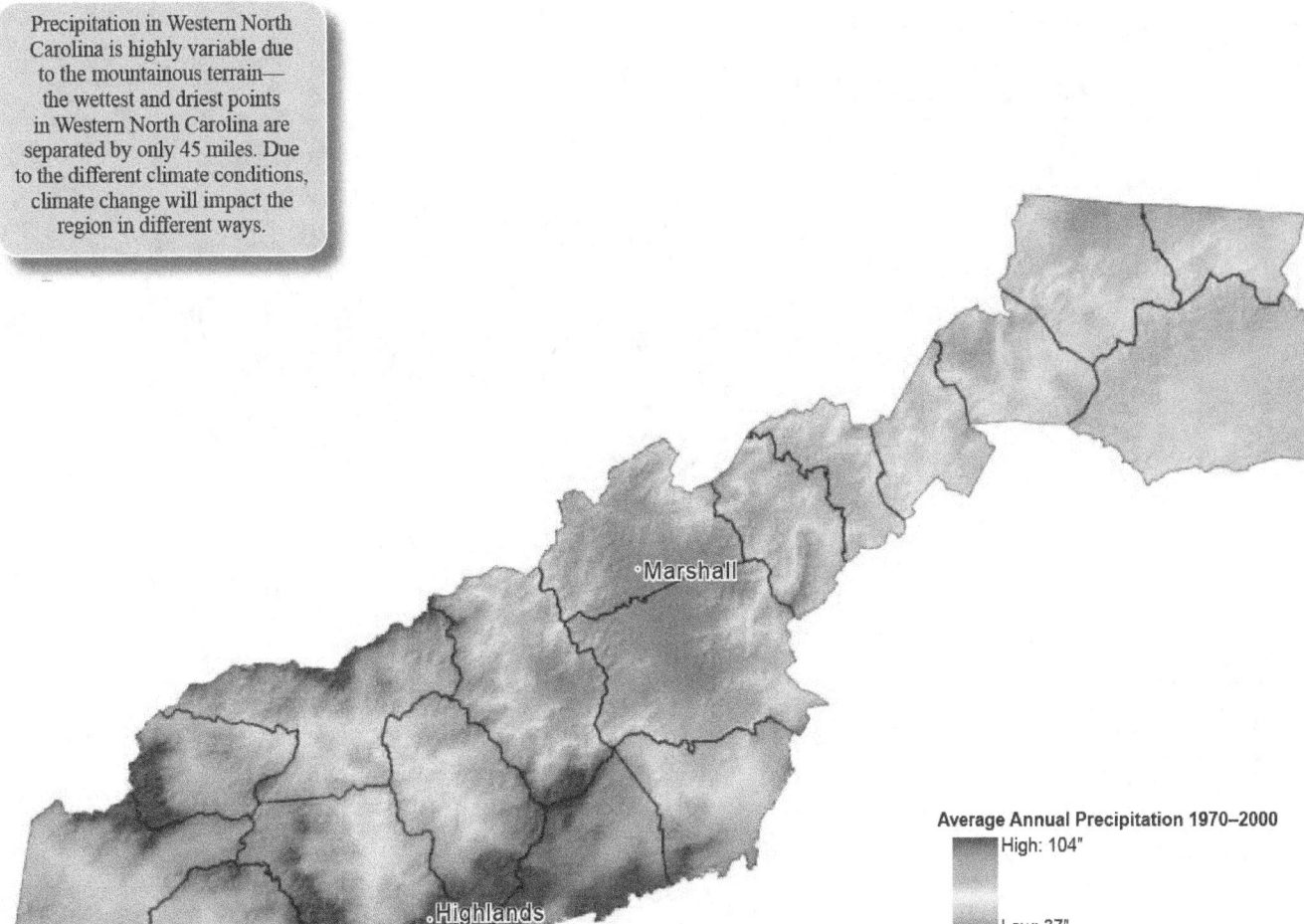

·Marshall

·Highlands

Average Annual Precipitation 1970–2000
High: 104"

Low: 37"

Average precipitation has remained constant over the past century.

Precipitation Patterns
Climate Change

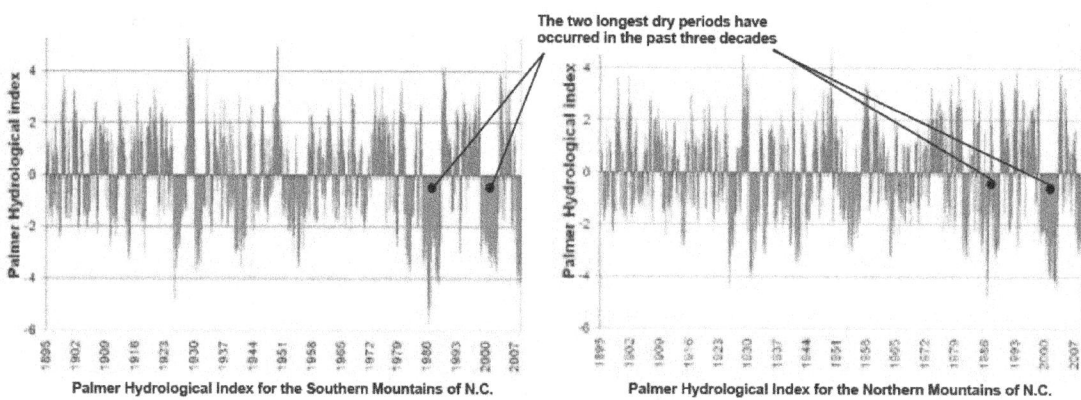

The two longest dry periods have occurred in the past three decades

Palmer Hydrological Index for the Southern Mountains of N.C.

Palmer Hydrological Index for the Northern Mountains of N.C.

Seasonal precipitation

The seasonal distribution or timing of precipitation is an important characteristic of climate. While average annual precipitation tells how much rainfall an area receives in a normal year, the seasonal distribution tells when it arrives. The timing of precipitation also indicates how often an area experiences drought and flooding. Both drought and flooding are natural occurrences in Western North Carolina, but changes in the frequency of these events have the potential to greatly impact water resources for forest ecosystems.

Western North Carolina receives most of its rainfall during the spring and summer months, while the fall and winter months are comparatively dry. This pattern in the distribution of rain throughout the year is essential to biological processes. Forests need more water in the

warmer growing season. Deciduous trees, especially, take up much more water in spring and summer when leaves are on the trees due to evapotranspiration (the process of water coming through the leaves of trees and then evaporating into the air). The timing of precipitation in Western North Carolina allows trees to leaf out in the spring and sustains the flow of water in streams.

Wet and dry periods

The Palmer Hydrological Drought Index (PHDI) is influenced by precipitation and shows long-term dry and wet conditions. The PHDI reflects how precipitation affects groundwater, water tables, and reservoirs. On the graphs above, the red indicates dry conditions while the green indicates wet conditions. Any green value above 2

indicates severe wet (flooding), while any red value below -2 indicates severe dry (drought). Uncharacteristically frequent or extended dry or wet periods indicate an interruption in the seasonal pattern of precipitation.

With climate change, there may not be any change in total precipitation, but there may be extended wet and dry periods that might result in more flooding or drought. The PHDI for Western North Carolina shows that the longest dry periods over the past century have occurred in the past three decades. While flooding and drought are natural disturbances in Western North Carolina, increased frequency or severity of these disturbances will negatively impact the forests.

Climate change alters the seasonal distribution of precipitation, changing the likelihood of droughts and floods.

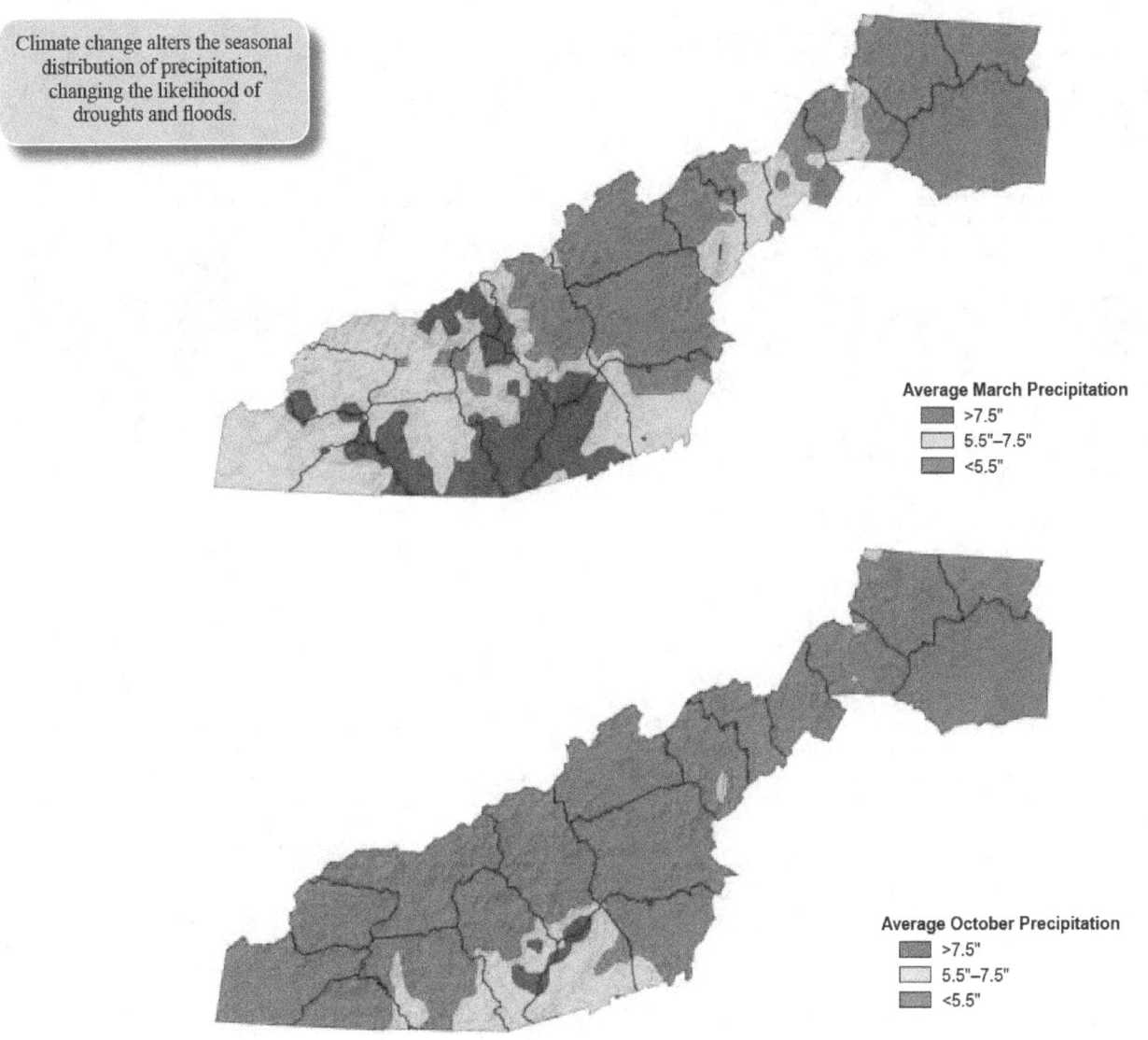

Average March Precipitation
- >7.5"
- 5.5"–7.5"
- <5.5"

Average October Precipitation
- >7.5"
- 5.5"–7.5"
- <5.5"

Climate Scenarios and Water Stress
Climate Change

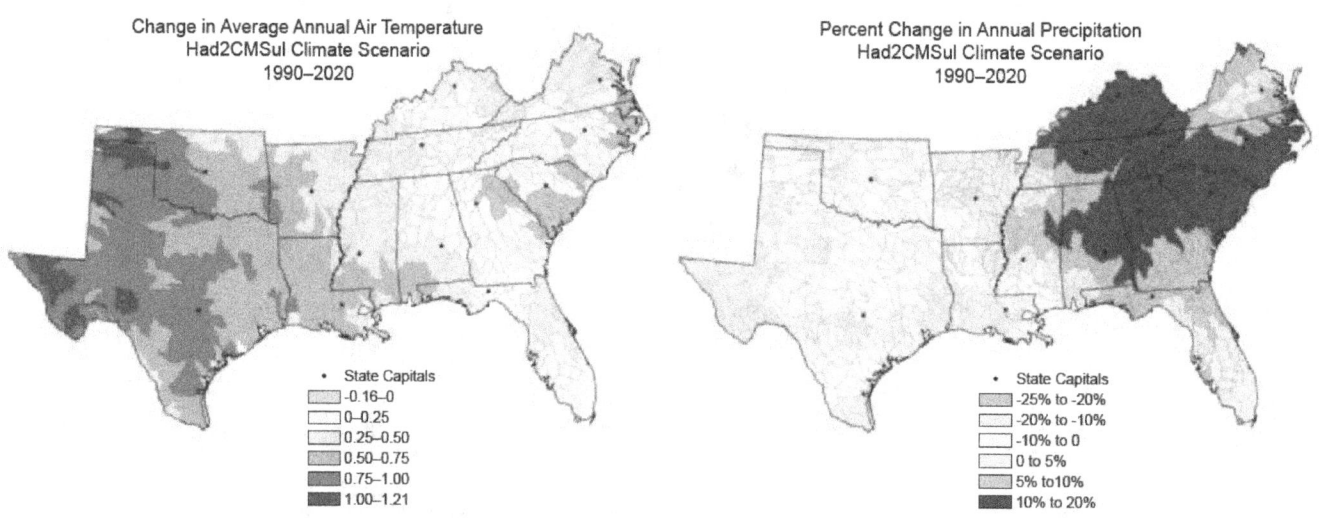

Change in Average Annual Air Temperature
Had2CMSul Climate Scenario
1990–2020

- State Capitals
  - -0.16–0
  - 0–0.25
  - 0.25–0.50
  - 0.50–0.75
  - 0.75–1.00
  - 1.00–1.21

Percent Change in Annual Precipitation
Had2CMSul Climate Scenario
1990–2020

- State Capitals
  - -25% to -20%
  - -20% to -10%
  - -10% to 0
  - 0 to 5%
  - 5% to10%
  - 10% to 20%

Climate models

Climate models are extremely important tools for simulating and understanding climate, and they can provide credible projections of future climate change. Climate model projections are not predictions, but rather scenarios of how the climate might change based on observed patterns. Multiple models are often used to illustrate a range of possibilities.

Every model has an inherent degree of uncertainty, because its projections provide only a general picture of what to expect. For a region such as Western North Carolina, changes in climate will be highly variable due to the range of microclimates; climate models do not necessarily account for the variability. This uncertainty

shows the importance of a regional approach to understanding the effects of changing conditions. With climate projections, uncertainty does not necessarily imply that change is unknown, but rather that future conditions involve variability.

The computer model developed by the Met Office Hadley Centre for Climate Change represents a "warm and wet" future scenario. In Western North Carolina, the Hadley model shows moderately warmer air temperature and increased average precipitation by 2020.

Hadley Model (Had2CMSul) and water stress

Water stress is defined by the availability of water. Water stress impacts forests primarily by its affect on

soil moisture. Soil moisture is important for biological processes and forest health, and soil moisture levels are determined both by temperature and precipitation. For Western North Carolina, soil moisture levels change due to the range of microclimates. The increases in precipitation for Western North Carolina with the Hadley model would generally increase soil moisture and, as a result, decrease water stress. However, while increasing precipitation alone would increase soil moisture, higher temperatures in some areas, resulting in greater evaporation, would offset the additional moisture. Some areas in Western North Carolina might experience more water stress conditions than others despite increased precipitation.

Continued...

Higher precipitation would decrease current water stress conditions, and fewer areas would be considered to have High stress.

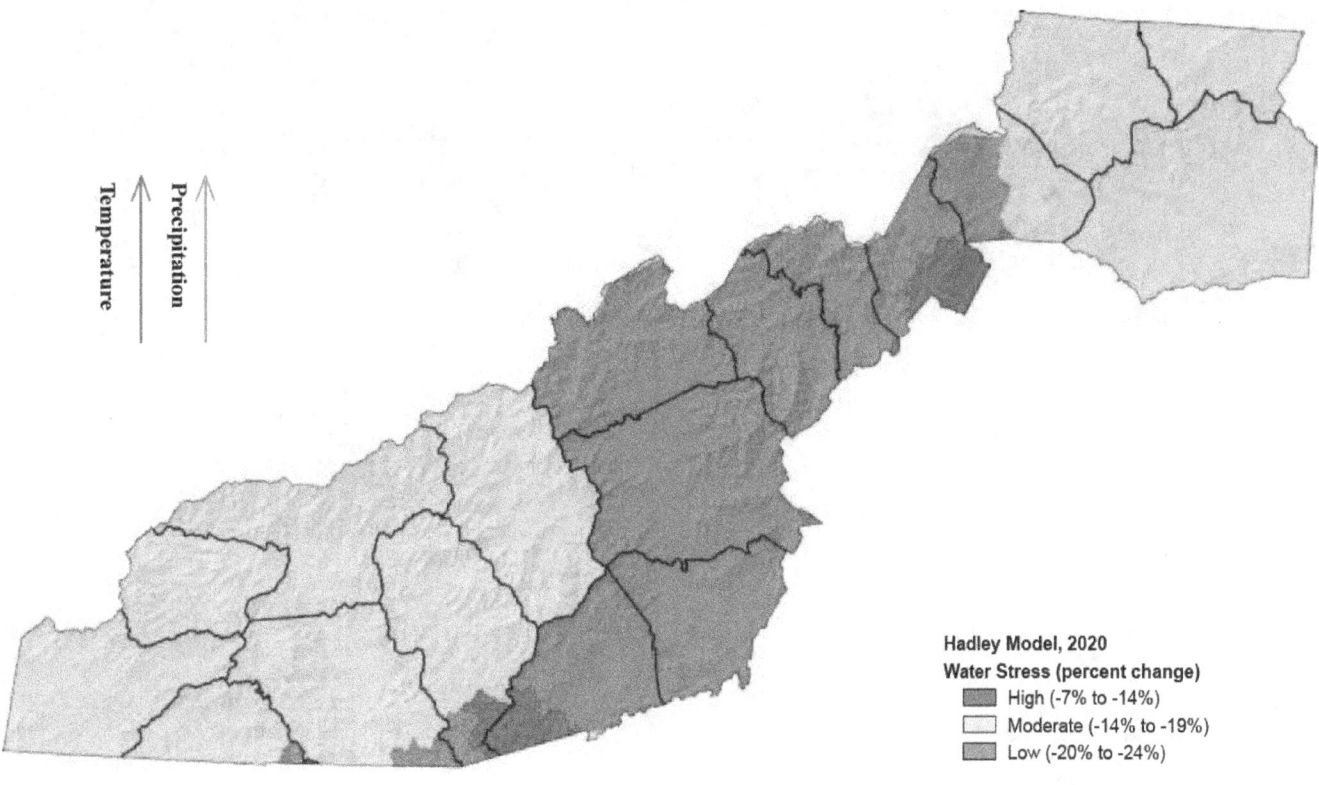

Temperature

Precipitation

Hadley Model, 2020
Water Stress (percent change)
- High (-7% to -14%)
- Moderate (-14% to -19%)
- Low (-20% to -24%)

Climate Scenarios and Water Stress
Climate Change

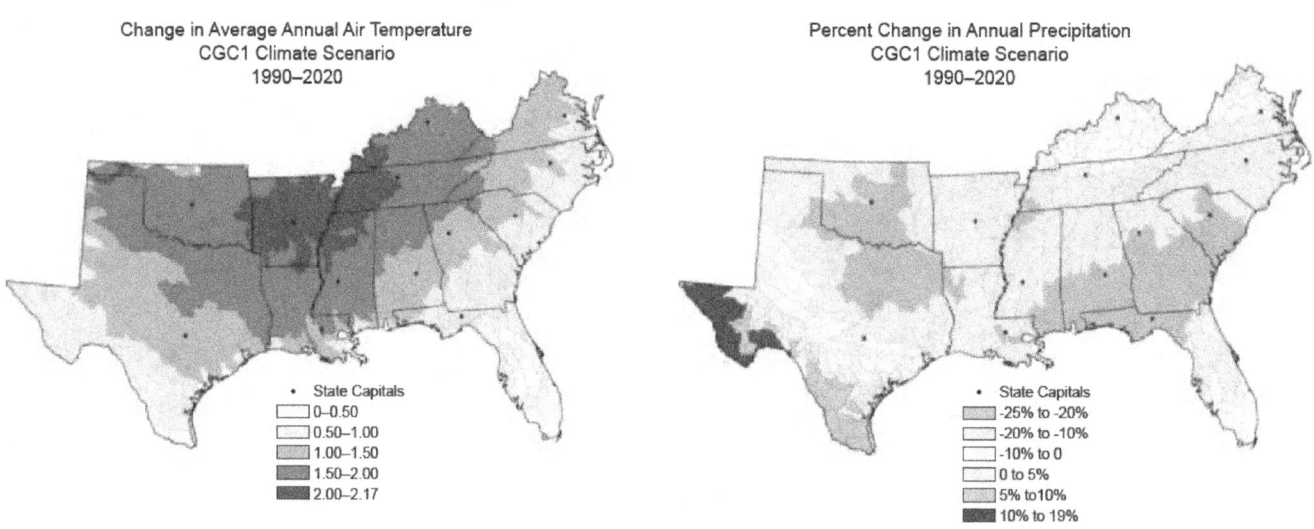

Change in Average Annual Air Temperature
CGC1 Climate Scenario
1990–2020

- State Capitals
  - 0–0.50
  - 0.50–1.00
  - 1.00–1.50
  - 1.50–2.00
  - 2.00–2.17

Percent Change in Annual Precipitation
CGC1 Climate Scenario
1990–2020

- State Capitals
  - -25% to -20%
  - -20% to -10%
  - -10% to 0
  - 0 to 5%
  - 5% to10%
  - 10% to 19%

The climate change model developed by the Canadian Centre for Climate Modelling and Analysis represents a "hot and dry" future scenario. For Western North Carolina, the Canadian model shows much higher average air temperature and decreased average precipitation.

Canadian Model (CGC1) and water stress
Water stress and soil moisture levels are determined by temperature and precipitation. Much of Western North Carolina would experience great declines in soil moisture. The Canadian model depicts increases in water stress and other effects, such as increased drought.

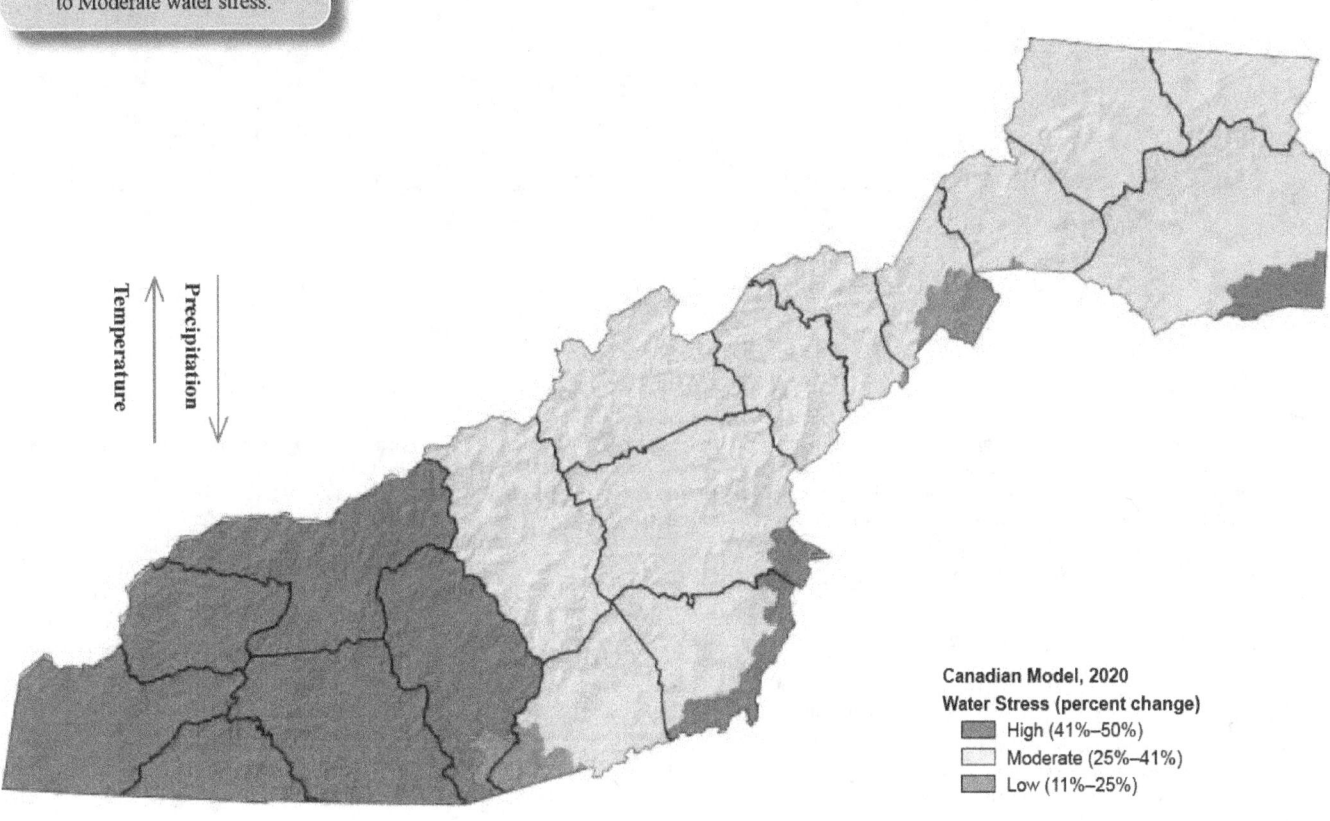

Increased temperature and decreased precipitation would increase water stress for the region. Most of Western North Carolina would experience High to Moderate water stress.

Precipitation

Temperature

Canadian Model, 2020
Water Stress (percent change)
High (41%–50%)
Moderate (25%–41%)
Low (11%–25%)

Impacts on Forest Sustainability
Climate Change

Because the forests of Western North Carolina may experience great change, how we use forest resources may also change. The ability to manage for disturbances affected by climate change varies greatly; therefore, strategies for coping with impacts from climate change in forests will vary regionally and by management area.

Integrating information about climate change and its potential impacts at a regional scale can help us answer the following questions about forest sustainability:

- How do forest disturbances interact with climate change?
- How should the forests be monitored to inform decisions?
- What information is needed to understand the response of a forest to changing conditions?
- What changes could forest managers make to reduce negative impacts of climate change?

Forests are acclimated to the climate zones in which they are found. Warming temperatures due to climate change will shift suitable conditions. With changing temperatures and precipitation, dominating forest types are likely to change. Warmer temperatures will shift suitable habitat for forests higher in elevation.

Drought
Decreased precipitation or increased temperature will lead to increased drought. Drought occurs in all forest types, and the general response of forests to drought is to reduce vegetation growth. Under severe drought, forests reduce vegetation growth and plants die. When drought occurs over multiple growing seasons, increased susceptibility to insects or pathogens is possible.

Fire
The frequency, size, and intensity of fires depend on climate as well as forest structure and composition. While fire is a natural occurrence in many forest types, increased frequency and severity of natural fires would greatly impact the forest. Decreased precipitation from climate change would increase fire risk in areas that become drier, and these changes could compound existing fire risks. While fire may be detrimental to some forest types, the vulnerability of the forest will depend on its resiliency and ability to adapt.

Insect infestations
Changes in temperature and precipitation also affect insect and pathogen survival, reproduction, and distribution. These changes can have a range of effects on forests and lead to increased tree mortality rates. The loss of certain tree species to disease or infestation can significantly reduce biodiversity and wildlife habitat.

Climatic Changes	Ecosystem Effects	Consequences for Forests
Warmer air temperatures	⬆ Water uptake from trees ⬇ Soil moisture	⬆ Drought ⬆ Invasive species ~ Forest species shifts
Lower average precipitation	⬆ Water stress ⬇ Stream flow ⬆ Susceptibility to pests and pathogens	⬆ Wildland fire ⬆ Tree mortality ⬇ Wildlife habitat ~ Forest species shifts
Higher average precipitation	⬇ Water stress ⬆ Flooding ⬆ Soil erosion	⬇ Water quality ~ Forest species shifts
Change in precipitation patterns	~ Water stress ~ Wet and dry periods	~ Water availability ~ Forest species shifts

Climatic changes, their effects on ecosystems, and consequences for forests.
⬆ = likely increase   ⬇ = likely decrease   ~ = likely change

Soil, Water, and Air
Conserving Our Natural Resources

Soil

The mountains of Western North Carolina today are only remnants of those formed long ago. Beginning about 500 million years ago, rifting and continental collision along what is now the East Coast of the United States created mountain ranges as high as the Rockies. Beginning 250 million years ago, these mountains eroded to almost nothing, and exceptionally warm temperatures led to the evolution and diversification of many new species. From 65 million years ago to present, the older mountain remnants re-formed and eroded to half of their original height, forming what we know as the Southern Appalachian Mountains.

Millions of years of geologic processes, weathering, and climate variability have resulted in a wide variety of soil types. Over the last two centuries, human-caused soil disturbance has increased considerably. During the early settlement period, subsistence farming on steep slopes, burning, and logging practices led to severe erosion and hydrologic changes across the landscape. Today, another more complex mix of practices threatens the soil resource.

Water

Nine river basins drain about 7,500 square miles in Western North Carolina. The New River, in the northeast corner of the region, is thought to be one of the oldest in the world. The largest basins in the region are the French Broad and the Little Tennessee, both of which flow north/northwest into Tennessee.

The region's river basins have some of the most outstanding and diverse aquatic systems within the State. However, the health of these systems is threatened by human actions such as pollution, impoundments, and poorly mitigated land management activities. Mussels, crayfish, snails, salamanders, and many species of freshwater fish, such as native brook trout, are at risk due to poor water quality and altered hydrology. The region has always had a bountiful supply of fresh water for residential, commercial, and industrial use; however, recent droughts have increased awareness of the need for water conservation.

Air

Beginning about 1860, fossil fuels became the primary energy source for the industrialization of the nation. Energy from coal and petroleum products greatly improved the quality of life for U.S. citizens, but combustion of these fuels led to large releases of air pollutants into the atmosphere. Consequently, there have been multiple impacts to the region, including a considerable reduction in how far and how well a person can observe scenic views (visibility impairment), as well as significant atmospheric and ground level deposition of acidic compounds in the region. Although improving, air pollution is still impacting the health of humans, wildlife, and vegetation, as well as water quality.

Soil Systems
Soil Resources

Soil formation

Soil is a critical support system for trees and other plants, and its variable properties play an integral role in all other biological systems. Soil is formed through processes that take thousands of years to complete.

Several factors have influenced the formation of the region's soil: topography, geology, climate, vegetation, elevation, and time. The parent material is predominantly crystalline rocks with varying degrees of mica content, and metasedimentary rocks. Precipitation levels across the region range widely from 40–80 inches annually. The interaction of these factors has led to unique and highly variable soil patterns and properties across the mountain region.

Soil types are further categorized by permeability, porosity, and texture. Permeability is how quickly water moves through soil and the ability of water to be held for plant use. Permeability is partially affected by porosity, which is the amount of empty space between soil particles. Soil texture (the proportion of sand, silt, and clay) is an important determinant of drainage, water-holding capacity, aeration, susceptibility to erosion, organic matter content, and buffering capacity.

Three major soil systems are found in Western North Carolina; their differing properties relate primarily to elevation change. A fourth type, the felsic crystalline system, is found here but to a much lesser extent. This latter system is similar to soils found in the Piedmont region.

Broad basins, river terraces, and floodplain system

This system is characterized by wide valleys and rounded, low hills with few steep slopes. Easy access, a temperate climate, and pleasant landscapes make these areas desirable for development and have historically been the region's urban, industrial, and agricultural centers. This is the youngest of the three systems.

Although prone to flooding in the river basins, these soils are ideal for agriculture, as higher elevation soils have shifted downward over time, increasing soil productivity. These soil profiles have relatively higher temperatures that enable microbes to break down organic material, thereby increasing nutrient supply and water-holding capacity while improving soil structure and preventing erosion.

Low and intermediate mountain system

Found between 1,400–4,600 feet above sea level, these soils are influenced by elevation, aspect, exposure, and forest cover. Typically taking hundreds of thousands of years to form, the predominant features include steep slopes and ridges, as well as steep, narrow, wet valleys. These are the most common soils below 3,000 feet and have well-developed profiles. They are acidic and highly weathered, and often colored red, orange, and yellow.

High mountain system

High mountain systems are generally found above 4,600 feet and have unique characteristics. Their formation is limited by frigid soil temperatures, resulting in less developed soil profiles with minimal microbial activity. Vegetative cover includes spruce-fir stands as well as heath and grassy balds.

Unique soil types
High-elevation frigid soils

High-elevation frigid soils are unique to the region. They are characterized by organic rich soils and cool, moist microclimates. Low temperatures significantly reduce the rate of decomposition and increase the amount of leaves and decaying vegetation. The difficult terrain and rocky soils limit their use for agriculture. Found at the highest peaks, these soils are forested and provide timber, wildlife habitat, and watershed protection. The forests on these sites contain northern hardwoods and conifers, resembling cool, moist, temperate forests of the Northeastern United States.

Southern Appalachian fens and bogs

Fens are high mountain wetlands that differ significantly from most soils found in the region. Fens are the result of groundwater seepage to the surface. High levels of calcium as well as other minerals are found in these soils, making it possible for only select vegetation to thrive.

Mountain bogs are generally wet and soggy. Groundwater seepage, rain, and snow are the sources of water that feed the bogs. Their primary location is valleys and gentle slopes. Predominant vegetation includes rhododendron thickets as well as mixed stands of red maple, eastern hemlock, and eastern white pine. Overgrazing has occurred in nearly all of the bogs. In addition, nonnative invasive species and flooding by beavers threaten their existence.

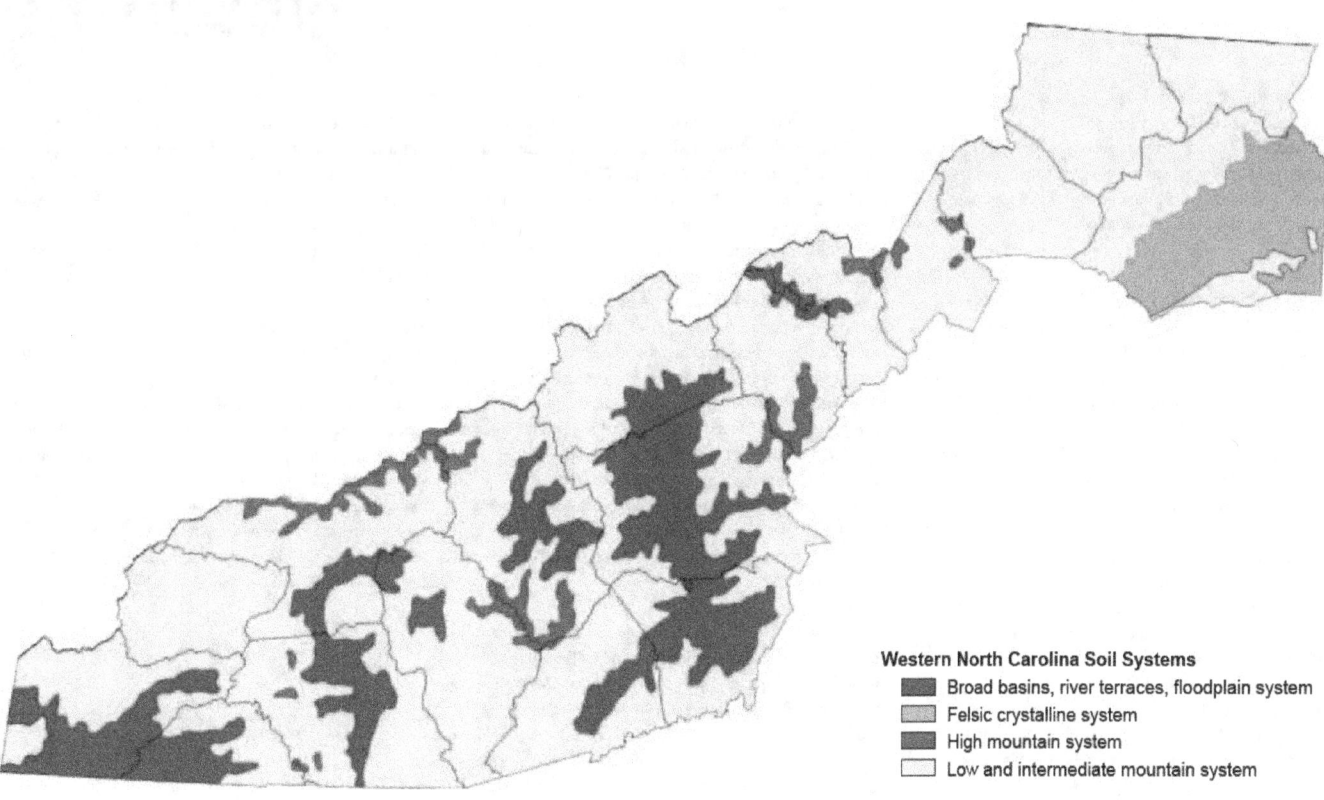

Mountain bogs in Western North Carolina are threatened by nonnative invasive species and flooding by beavers.

Western North Carolina Soil Systems

- Broad basins, river terraces, floodplain system
- Felsic crystalline system
- High mountain system
- Low and intermediate mountain system

Erosion and Sedimentation
Soil Loss and Degradation

Causes and effects of soil loss

Soil loss is caused by a variety of factors, including erosion from wind and water, mechanical tilling, logging, agricultural practices, and poor water management. Erosion and sedimentation, the major effects of soil loss, are widespread and can be devastating.

Erosion

Erosion is a natural process on hill slopes. The rate of erosion is determined by several factors, including soil type, rainfall, and length and percent of slope. Generally, human-induced changes in the landscape lead to higher levels of erosion than would occur naturally. While there are many ways to minimize erosion, vegetative cover is the most effective over the long term. When vegetation is removed, the rate of soil erosion is greatly accelerated, often beyond sustainable levels.

Sedimentation

Eroded soil deposited downslope is referred to as sedimentation. When severe rain or wind events occur or soils are disturbed by human activities, soils are moved off site and deposited on land and in lakes, wetlands, and streams. Sediment, the single largest nonpoint source pollutant, contributes to the decline of surface water quality, imperils aquatic wildlife, and leads to increased stream bank erosion and flooding. Levels of sedimentation increase due to roads, residential and commercial development, agricultural practices, timber harvesting, and any other land-disturbing activity.

The Sedimentation Control Act of 1973 requires operators to implement short- and long-term mitigation measures to reduce erosion on- and off-site. Forest landowners who wish to harvest trees are exempt from these regulations if they comply with forestry practice guidelines, which include erosion control measures and mitigation. Best management practices (BMP's) are voluntary practices that reduce sources of sedimentation and runoff, confine sediment on site, and trap the movement of sediment so that it settles. Although these practices are not required by law, it is estimated that about 85–90 percent of landowners and loggers voluntarily comply with BMP's and regulations. If loggers/landowners are found to be out of compliance, the North Carolina Division of Forest Resources (NCDFR) works with operators to correct problems. If not resolved, the operator may forfeit their exemption under the Sedimentation Control Act and must seek a permit to continue the activity.

Forest road erosion

Forest road erosion and eventual sediment delivery to nearby streams largely depends on soils, climate, traffic intensity, and topography. Erosion rates from forested roads range from about 0.5 to 100 tons per acre per year, while the geologic or natural erosion rate is estimated at 0.1 tons per acre per year. A sustainable range of erosion from disturbance is estimated at 0.4 to 2.0 tons per acre per year. Sediment control can be significantly improved through appropriate road location, drainage systems, and reestablishment of vegetation. These practices effectively trap eroded road sediments and isolate or essentially disconnect roads from stream systems.

In the Southern Appalachians, cut slopes (as opposed to fill slopes) and road beds have been found to account for as much as 75–80 percent of soil loss from the road area, the majority of which occurs during the establishment period for vegetation. These rates decrease significantly, however, following complete reestablishment of vegetative cover.

Steep slopes and development

Because building construction was easier and less costly and crop cultivation better in the fertile valleys, human development historically was limited to broad basins, terraces, and floodplains. However, as land became scarcer in the valleys and the demand for uninterrupted mountain views increased, residents slowly began building uphill toward the intermediate and even high mountains. This preference has led to development on steep slopes with few regulations in place to protect those located downslope from soil erosion and landslides.

Case Camp Ridge forest road, a stable road site.

Home destroyed when an upslope embankment failed, contributing to a debris flow, January 7, 2009, in Maggie Valley, NC.

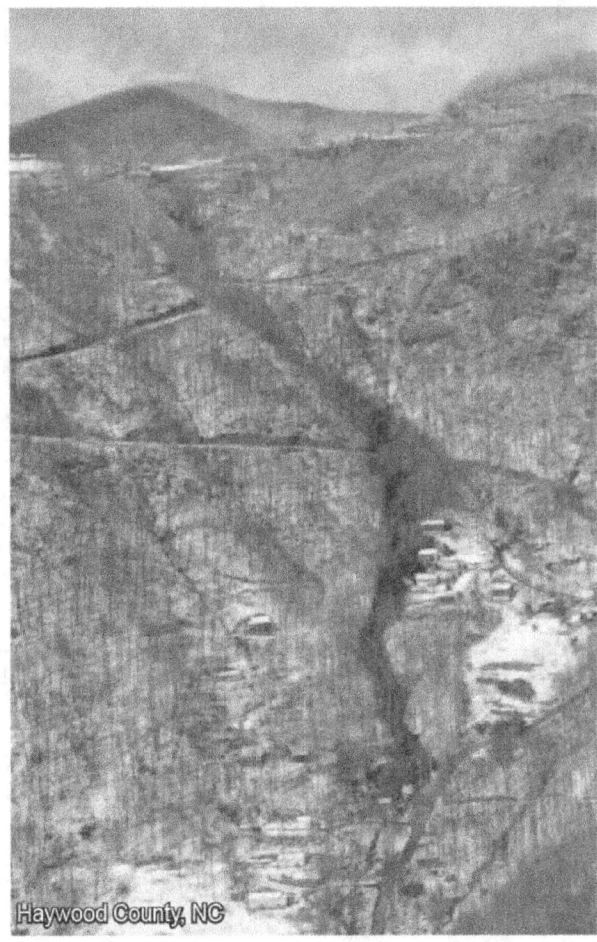

On February 5, 2010, a retaining wall in Haywood County failed, sending 27,500 cubic yards of soil, rocks, and large woody debris along a 3,000-foot path to the stream valley below. Three homes were damaged. Stabilization of remaining unstable retaining walls will cost $1.4 million to reinforce.

Soil Subsidence and Landslides
Soil Loss and Degradation

A damaging landslide occurs nearly every year in the region. As of April 2010, over 6,000 landslides and landslide deposits have occurred in Western North Carolina.

Soil subsidence and landslides

Causes and triggers of soil and debris slides are omnipresent in the region. Causes are those conditions leading to instability of slope, while triggers are those events that initiate slope movement. Slides are influenced by geology, geomorphology, weather, climate, and slope. Mountainside disturbances can result in embankments or slope angles that are too steep or too high and, therefore, inherently unstable. The most common trigger of slides in the region is frequent or high-intensity storms. Other triggers include repeated freezing and thawing of the soil, blasting, and earthquakes. Landslides present an ever present danger in the region. Their likelihood is increased by weather events, vegetation removal, and poorly designed access.

Regional soils prone to landslides are those high in mica (>30 percent), especially when used in embankments, as mica is difficult to compact. Most debris flows, however, initiate in soil types made up predominantly of silt and sand, often with gravel to cobble-sized stones. An increase in water content increases the pore-water pressure, which causes a decrease in shear strength. Hence, these soils are more prone to move downhill, especially after large rain events. When a landslide occurs, debris is moved downhill quickly, and includes anything generally larger than coarse sand, often destroying whatever is in its way and moving those materials downhill with it.

Sulfidic rock is common in the region, particularly in certain formations, generally owing to high pyrite content. Unless properly mitigated, excavation of this rock can lead to acidic runoff leading to stream degradation. Furthermore, untreated acidic bedrock used in embankments can become unstable and result in landslides.

A damaging landslide occurs nearly every year in the region. Since 1916, eight major storm events have triggered numerous landslides across Western North Carolina. In 1985, a major rockfall crushed a tunnel portal. In 2009, a bedrock landslide, the most destructive in more than a decade, closed Interstate 40 in Haywood County for over 6 months, with a repair cost of $12.9 million. Soil movement, a downhill slide of soil only, can be equally destructive. In 2004, intense rain events from hurricanes Frances and Ivan led to at least 400 slides, causing five deaths, wiping out 27 houses, and disrupting transportation throughout the region.

As of April 2010, over 6,000 landslides and landslide deposits have occurred in Western North Carolina. In Buncombe County alone, geologists found evidence of over 1,253 landslide features, 314 landslides, and 938 landslide deposits. Over half of these occurred where slopes had been modified by people.

Currently, a seller is not required to tell a potential purchaser if the property under consideration may be in the path of a potential landslide. Legislation is being considered in the North Carolina State legislature that would limit steep slope development. The proposed legislation requires a licensed general contractor to supervise construction on any activity occurring on slopes greater than 22 degrees. It would also require retaining walls over 8 feet in height be prepared by an engineer.

Conservation and mitigation of soil resources

Techniques that prevent or reduce soil loss include surface water runoff control, vegetative cover, sedimentation catch basins, and buffer zones. Practices that reduce the speed of runoff will reduce erosion significantly and can be used in forestry, agriculture, and construction operations. Plant cover significantly reduces erosion because root systems securely hold soil in place. Buffer zones—designated areas of trees, shrubs, and herbaceous vegetation—act as filters to keep sediment from water bodies.

To minimize landslides and soil movement, it is imperative that slope modifications stay within stable limits. Controlling drainage and reducing the slope angle reduces landslide potential. Drains can be constructed to contain runoff and prevent infiltration. Steep slopes can be graded into gentler slopes, and a series of "stair-steps" can be created on very steep slopes. Many engineering techniques are available to prevent water entry and inhibit slope failure. Wire cables and wire fences minimize the danger of rockfall. Correction of some landslides can be accomplished by installing a drainage system, which reduces water pressure in the slope, thereby preventing further movement.

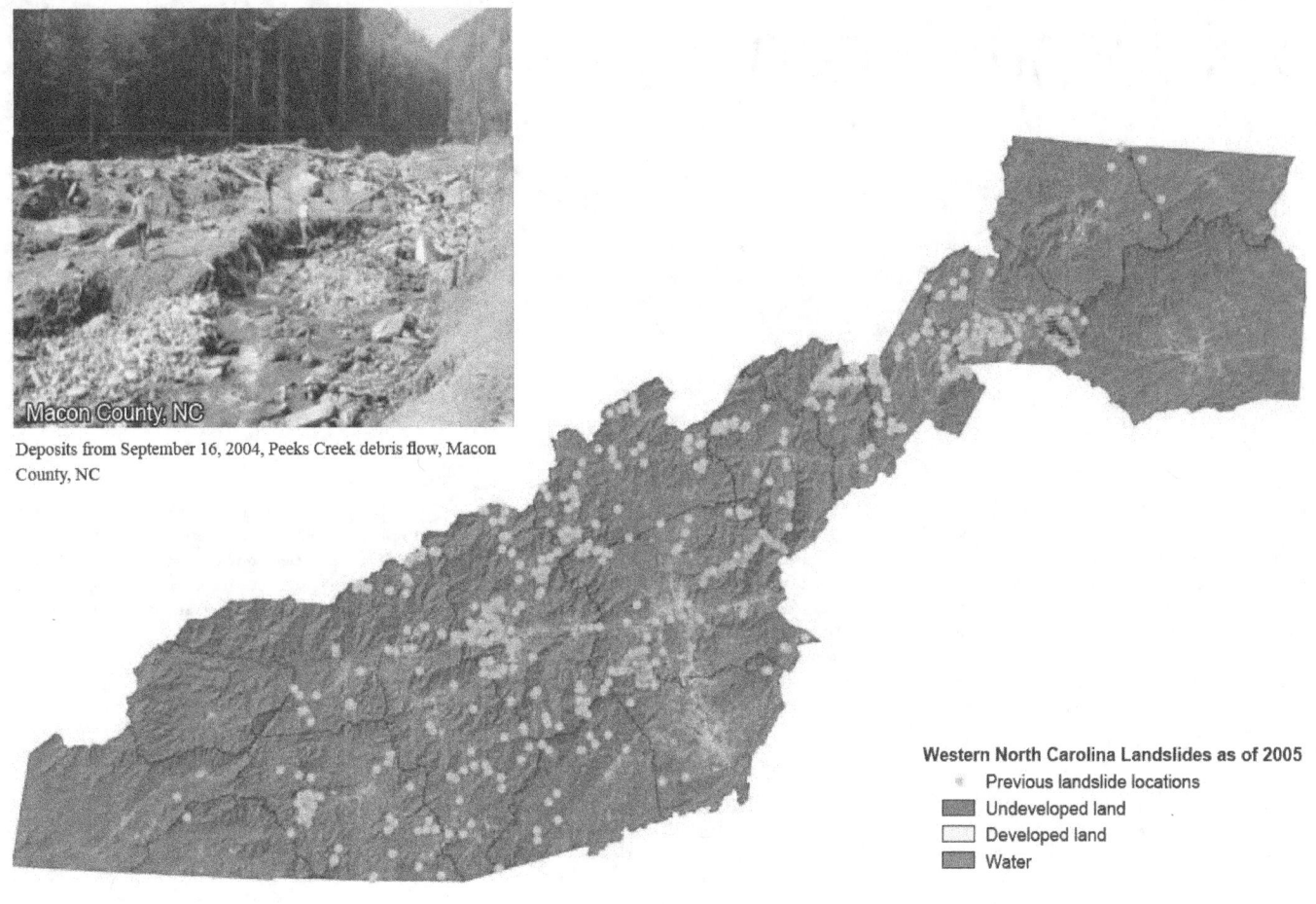

Deposits from September 16, 2004, Peeks Creek debris flow, Macon
County, NC

Western North Carolina Landslides as of 2005
* Previous landslide locations
Undeveloped land
Developed land
Water

Acidic Deposition
Soil Degradation

Human-caused acidic deposition of sulfates from the atmosphere have had a negative impact on sensitive soils in the region.

Acidic deposition

Human-caused acidic deposition of sulfates from the atmosphere have had a negative impact on sensitive soils in the region. Several factors interact to increase this effect. Forests soils associated with pines, spruce, and fir are naturally more acidic than areas dominated by hardwoods such as oak, hickory, maple, or poplar. Elevation is also an important factor when assessing the risk of acidification, as some soils, especially high mountain systems, are more sensitive to acidic deposition due to increased deposition levels, decreased soil depth, and decreased microbial activity.

Bedrock geology, however, has the greatest influence on soil sensitivity to acidic deposition. In Western North Carolina, soils that develop from bedrock classified as siliceous are more sensitive to acidification than soils that have developed from carbonate rocks.

Under natural conditions, soil acidity remains relatively stable, with the ability to balance normal increases in acidity by weathering rocks or deposition of dust from the atmosphere. This balance is essential to maintaining healthy terrestrial and aquatic ecosystems.

However, with increased deposition of sulfur, sensitive soils become too acidic, releasing biologically toxic levels of aluminum. Aluminum penetrates the fine roots of vegetation and exacerbates nutrient (especially calcium) deficiencies. At high enough concentrations, aluminum can kill roots, reducing the amount of area from which nutrients and water can be absorbed into the vegetation. Consequently, tree and plant mortality may increase during periods of drought.

High soil acidity and toxic levels of aluminum have been recorded at Shining Rock Wilderness Area, where the soil is at near maximum capacity to retain future deposition of sulfates. Therefore, any reduction in sulfur dioxide emissions will have a delayed benefit in improving ecosystem health because it will take a long time for the accumulated sulfur to be removed from the soils. In addition, aluminum can be transported from the soil to streams, where high acidity and high concentrations of aluminum can be lethal to sensitive aquatic organisms.

The addition of nitrogen from air pollution is believed to be utilized biologically by forest organisms (with the exception of high elevation old growth spruce-fir forests), since nitrogen is typically a nutrient in short supply and is not currently believed to be negatively impacting the region's forests.

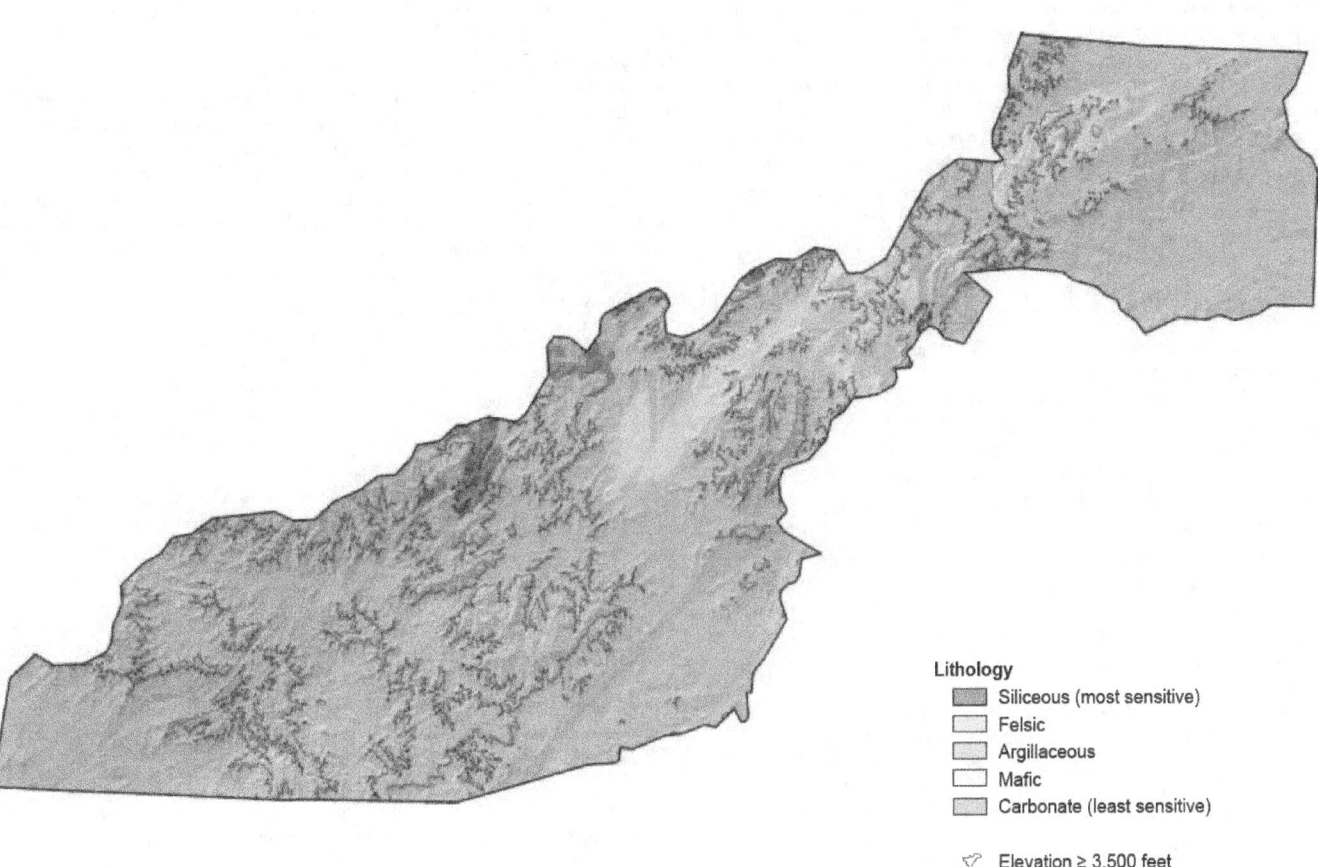

Lithology

■ Siliceous (most sensitive)
□ Felsic
▨ Argillaceous
□ Mafic
▨ Carbonate (least sensitive)

▽ Elevation ≥ 3,500 feet

Western North Carolina River Basins
Water Resources

River basins in Western North Carolina

A river basin catches all the water flowing downhill into streams and creeks and, eventually, sends it out to sea. In Western North Carolina, there are nine basins split by the Eastern Continental Divide, five draining to the Gulf of Mexico (New, Watauga, French Broad, Little Tennessee, and Hiwassee) and four draining to the Atlantic Ocean (Yadkin, Catawba, Broad, and Savannah). These basins contain the headwaters of streams and rivers that provide a critical supply of fresh water to towns and cities in and outside of the region.

Hiwassee River Basin

The Hiwassee River basin drains 641 square miles in Clay and Cherokee Counties. The Hiwassee is located in the homeland of the Cherokee, flowing generally to the northeast into the Tennessee River. The basin is about 70 percent forested, 23 percent agriculture, 3 percent urban, and is predominantly in private ownership. Its two major tributaries, the Nottely and Valley Rivers, feed scenic, man-made lakes including the Apalachia, the Hiwassee, and the Chatuge.

Little Tennessee River Basin

The Little Tennessee River basin encompasses about 1,800 square miles in Swain, Macon, Clay, Graham, Jackson, and Cherokee Counties. More than half of the land within the basin is federally owned; much of it located in the Nantahala National Forest (including the Joyce Kilmer-Slickrock Wilderness) and the Great Smoky Mountains National Park. The basin also drains portions of the Cherokee reservation. The Little Tennessee River basin has one of the most outstanding and diverse aquatic communities within the entire State.

Savannah River Basin

Only two percent of the Savannah River basin is located in Western North Carolina, draining 172 square

miles in Macon, Jackson, Transylvania, and Clay Counties. Much of the basin is in public ownership, including portions of the Nantahala National Forest and the North Carolina Gorges State Park. With no impaired waters in the basin, the Savannah exhibits excellent water quality, with the exception of a few small headwater streams impacted by developmental runoff.

French Broad River Basin

The French Broad River basin drains 2,830 square miles in North Carolina, going from the high mountains through the broad, flat Asheville basin. The basin includes land in Haywood, Madison, Buncombe, Transylvania, Henderson, Yancey, Mitchell, and Avery Counties. The basin is subdivided into three sub-basins—the French Broad River, the Nolichucky River, and the Pigeon River —none of which merge in North Carolina. Approximately 50 percent of the basin is forested, with extensive portions found in the Pisgah and Cherokee National Forests. Agriculture covers 17 percent of the basin, and 10 percent is considered urban.

The French Broad River headwaters start in the mountains of Transylvania County and flow north to Tennessee. The Pigeon River parallels Interstate 40 north of Canton, NC, and also flows into Tennessee. The Nolichucky River is formed by the convergence of the North Toe River and the Cane River north of Burnsville, NC. This sub-basin drains the western slope of the Blue Ridge Mountains north from Mount Mitchell to the Tennessee State line. The Nolichucky and Pigeon Rivers merge with the French Broad in Douglas Lake, east of Knoxville, TN.

Broad River Basin

The Broad River Basin is located mostly in South Carolina. The 150 square miles of the Broad River basin located in North Carolina contain the headwaters of the basin. Many small forest streams in Henderson, Buncombe, and

McDowell Counties combine to form the Green and Broad Rivers.

Catawba River Basin

The Catawba River basin begins on the eastern ridge of the Blue Ridge Mountains and quickly moves off the escarpment into the Piedmont. The basin drains 3,343 square miles of land, but 93 square miles of it is in Western North Carolina. The Catawba River originates in the forested streams found between Blowing Rock and Old Fort. Flow from the Linville River merges with the Catawba in Lake James, in McDowell County.

Watauga River Basin

The headwaters of the Watauga River basin are located in the mountains of Watauga and Avery Counties. Predominantly forest land, the Elk and Watauga Rivers drain 205 square miles in North Carolina and flows northwest into Watauga Lake in Carter County, TN.

New River Basin

Stretching through Ashe, Alleghany, and Watauga Counties, the New River Basin drains 753 square miles in Western North Carolina. With a rural mountainous landscape, half of the basin's land usage is forested, 33 percent pasture, and 6 percent urban. In 1976, the New was dedicated as a National Scenic River. Most development occurs in the valleys, though in recent years rates of steep slope development are rising. With an estimated age of 300 million years, the New River is thought to be one of the oldest rivers in the world, and hosts rare mountain bog habitats that require ample soil moisture to exist.

Yadkin River Basin

Only the forested headwaters of the Yadkin River are located in Western North Carolina, with 838 square miles predominantly in Wilkes County. The vast majority of the basin is located in the Piedmont. Three of North Carolina's major cities depend on this basin for water supply.

Area of river basins, portion in Western North Carolina

River basins	Square miles
French Broad	2,830
Little Tennessee	1,797
Yadkin	838
New	753
Hiwassee	641
Watauga	205
Savannah	172
Broad	150
Catawba	93

In Western North Carolina, there are nine basins split by the Eastern Continental Divide, five draining to the Gulf of Mexico and four draining to the Atlantic Ocean.

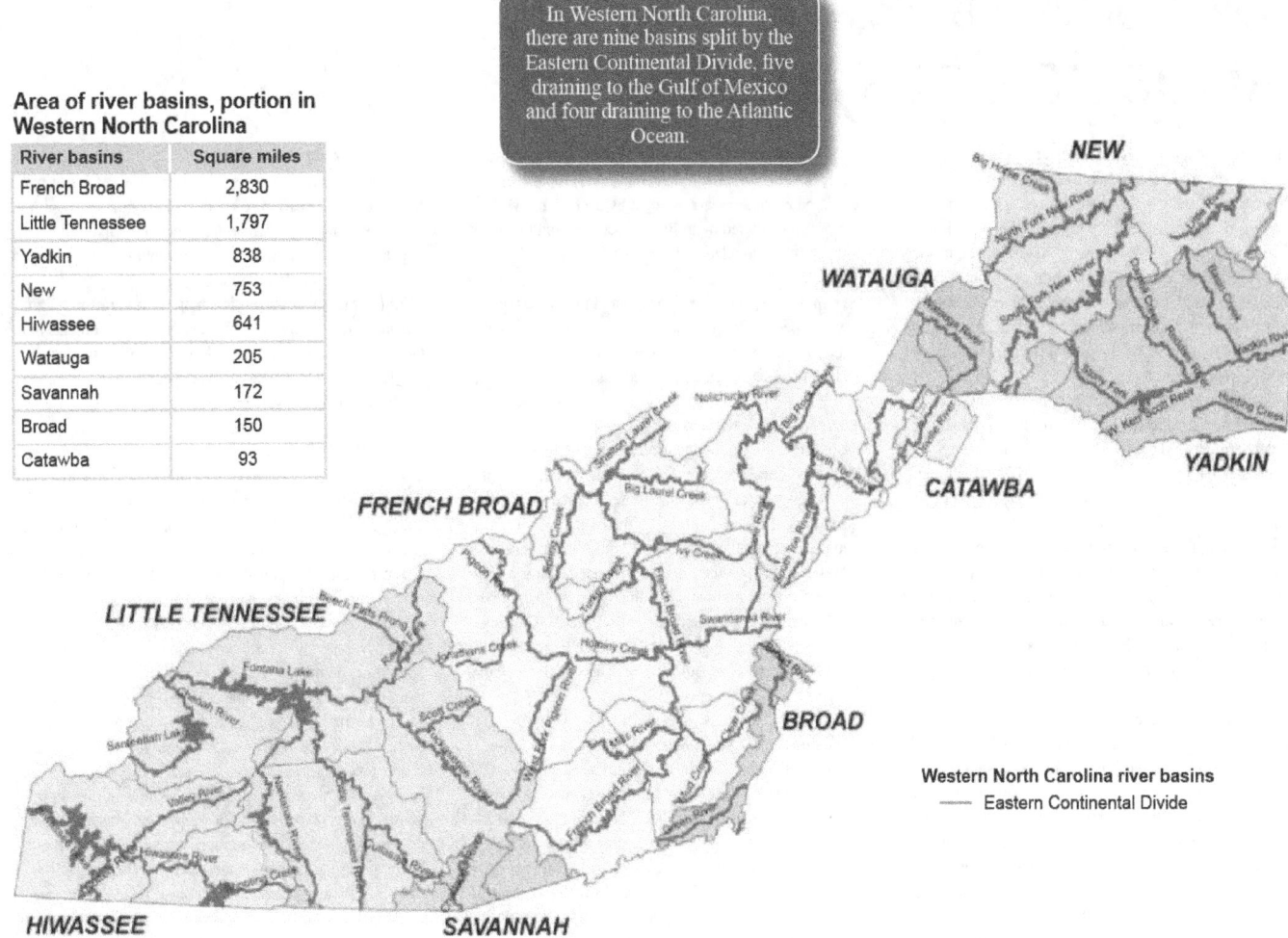

Western North Carolina river basins
—— Eastern Continental Divide

Health of River Basins
Aquatic Ecosystems

The health of aquatic ecosystems in the region can be adversely impacted by habitat destruction due to development, point and nonpoint source pollution, hydrologic alteration, and poorly managed agriculture and forest lands. Though water quality has improved in the past few decades, habitat degradation continues to threaten the overall health of these unique aquatic ecosystems. Other threats include impoundments on major rivers and tributaries that block fish migration patterns and cause habitat fragmentation.

Fortunately, increasing attention is being focused on analyzing aquatic systems, identifying the causes of endangerment, and applying conservation strategies. From national groups such as the World Wildlife Fund and the Nature Conservancy to more locally based organizations like the North Carolina Wildlife Resources Commission, there is research being conducted with the goal of preserving these valuable aquatic ecosystems. The following evaluations of the river basins in Western North Carolina are a brief summary of the threats identified in the North Carolina Wildlife Resources Commission Action Plan for Aquatic Habitat Conservation.

Hiwassee River Basin
The Hiwassee River basin is relatively stable with good water quality. It is impacted from nonpoint sources, primarily erosion, which increase as streams flow into the more developed valleys and merge into larger water areas. Erosion and sedimentation are primarily from ground disturbance from development activities (residential, commercial, transportation, and utility) and agriculture (erosion from poorly managed pastures and row crops). Timber harvest with insufficient erosion controls may be another contributor of sediment to the basin, along with other nonpoint source pollutants, such as runoff from built-up areas and roadways. Pointsource discharges are not a current major pollutant of the Hiwassee River basin.

Hydropower development has altered and degraded many habitats for most indigenous aquatic species. Un-impounded areas are affected by decreasing water temperature, altered hydrologic processes, and low levels of oxygen due to releases from the Chatuge and Nottely Dams.

Invasive species are also potential threats to the native aquatic species living in the basin. The blueback herring appears to have an impact on game species in the area, as well as the Asian clam and striped bass.

Little Tennessee River Basin
Major problems affecting species and habitats within the Little Tennessee River basin include impoundment and excessive erosion and stream sedimentation from development and agriculture. Of the entire 144-mile Little Tennessee River, there are only 47 miles in Georgia and North Carolina that remain un-impounded. Portions of the basin are currently at good quality levels, but it does have some impaired waterways, including the Cullasaja River, Mill Creek, upper Little Tennessee River, Beech Flats Prong, and West Buffalo Creek arm of Santeetlah Reservoir.

Invasive, nonnative species like the yellowfin shiner, which is expanding downstream from Franklin, are a potential problem to the basin. The Asian clam is established in both the Little Tennessee and Tuckasegee Rivers, Chinese snails have been found in Cowee Creek, and the rusty crayfish is established in at least one area downstream from Fontana Reservoir. The native spotfin chub was recently found to be infested with a tapeworm from Asia. Exotic pathogens and parasites pose serious threats to the rare species inhabiting the Little Tennessee River basin.

Savannah River Basin
National forest and State park lands occupy the majority of the Savannah River basin, but development is increasing on private lands. Land clearing, removal of riparian vegetation, and rural roads are all potential nonpoint source problems. Numerous small impoundments fragment headwater regions. The basin's major tributaries in North Carolina are also upstream from larger impoundments in Georgia and South Carolina. More monitoring is needed to address to what extent invasive species have become established in the Savannah River basin.

French Broad River Basin
The most widespread problem facing the French Broad River basin is habitat degradation from nonpoint source pollution. Large development, urbanization, and agriculture are also evident nonpoint sources of pollution and sedimentation. Highway development and construction pose significant threats to many areas of the French Broad River basin, along with poorly managed steep slope development contributing runoff and sedimentation. Nutrient enrichment is a more serious issue in this basin than in any other basin in the region. Increasing in severity are threats from hydrologic modifications, from activities such as impervious surfaces, floodplain filling, and stream channel alterations.

Not as widespread as nonpoint sources of pollution, point sources are still a significant problem causing habitat degradation in the basin. Impoundments pose a smaller threat to this basin than to other basins in Western North Carolina, but are still cause for concern in some portions of the basin. Specifically within the French Broad River sub-basin, point source pollution, including both current and lingering effects from past pollution, contributes significantly towards habitat degradation and the extirpation of priority species.

The Pigeon River sub-basin has a long history of point source pollution. Toxic wastes were discharged directly to the Pigeon River for much of the 20th century, eliminating many priority aquatic species. Treatment began in the early 1990s to improve water quality and the recovery of many native species has been favorable, though the River continues to be heavily monitored.

More research is needed to fully assess effects of invasive species in the French Broad River basin. The native longear sunfish has been displaced entirely by the nonnative redbreast sunfish, and a few other invasive species have been established in segments of the basin, but exact influences on game versus non-game communities are not known.

Broad River Basin

The predominant impact on water quality in the Broad River basin is habitat degradation from sedimentation originating from construction, row crop agriculture, timber harvest, mining, stream bank erosion, and runoff from unpaved rural roads. Stream bank vegetation is either significantly or entirely lacking throughout the basin, leaving the waters more susceptible to runoff. Water quality is declining due to channel alterations in both rural and urban areas of the basin, combined with the escalating amount of impervious surfaces which lead to drainage problems.

Waste water treatment plants and industrial discharges are the primary point source polluters. Aquatic communities are impacted from impoundments at Lake Lure, Kings Mountain, and Lake Adger. With a steadily increasing human population, demand is growing for water supply from surface waters. Water withdrawals, impoundments, and interbasin water transfers will have a serious effect on species in these aquatic areas.

Catawba River Basin

The most severe threat facing the Catawba River basin is impoundment. Almost the entire basin is either impounded or regulated by hydropower projects. The release of colder water causes wildlife degradation, as many native species are unable to adapt to the abrupt changes in water temperature. Migration routes are limited, if not completely impassable, due to dams. Other causes of degradation in the basin include sedimentation from ground disturbance from development and agriculture, loss of streamside vegetation, water withdrawals, point source pollutants (waste water treatment plants and permitted industrial dischargers), and nutrient loading.

The numerous nonnative species inhabiting the basin includes Asian clams; grass carp; blue, channel, and flathead catfishes; smallmouth bass; muskellunge; white bass; yellow bass; and rainbow and brown trout. Blueback herring, alewife, and white perch are also known from several impoundments. There are nonnative flora species present in the Catawba River basin as well, particularly in the reservoirs, but the specific effects on the native communities require further research.

Watauga River Basin

At present, water quality conditions of the Watauga River basin are very favorable, but there are lingering effects from past pollution occurrences. Sedimentation and erosion from nonpoint sources is a primary threat affecting the basin. The drastic lack of streamside vegetation and overly narrow riparian corridors have caused excessive erosion and habitat loss due to sediment deposition and the over-widening of water channels. Residential and agricultural development is on the rise, which also raises the threat of habitat loss through increasing erosion. Christmas tree farming in the basin may also add pesticide and herbicide pollution to streams.

New River Basin

Although it exhibits overall good water quality, the New River basin is affected by localized problems and habitat degradation in many of the streams inhabited by priority aquatic species. Development and land clearing, poorly managed livestock grazing, unpaved rural roads, and loss of streamside vegetation all contribute to ecosystem degradation. New home construction, primarily on steep slopes, is increasing steadily. Sedimentation impacts are very serious, particularly in larger tributaries and in the main stem of the New River. There are also increases in water withdrawals as a result of larger populations moving into the area, a problem primarily in the upper South Fork New sub-basin.

Degradation in water quality is a result of acid mine drainage, urban runoff, and discharges from waste water treatment plants. Like the Watauga River basin, herbicides and pesticides used in Christmas tree production also impact the New River basin, but to what degree is still uncertain. Threats also emerge from the numerous nonnative aquatic species established throughout the basin.

Yadkin River Basin

There is limited information and inadequate surveys on aquatic species distribution in the upper region of the Yadkin. Invasive species have undoubtedly become established in the basin and are likely having a negative impact on native populations, though the exact effects are unknown. Dams and impoundments to the east of the region pose a serious threat to the Yadkin River basin.

Atmospheric Deposition
Aquatic Ecosystems

About 53 percent of Western North Carolina streams sampled between 2000 and 2005 were classified as potentially, episodically, or chronically sensitive to acidification.

Atmospheric deposition impacts to streams

The atmospheric deposition of acidic compounds (sulfates and nitrates) and ammonia, originating predominantly from the combustion of fossil fuels and livestock production, can impact water quality. The acidifying compounds are deposited on soils and can be transported into the soil water in the watershed before traveling downslope into the stream or groundwater. All watersheds in the region have been impacted by acidic deposition; however, some streams have a significantly higher ability to buffer or neutralize acidic compounds than others. Stream buffering capacity is determined by surrounding soil types and underlying bedrock. For example, stream beds which develop from carbonate rocks (those high in calcium, magnesium, potassium, and sodium) have a high capacity to mitigate acid inputs, and are not currently vulnerable to the effects of increased acidity.

Some aquatic organisms, such as aquatic insects, are highly sensitive to changes in stream water chemistry, while native brook trout, in particular, are somewhat tolerant of acidic conditions. The relationship between brook trout health and survival has been studied in streams with differing buffering capacities. Streams with adequate buffering capacity will have healthy trout populations if other habitat factors are favorable for their survival. However, negative impacts on native trout populations increase as stream water becomes more acidic and toxic metals such as aluminum appear.

Between 2000 and 2005, the USDA Forest Service found that, of streams sampled, 47 percent had adequate buffering capacity to mitigate future acidic deposition. However, about 53 percent of sampled streams were classified as potentially, episodically, or chronically sensitive to acidification. These vulnerable headwater streams were found predominantly at elevations greater than 3,500 feet on soils with low buffering capacity.

By the year 2100, while sulfate deposition from the atmosphere is predicted to decrease significantly, stream sulfate concentrations are predicted to decrease only in streams currently classified episodically or chronically acidic. Sulfate concentration in potentially sensitive streams is predicted to remain constant or increase slightly during the same time period. The lack of responsiveness of stream sulfate concentrations is attributed to soil retention of a portion of sulfate depositions. It may take centuries for stream sulfate concentrations to decrease significantly, even though the total sulfate deposition has decreased and is predicted to decrease in the future. A significant decrease in stream water sulfate concentration will not occur until historical sulfates bound to the soils are removed through natural processes.

Brook trout health in differing buffer regimes

Brook trout category	Buffering capacity	Brook trout response
Suitable	Adequate buffering	Reproducing populations expected in suitable habitat
Indeterminate	Potentially sensitive	Extremely sensitive to acidification, response variable
Marginal	Episodically sensitive	Sublethal or lethal effects possible
Unsuitable	Chronically acidic	Lethal effects probable

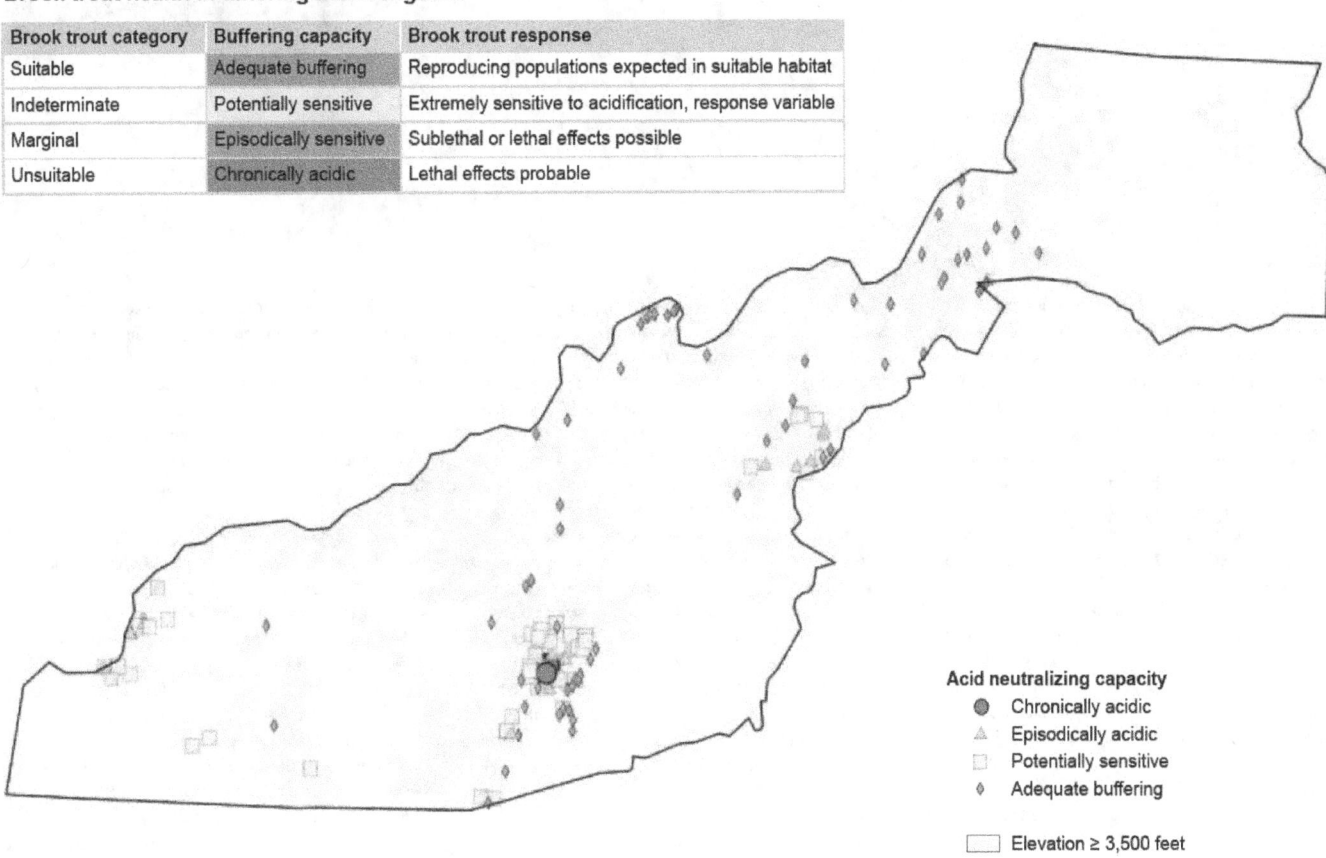

Acid neutralizing capacity
- ● Chronically acidic
- △ Episodically acidic
- ◻ Potentially sensitive
- ◇ Adequate buffering

◻ Elevation ≥ 3,500 feet

Species at Risk
Aquatic Ecosystems

The dense network of rivers and mountain streams in Western North Carolina supports highly diverse aquatic ecosystems, including many species of fish, mussel, snail, crayfish, amphibian, and reptile.

The increasing threat to aquatic communities in the region is primarily due to habitat degradation and destruction, point and nonpoint source pollution, dams and impoundments, and the introduction of nonnative species.

Fish commonly found in the region include native brook and nonnative brown and rainbow trout, bass, crappie, many species of perch, catfish, minnow, darter, and sucker.

Native brook trout, which once thrived in cold mountain streams across the region, have been severely impacted and are now found in less than 80 percent of their historic range. The majority of populations are currently found in the Nantahala and Pisgah National Forests and the Great Smoky Mountains National Park. Sensitive to changes in stream chemistry, stream temperature, competition from other trout species, and land use change, native brook trout continue to need protection and restoration.

Freshwater mussels, found in the shallows of streams and rivers, require cool, clean, well-oxygenated water with riffles, runs, and shallow flowing pools with stable, silt-free, rocky stream beds. Stream bed stability is critical to mussel survival, and they are seldom found in areas with accumulations of silt or shifting sand. Freshwater mussels, especially in their early life stages, are extremely sensitive to chemicals found in wastewater, such as chlorine, ammonia, heavy metals, or high concentrations of nutrients. The destruction of river habitats by dams, channelization, erosion, and pollution has left several species of mussel on the brink of extinction.

Crayfish are freshwater crustaceans found in streams, rivers, swamps, ponds, and other aquatic habitats with flowing water and cover. The small range of many crayfish species is a primary factor in their vulnerability to habitat loss and competition. Threats to crayfish include pollution, impoundment, and competition with nonnative species.

The Southern Appalachian region is the world's center for salamander diversity. According to the Southern Appalachian Biodiversity Institute, nearly 10 percent of global salamander diversity and 10 percent of freshwater mussel diversity occur here. Salamanders are inhabitants of springs, seepages, and streams. They live in bottomland as well as high elevation forests throughout the region. Species diversity is high because many species are at the southern limit of their distribution and gradients in elevation, aspect, slope, and rainfall contribute to a range of available niches and habitats.

Snails play a dominant role in the ecology of the region's freshwaters by providing food for many other animals and by grazing on vast amounts of algae and debris. They are critical to normal ecological processes in rivers and as indicators of water quality. Freshwater snails are in decline, especially those that inhabit streams and rivers. Dam construction and other channel modifications, siltation, and industrial and agricultural pollution have degraded the river habitats on which most species depend.

The continued loss and decline of freshwater snails, mussels, fish, crayfish, amphibians, and reptiles demonstrates that, despite significant water quality improvements made in the last 28 years since the passage of the Clean Water Act, species loss is still a critical concern in the region.

The U.S. Fish and Wildlife Service currently lists 11 fish, 7 mussels, 2 crayfish, 4 salamanders, and 5 snails as federally threatened, endangered, or species of concern in river basins across the region. Many of these are found in the Hiwassee, Little Tennessee, and French Broad basins. Additionally, the State of North Carolina has identified at least 50 additional aquatic species of priority concern in the nine river basins in Western North Carolina.

Federally Listed Threatened Species, Endangered Species, and Species of Concern in Western North Carolina, 2010

Fish
Blotchside logperch
Kanawha minnow
Olive darter
Sharphead darter
Sickle darter
Wounded darter
Smoky dace
Paddlefish
Sicklefin redhorse
Blotched chub
Spotfin chub

Mussels
Carolina heelsplitter
Tennessee clubshell
Tawny crescent
Green floater
Appalachian elktoe
Cumberland bean
Little-wing pearly

Snails
Fragile glyph
Clingman covert
Noonday globe
Roan supercoil (land)
Sculpted supercoil (land)

Salamanders
Pygmy
Seepage
Hellbender
Junaluska

Blotched chub

Appalachian elktoe

Noonday globe

Pygmy salamander

Smoky dace

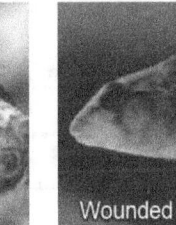

Little-wing pearly

Wounded darter

Water Supply and Use
Water Quantity

Shortly after passage of the Clean Water Act, the Safe Drinking Water Act of 1974 was passed to protect public health by regulating the Nation's drinking water supply. The Federal law, augmented by amendments as well as State laws and regulations, requires many actions to protect water and its sources, including rivers, lakes, reservoirs, springs, and groundwater wells. Originally focusing on water treatment, it now also focuses on source water quality and conservation.

Overall, Western North Carolina has abundant rainfall, surface water, and groundwater. The headwaters of the river basins in the region provide water to local residents and to distant southeastern cities. While supply has historically been more than adequate, recent droughts have raised public awareness of the issues of water use and conservation.

In 1990, data was collected for commercial, domestic, industrial, and agricultural water withdrawals. The average water withdrawal per day was 172 million gallons (this data does not account for water returned to the source after use). Buncombe, Henderson, and Wilkes counties had

relatively high commercial, domestic, and industrial use, while Haywood and Transylvania Counties had the highest industrial use.

In 2005, data collection methods changed, resulting in the collection of several more water withdrawal categories in addition to changes in the definitions of categories. In the most recent data, the public water supply category includes all uses supplied by residential, commercial, industrial, and institutional uses in the public water systems. Domestic self-supplied captures residential well usage. The average water withdrawal per day in 2005 was 136 million gallons. Due to collection method changes, the charts presented here should not be compared on a one-to-one basis; however, water use trends have been showing decreases in many areas due to changes in the manufacturing base of the economy, conservation practices, treatment efficiencies, leak detection, incentive programs, and public education. Also collected but not shown here are withdrawals for aquaculture (961 million gallons per day) and thermoelectricity (262 million gallons per day). In these operations also, much of the water withdrawn is returned to the source after treatment a short distance downstream.

Many municipal water supplies in the region depend, at least partially, on watersheds in the Pisgah, Nantahala, and Cherokee National Forests—lands that were set aside a century ago for the purpose of protecting water supply. The national forests are high-quality sources of clean water because these forests mainly grow under conditions that produce relatively reliable water runoff and yield water relatively low in contaminants when compared with many urban and agricultural land uses.

In much of the rural parts of the region, groundwater is the sole resource for drinking water. The depths of wells normally range from 20 to 1,200 feet. With increasing population, many more wells are being drilled, and information on this important resource is not well documented. Small towns dependent on wells from local fractured-bedrock aquifers are concerned about sufficient water supply to support economic development and population growth.

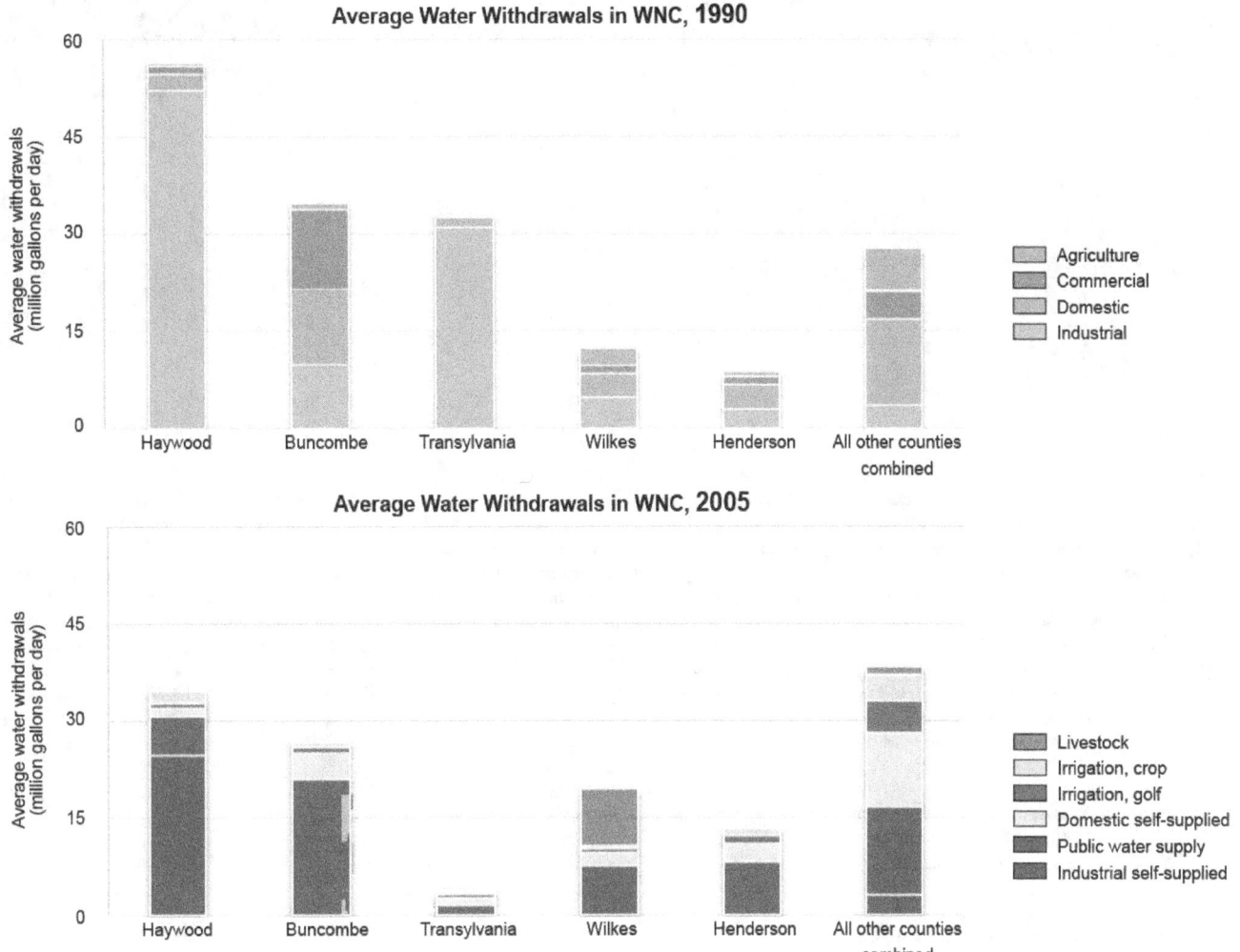

Visibility and the Clean Air Act
Air Quality

Clean Air Act of 1970

Air pollution in Western North Carolina, specifically total sulfate and nitrate deposition, has been intensely studied on 44 sites for over a century. Study sites demonstrate a significant increase in total sulfate deposition from 1860–1970 followed by a significant decline after the Clean Air Act of 1970 (CAA). The CAA mandates pollution control devices and other techniques be adopted to meet targeted reduction levels. In 1977, an amendment to the CAA set a national goal to prevent any future, and remedy any existing, impairment of visibility in mandatory Class I areas, which are a result of human-caused air pollution.

Visibility conditions

There are four federally mandated Class I areas in Western North Carolina: Joyce Kilmer-Slickrock Wilderness, Linville Gorge Wilderness, Shining Rock Wilderness, and the Great Smoky Mountains National Park. To achieve the visibility goal set by the CAA, a Regional Haze Rule has been implemented to achieve natural background visibility (following reasonable progress) by the year 2064.

The first year to determine if reasonable progress is being achieved is 2018. The initial emissions reductions will focus on reducing sulfur dioxide emissions in order to improve visibility by 2018 in comparison to the 2000–2004 baseline conditions. Information collected from study sites predict a decrease in total sulfate deposition between 2010 and 2018, and it is reasonable to assume that further sulfur dioxide emission reductions will be required to achieve natural background visibility at the four Class I areas by 2064.

Man-made emissions of sulfur dioxide, nitrogen oxides, and ammonia are converted in the atmosphere and deposited on the ground. The deposition of sulfates, nitrates, and ammonia can occur in three forms: wet, dry, and cloud water. Before dry deposition can occur, sulfates and nitrates, along with other pollutants, contribute to a uniform haze that obscures scenic views in Western North Carolina.

At most low elevation locations in the Eastern United States, the annual amount of wet and dry deposition is similar. Fog may be an additional source of deposition below 3,500 feet elevation, but is considered a minor component, contributing less than 10 percent of the annual total. Cloud water, however, is a significant contributor at elevations above 3,500 feet, and the region's forests may be immersed in clouds 30–50 percent of the year. Moreover, elevations above 3,500 feet may have twice as much deposition as lower elevation sites as a result of the larger amount of acid compounds deposited from the cloud water.

Visibility Simulations

Natural Background (1860)

Worst Baseline (2000–2004)

Worst (estimated progress for 2018)

Natural Background (2064)

Airborne Particulates
Air Quality

In Western North Carolina, there are six locations measuring fine particulates. In all six locations, neither the daily average nor the annual average has exceeded EPA's standards.

Airborne particulates

Tiny particles of matter originating from land and sea are continually emitted directly into the atmosphere and suspended in either gas or liquid form. Particulates are also formed in the atmosphere, for example, when sulfur dioxide is converted to ammonium sulfates.

Fine particles are responsible for visibility impairment, but they can also negatively impact people's health. High concentrations of fine particulates on a daily or annual basis can increase the likelihood of respiratory or cardiovascular disease, especially for children and the elderly.

On most days in rural areas of Western North Carolina, especially when visibility is poor, ammonium sulfates make up the majority of fine particles suspended in the atmosphere. In urban areas, the addition of organic particles (sodium chloride, magnesium, sulfates, nitrates, calcium, ammonia) makes adverse health effects greater in these areas.

The U.S. Environmental Protection Agency (EPA) has established two National Ambient Air Quality Standards (NAAQS) to protect people's health. In Western North Carolina, there are six locations measuring fine particulates. In all six locations, neither the daily average nor the annual average has exceeded EPA's standards. Furthermore, the 3-year average trend in fine particulates has been decreasing at most of the monitoring sites.

Clear day: little uniform haze, no cloud deposition

Cloud deposition

Uniform haze: visibility impairment before dry deposition pollutants

Fine particulates, Shining Rock Wilderness Area, August 2007

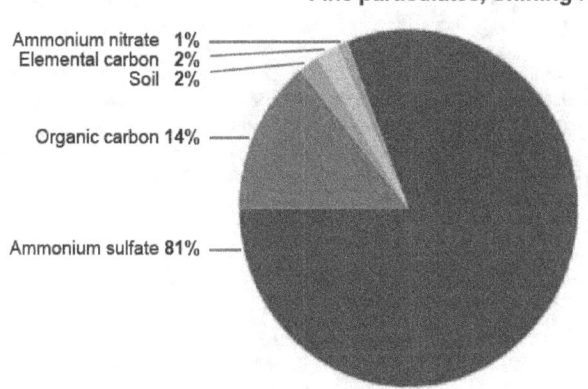

Ammonium nitrate 1%
Elemental carbon 2%
Soil 2%
Organic carbon 14%
Ammonium sulfate 81%

Total fine particulates (22.22 µg/m^3) measured near Shining Rock Wilderness and the corresponding digital photograph at 3 p.m. on Aug. 1, 2007, when visibility was poor.

Ground-LevelOzone
Air Quality

Recent monitoring indicates that ground-level ozone is currently not exceeding EPA standards at low and medium elevation sites, but standards are exceeded at most high elevation sites.

Ground-level ozone

Ozone is an oxygen molecule with three oxygen atoms (O_3). A gas found high in the atmosphere, ozone protects the planet against the harmful effects of ultraviolet radiation. Ozone also naturally occurs at ground level. However, ground levels of ozone can increase substantially when nitrogen oxides, emitted mostly from vehicles and coal-fired power plants, combine with volatile organic compounds released primarily from trees.

The greatest amount of ground-level ozone formation occurs on hot, sunny days when wind speeds are low and the air becomes stagnant. Both chronic and acute ozone exposures at ground level can be harmful to sensitive humans and vegetation.

Ground-level ozone is continuously monitored at 11 sites in Western North Carolina. The sites are distributed across low-, medium-, and high-elevation sites. At low- and medium-elevation sites, ground-level ozone varies throughout the day. Typically, ozone levels begin to increase at about 8:00 a.m., reaching the highest concentrations at 11:00 a.m. and remaining elevated until about 5:00 p.m. Ozone begins to decrease in the evening hours and continues to decrease until the early morning hours of the next day.

Ozone patterns mirror daily weather patterns of temperature and solar radiation, increasing during the day and decreasing during the night. The daily pattern also mirrors fossil fuel use. Nitrogen oxide emissions increase in the morning when people use electricity to get ready for work and gasoline to travel to work. Fossil fuel combustion, and thus nitrogen oxide generation, is also greatest at the end of the day; however, with decreasing solar radiation, the nitrogen oxides react with the ozone

(instead of volatile organic compounds) and decrease the ozone concentrations in the atmosphere. Typically, the total amount of ozone exposure is less at lower elevation sites (except for the monitoring site adjacent to Asheville) when compared to the medium elevation site at Linville Falls.

Recent monitoring indicates that ground-level ozone is currently not exceeding EPA standards at low- and medium-elevation sites, but standards are exceeded at most high-elevation sites. Therefore, people outdoors and sensitive plant communities above 4,000 feet elevation are likely to be negatively impacted by ground-level ozone.

The EPA continually reviews the scientific literature and is considering a revision in ground-level ozone standards. If EPA decides to lower the standard to 0.06 parts per million, all 11 sites in Western North Carolina will exceed the National Ambient Air Quality standard. EPA may also reduce secondary ozone standards, such as hourly averages over time and peak concentrations. If this change occurs, most of the study sites will exceed the new standards.

Ground-level ozone and growth rate of trees

Controlled studies indicate that reductions in vegetation biomass (the dry weight of stems, leaves, and roots) occur with chronic exposures of peak concentrations at high-elevation sites. Although scientists disagree on the effects of ozone exposure to vegetation during the night, it has been argued that vegetative defense mechanisms to ozone exposure may decrease during the night and, therefore, peak ozone concentrations could cause physiological damage to vegetation.

Other factors have to be considered as well. The Southern Appalachian Mountains have the highest number of plant species of any temperate forest in the United States. While only a few species have been studied, scientists have demonstrated that there is a continuum of plant tolerance to ozone exposure both between and within species. Recent studies have shown that northern red oak was unresponsive to increases in ozone exposure; however, tulip-poplar experienced reduced biomass formation. Overall, the total amount of area occupied by trees in a forest stand is likely to remain unchanged with variable ozone levels, but species composition may change.

Additional factors, such as the amount of sunlight hitting the leaves or the amount of available soil nitrogen, can influence the level of gaseous uptake from the atmosphere in sensitive species. Soil moisture, however, has the greatest influence on whether ozone will penetrate the leaves, because plant cells used for gas exchange close during periods of drought.

Sensitive		Tolerant
Black cherry	Sugar maple	Northern red oak
Tulip-poplar	White pine	Virginia pine
Winged sumac	Loblolly pine	Eastern hemlock
American sycamore	Red maple	Red spruce

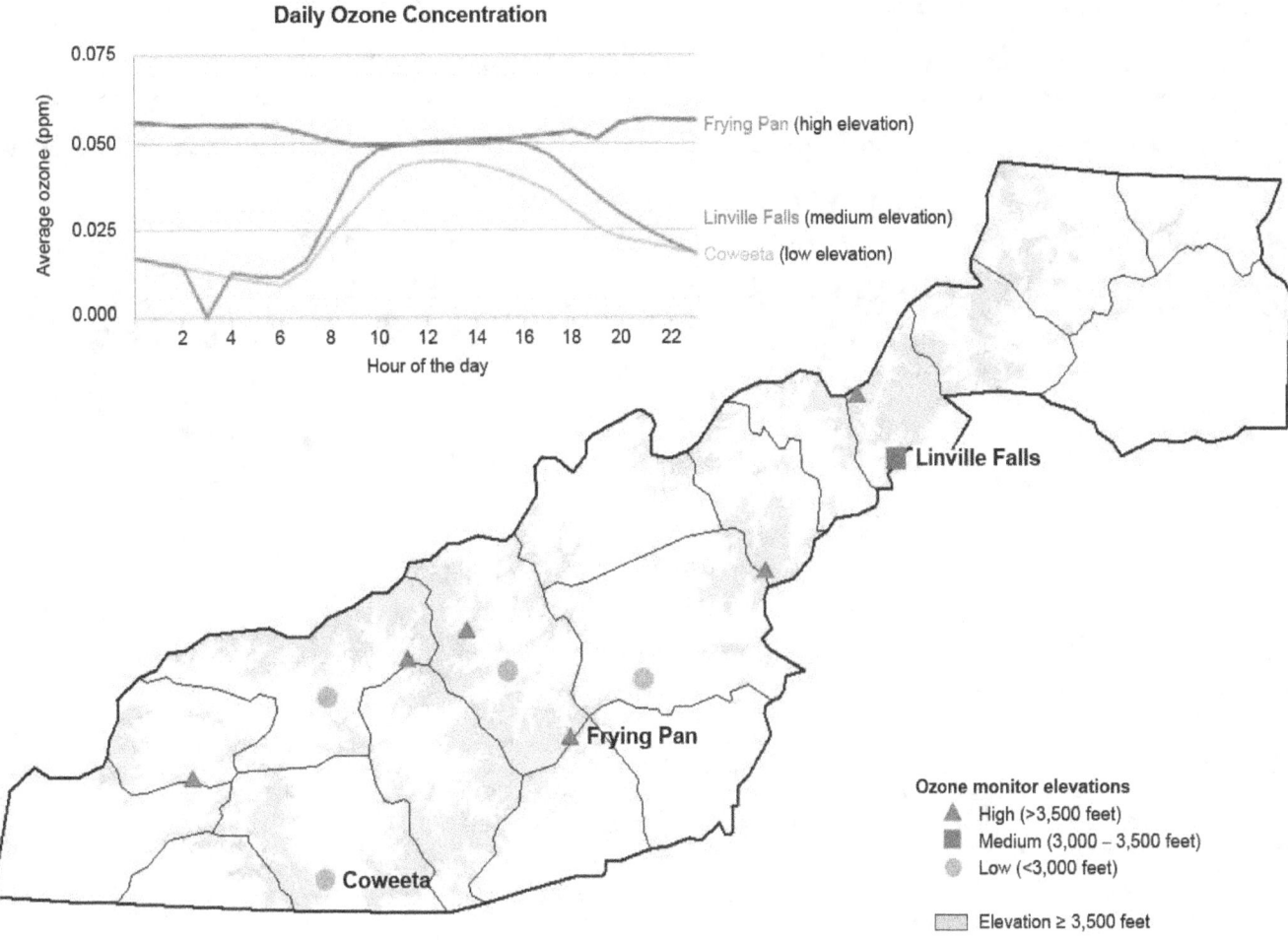

Daily Ozone Concentration

Frying Pan (high elevation)

Linville Falls (medium elevation)

Coweeta (low elevation)

Linville Falls

Frying Pan

Coweeta

Ozone monitor elevations
- ▲ High (>3,500 feet)
- ■ Medium (3,000 – 3,500 feet)
- ● Low (<3,000 feet)

Elevation ≥ 3,500 feet

NO and SO$_2$ Emissions
Air Quality

Nitrogen oxide emissions from coal-fired power plants

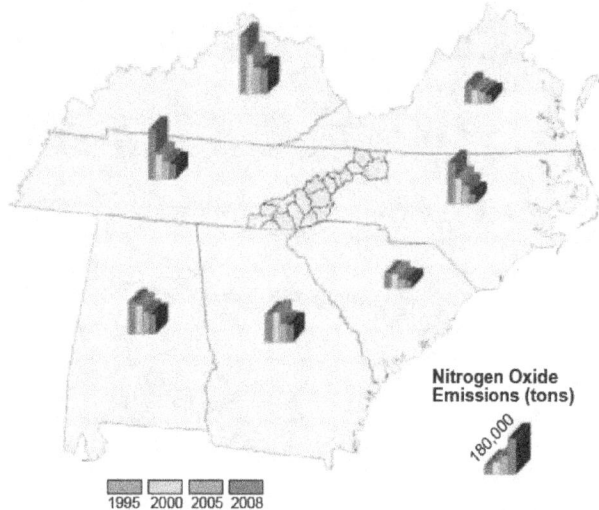

Nitrogen Oxide
Emissions (tons)

180,000

1995 2000 2005 2008

Sulfur dioxide emissions from coal-fired power plants

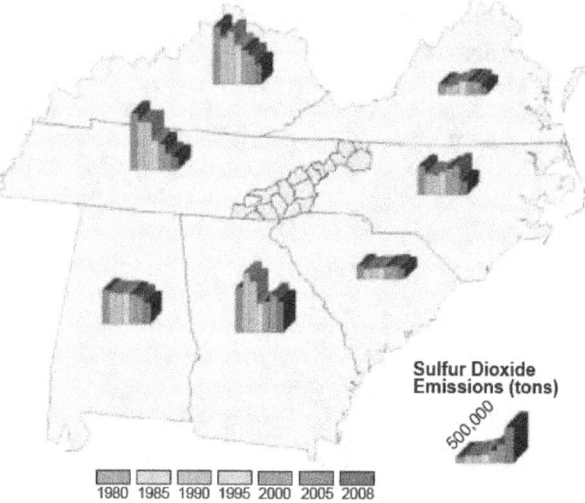

Sulfur Dioxide
Emissions (tons)

500,000

1980 1985 1990 1995 2000 2005 2008

Nitrogen oxides and sulfur dioxide reduction
Nitrogen oxide emissions have been decreasing in States near Western North Carolina, and it is anticipated that they will continue to decrease in the future. This reduction will lower ozone exposures, especially peak concentrations from ground-level sources (primarily vehicles) and elevated sources (primarily coal-fired power plants).

In a recent six-State analysis by the Southern Appalachian Mountains Initiative, nitrogen oxide reductions from ground-level and atmospheric sources were studied, one State at a time. Resulting ozone concentrations were then predicted for Joyce Kilmer-Slickrock, Linville Gorge, and Shining Rock Wilderness Areas (these three Wilderness Areas represent the range of responses to ozone reduction that could occur throughout

Western North Carolina). Findings indicate that ozone exposures will be lowered if nitrogen oxides are reduced from both sources. However, the greatest benefit would occur if ground-level emissions of nitrogen oxides were reduced. Also, Western North Carolina would receive the most benefit if nitrogen oxide emission reductions occurred in eastern Tennessee, North Carolina, South Carolina, and Georgia.

The major source of sulfur dioxide emission is coal-fired power plants. In 1990, the utility industry contributed about one-half of all nitrogen oxide emissions. From 1980–2008, in States adjacent to the region, the implementation of various emission reduction strategies led to decreased emissions of both sulfur dioxide and nitrogen oxides. Additionally, from 1993–2008, the reduction in

sulfur dioxide led to an overall reduction in wet sulfate deposition. In the same period, the annual wet nitrate deposition decreased, but the ammonia deposition from rainfall remained level or perhaps increased slightly.

The Southern Appalachian Mountains Initiative conducted a study in 2002 to find out where air pollution affecting the region originates. Estimates were provided for three locations in Western North Carolina: Joyce Kilmer-Slickrock, Linville Gorge, and Shining Rock Wilderness Areas. Fossil fuel emissions from the States of Tennessee, North Carolina, Georgia, and Alabama are major contributors to visibility impairment and unsustainable acidic deposition in these areas of Western North Carolina.

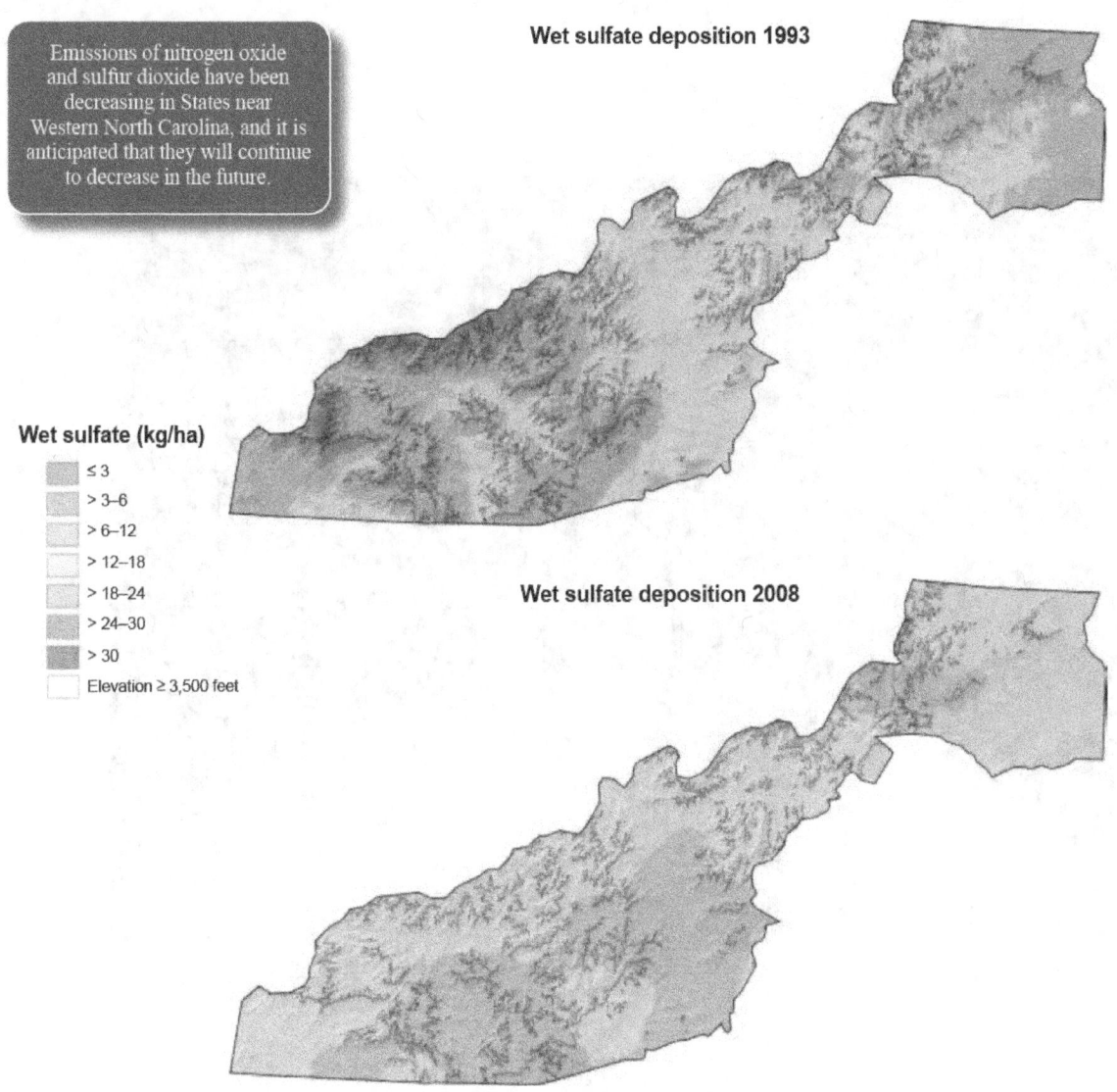

Emissions of nitrogen oxide and sulfur dioxide have been decreasing in States near Western North Carolina, and it is anticipated that they will continue to decrease in the future.

Wet sulfate deposition 1993

Wet sulfate deposition 2008

Wet sulfate (kg/ha)

≤ 3
> 3–6
> 6–12
> 12–18
> 18–24
> 24–30
> 30
Elevation ≥ 3,500 feet

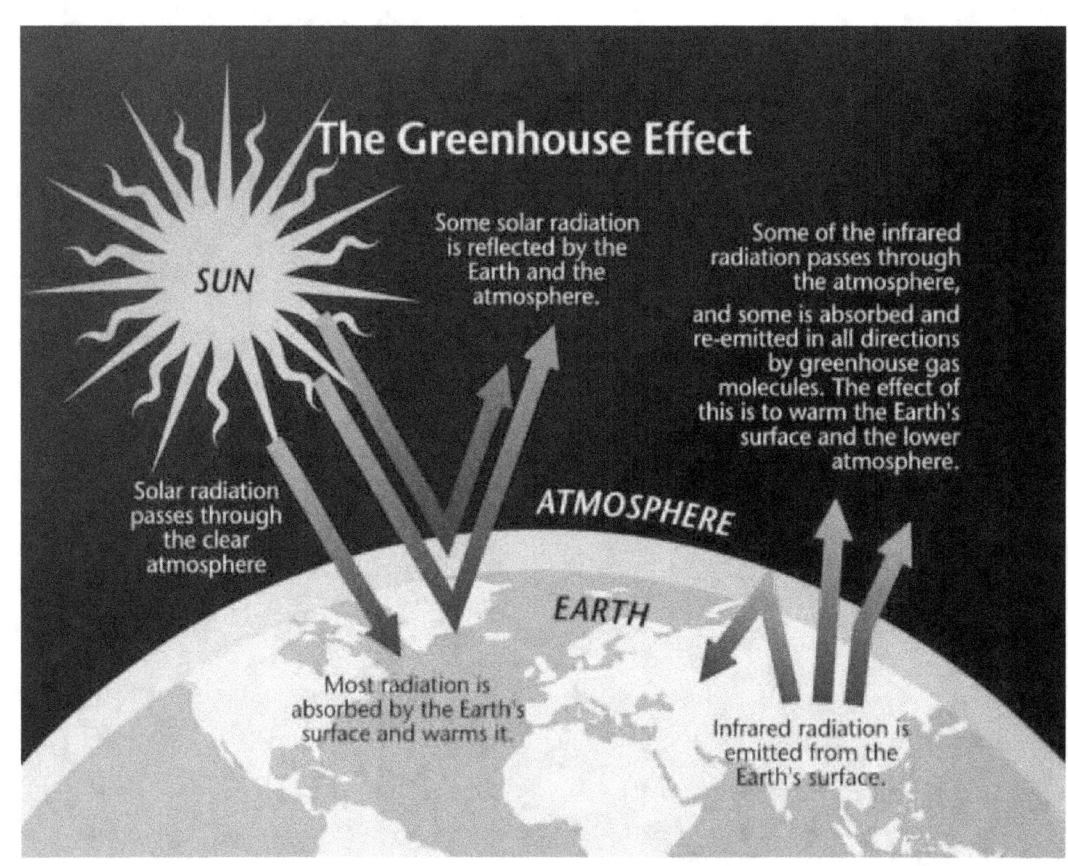

The Greenhouse Effect

Some solar radiation is reflected by the Earth and the atmosphere.

Some of the infrared radiation passes through the atmosphere, and some is absorbed and re-emitted in all directions by greenhouse gas molecules. The effect of this is to warm the Earth's surface and the lower atmosphere.

SUN

Solar radiation passes through the clear atmosphere

ATMOSPHERE

EARTH

Most radiation is absorbed by the Earth's surface and warms it.

Infrared radiation is emitted from the Earth's surface.

Carbon Cycle
Carbon Cycle, Carbon Pool, Carbon Market

Carbon is the key element in all living things. It continuously cycles through the earth's plants, animals, atmosphere, land, and oceans. The vast majority of carbon is stored in sedimentary bedrock and seawater. At current levels, atmospheric carbon threatens to alter climate conditions on Earth.

Carbon dioxide (CO_2), often called a "greenhouse gas," traps heat within the atmosphere in much the same way as glass traps heat in a greenhouse. The accumulation of greenhouse gases has led to rising global average temperature which, in turn, has led to changes in precipitation patterns, storm severity, and sea level. A high level of uncertainty exists as to the magnitude of projected changes. This phenomenon is commonly referred to as "climate change."

Technological advances and conservation measures are needed to reduce the human-caused contribution of atmospheric carbon. Technological innovations that may one day transform our energy sources are already in place and will likely become more widespread in the future. Alternative methods include wind, solar, and nuclear power. The use of these sources could eventually reduce or replace the combustion of fossil fuel, although significant challenges must be overcome for them to become established in the United States at large.

Carbon is stored in forests and "carbon markets" are financial instruments used to counteract emissions through the conservation of forest land. Specifically, landowners may be paid to keep their forests intact.

In the short term, a 25-percent decrease in atmospheric carbon could be achieved by voluntary conservation measures, such as turning off home computers when not in use, replacing light bulbs with compact fluorescents, and driving less in more fuel-efficient vehicles.

Global Carbon Exchange
Carbon Cycles

Carbon cycling in the atmosphere

The earth's atmosphere is a mixture of nitrogen (78 percent), oxygen (21 percent), and trace gases (1 percent). CO_2, a trace gas, and other greenhouse gases, including methane, water vapor, and nitrous oxide, are important because they form a layer in the atmosphere that prevents infrared energy (heat) from circulating back into space.

Historically, natural fluctuations in atmospheric CO_2 occurred due to temperature fluctuation or volcanic eruptions. Since the mid-1800s, however, atmospheric concentrations of CO_2 have risen at a much faster rate than at any time within the previous 650,000 years. The 20th century, especially, has seen massive increases in emissions, due predominantly to increased combustion of fossil fuels. To release their stored energy, fossil fuels are burned to serve growing energy needs, such as electricity, transportation, and manufacturing. During the combustion process, a variety of gases and particulates are released into the atmosphere. Primary releases include carbon, sulfur, and nitrogen. Carbon molecules combine with water vapor to form atmospheric CO_2.

Carbon cycling on land

Carbon is cycled on land through various processes. Trees and all other plants absorb carbon dioxide (CO_2) through photosynthesis and store the carbon-based sugars in their trunks, leaves, and roots. On the forest floor, carbon is pooled in leaf litter. Soils store carbon in organic matter made up of plant and animal materials in various stages of decay. Coal, oil, and natural gas, formed hundreds of millions of years ago from the decomposition and remains of organisms, store carbon beneath the earth's surface. Lastly, sedimentary rock stores large amounts of carbon in deposits of limestone, dolomite, and chalk. All living organisms (plants, animals, fungi, and bacteria) release CO_2 through the process of respiration and decomposition.

While changes in land use have resulted in the release of carbon to the atmosphere, the most significant release has been through the extraction and combustion of coal, oil, and natural gas.

Carbon cycling in the oceans

Ocean organisms also use CO_2 in the process of photosynthesis. Sea creatures feed on carbon-rich plants and release CO_2 into the water through respiration and decomposition. Carbon from the remains of aquatic plants, animals, and plankton dissolve or is buried in sediment on the ocean floor. Deep ocean water and its underlying bedrock also comprise a rich carbon sink.

Additionally, surface waters chemically react with atmospheric CO_2. The rate at which oceans uptake atmospheric CO_2 varies with water temperature and wind-driven currents. The warmer the surface water becomes, the harder it is for winds to mix surface layers with deeper layers. Stagnant waters support fewer plankton and CO_2 uptake from photosynthesis slows. In short, stratification decreases the amount of carbon the ocean can sequester.

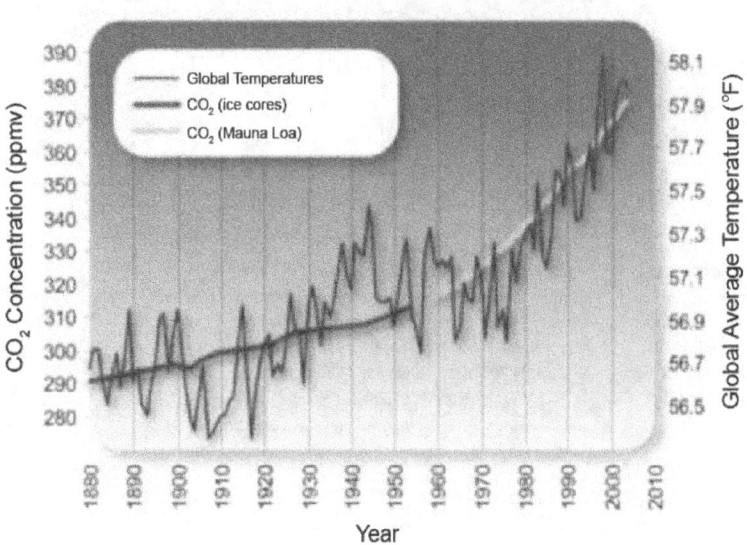

Global Average Temperature and
Carbon Dioxide Concentrations, 1880–2004

Carbon Storage

> The forests of Western North Carolina currently represent a significant carbon pool, but in the future carbon losses will almost certainly outpace carbon gains.

Carbon storage

In addition to existing benefits such as scenic beauty, biodiversity, water quality, and recreation opportunities, our region's heavily forested landscape stores a significant amount of carbon. The USDA Forest Service Forest Inventory Data Online (FIDO) EVALIDator 4.01 tool estimates the total amount of carbon currently stored in Western North Carolina to be 240 million tons. Carbon is primarily stored in live trees (58 percent) followed by soil (31 percent).

Storage capacity

Under normal growing season conditions, the process of photosynthesis leads to an increase in the amount of carbon stored in forests, while metabolic changes (respiration, decomposition) and physical changes (wildfire, harvest, insects, and disease) decrease this amount. Moreover, the rate of carbon accumulation varies significantly with forest age, type, location, soil type and depth, as well as leafy and wood biomass.

Because the rate of growth in young forests is relatively high, carbon accumulates quickly in the first several decades. However, as a forest matures—such as the forests here in Western North Carolina—the rate of growth slows and the ability to sequester new carbon declines and eventually falls off precipitously. The predominant forest type in Western North Carolina is upland hardwoods. After these forests surpass 80 years of age, the trees are more likely to lose vigor and the ability to uptake carbon from the atmosphere.

This loss in vigor also drives the incentive to harvest trees while they are at peak market value. The forests of Western North Carolina currently represent a significant carbon pool, but in the future carbon losses will almost certainly outpace carbon gains.

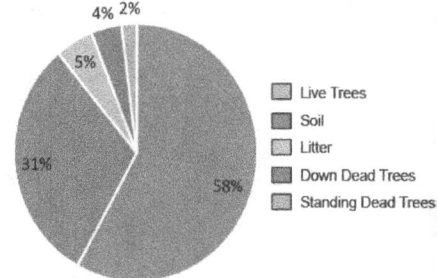

Carbon storage in Western North Carolina

- Live Trees
- Soil
- Litter
- Down Dead Trees
- Standing Dead Trees

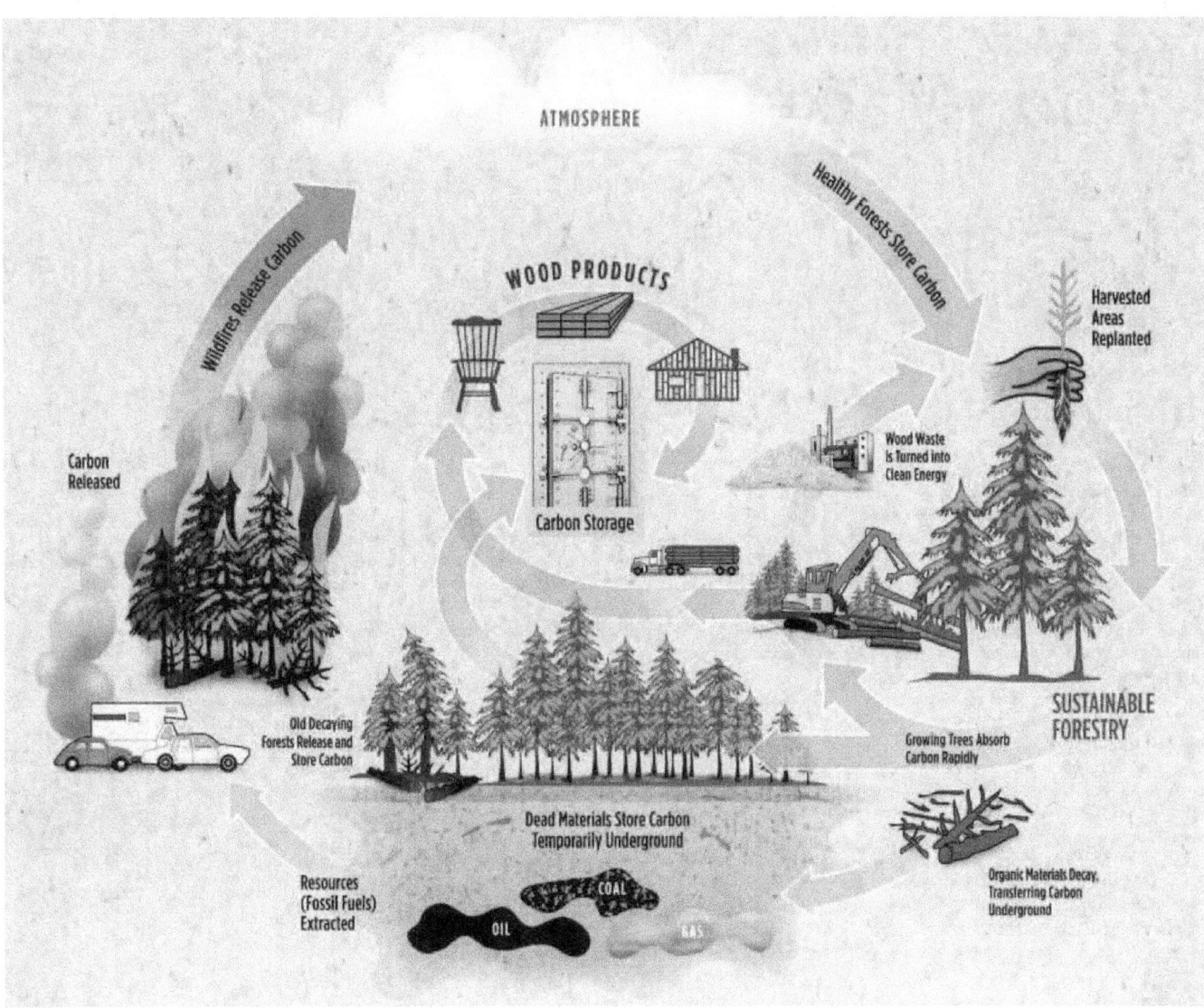

ATMOSPHERE

WOOD PRODUCTS

Carbon Storage

Wildfires Release Carbon

Carbon Released

Old Decaying Forests Release and Store Carbon

Dead Materials Store Carbon Temporarily Underground

Resources (Fossil Fuels) Extracted

OIL

COAL

GAS

Healthy Forests Store Carbon

Harvested Areas Replanted

Wood Waste is Turned into Clean Energy

SUSTAINABLE FORESTRY

Growing Trees Absorb Carbon Rapidly

Organic Materials Decay, Transferring Carbon Underground

Carbon Markets

Two market-based initiatives exist to reduce pollutants in the atmosphere: a carbon emission tax and a "cap and trade" program.

What is a carbon market?

Historically, regulations to lower air pollution were designed to control specific emissions from designated sources. However, early regulatory programs were found to be inefficient and did not serve their purpose of improving air quality. Recently, the U.S. Environmental Protection Agency has listed carbon dioxide as a pollutant. Regulatory programs and market-based options are under consideration in response to calls for emission reduction.

Market-based options create a public venue where buyers and sellers come together to exchange goods and services at prevailing prices. Two market-based initiatives exist to reduce pollutants in the atmosphere: a carbon emission tax and a "cap and trade" program.

Carbon tax

A carbon tax levies a tax per unit of emissions. The tax can be added as a surtax to existing tax structures, which is relatively easy; however, the use and dispersion of the generated funds is often complicated. A tax may significantly increase revenue, which can be used to decrease other inefficient taxes, or to provide subsidies for more sustainable investments. Applied effectively, a tax would encourage firms to reduce emissions and provide revenue for the government. Several European countries —including Finland, Sweden, Denmark, the Netherlands, and Norway—have successfully implemented a carbon emission tax.

"Cap and Trade" System

A "cap and trade" system sets an aggregate limit, or cap, on emissions and creates permits for this amount. Permits are issued for free or auctioned off by regulatory agencies to be traded among firms as a part of their strategy to meet emission requirements. Often, companies with high pollution abatement costs purchase permits from those with low costs. A "cap and trade" system doesn't put a specific price on emissions; it allows the market to set the price, thus eliminating the difficulties associated with policy makers attempting to do this. Significant cost savings have been observed under existing "cap and trade" systems, but long-term results are not yet known.

"Avoided Deforestation" Carbon Offset Market

Offsets are the result of an action taken to avoid, sequester, or displace emissions of carbon. A successful carbon offset program begins with the creation of a market for entities producing atmospheric carbon and those sequestering it. Emission rates are determined for carbon producers, such as regional energy utilities, as well as their willingness to buy carbon offsets. Likewise, carbon sequestration rates are calculated for forest land whose owners agree to keep their forests intact. Through third-party auditors, the amount of carbon that can be sequestered through "avoided deforestation" is certified and becomes available for an offset purchase.

Carbon offset market in Western North Carolina

At some point in the future, voluntary guidelines and/or mandatory regulations are expected to be put in place to limit CO_2 emissions. The decision to regulate greenhouse gas emissions will undoubtedly have large political and economic ramifications, and the time frame for passage of such legislation is unknown. If guidelines are adopted or regulations are issued and a "cap and trade" system is established, "avoided deforestation" is an offset option that should be analyzed further. The value of such an offset may rise due to increased demand, which may attract forest landowners to participate.

The establishment of such a market would entail the identification of buyers and sellers as well as the appointment of regulatory oversight responsibilities. A number of monitoring issues must be addressed for any carbon-based project. These include natural or man-made events that reduce or increase carbon storage, as well as changes in land use patterns in and outside the region.

Sellers of carbon offsets

Landowners must certify their forest to participate in the market; but after initial inventory requirements are met, the offset allowance should be straightforward to maintain. Sustainable harvesting should be allowed, even encouraged, as it would increase multiple values and help maintain the health and vitality of a maturing forest. In addition, management practices, such as group selection harvests under an uneven aged management system, would result in increased carbon storage capability and provide early successional habitat for wildlife.

Presently, few financial incentives are available to private forest landowners who want to maintain and manage their forest land. Often, the most profitable action a landowner can take is to harvest their timber resource and develop the land. Market prices do not take into account consequences that may be associated with land use change and/or unsustainable harvesting regimes, such as impaired water quality, increased levels of erosion, and reduced biodiversity, for which no compensation is paid. The single largest threat to forest land in the region continues to be fragmented residential and commercial development. The economic returns from development are significant and will be hard to match. Any and all monetary incentives available to forest landowners may help deter them from converting their forest land to nonforest land uses.

Buyers of carbon offsets

Several large entities in Western North Carolina, such as the City of Asheville and the University of North Carolina at Asheville, have calculated the amount of carbon they are currently emitting. Many others are already in the process of creating emission reduction programs and have expressed interest in a local carbon offset market. There may also be buyers located outside of the region.

Continued...

Carbon Markets

Challenges and implications

Western North Carolina forests are no longer experiencing high growth rates, and their ability to sequester carbon will continue to diminish as they age. Areas outside the region that have the capability to sequester large amounts of carbon in short rotation forests in more nutrient-rich soils may provide a more profitable offset market. In addition, our existing regional timber markets will likely experience growth as demand strengthens for mature high-quality hardwood and softwood products. If a viable infrastructure for small diameter wood emerges, a market for wood biomass may also develop.

However, if an "avoided deforestation" offset market were found to be economically feasible, it would position the region to adopt regional or national regulations in a more cost-effective manner and help landowners conserve their forests while providing abundant collateral benefits.

In any case, in order to avoid the detrimental effects of global climate change, it is necessary to begin the hard process of reducing and mitigating the effects of burning fossil fuels. Although the extent of change is yet to be determined, overall welfare is expected to be permanently reduced. A variety of mitigation strategies will be needed, and Western North Carolina policy makers should take a closer look at regional forest and wood product accounting as they relate to carbon flows, as well as working to conserve and manage our existing forests as a valuable carbon pool.

Avoided Deforestation Carbon Offset Market

Historic Cabin, Nantahala National Forest

Socioeconomic Benefits
Recreation, Tourism, and the Forest Economy

Social, cultural, and economic factors in Western North Carolina have changed dramatically in the years since 1960. The large metropolitan areas have grown faster than the rural counties and have been better able to withstand economic downturns as their economies became more diversified. Arts, entertainment, and recreation represent a significant growth sector in the region, with Buncombe, Watauga, Henderson, and Jackson Counties being the major centers for these endeavors. Western North Carolina is also recognized for its wilderness and roadless areas, resources limited in both the Southern Appalachians and the Eastern United States.

Forest products are an important contributor to the regional economy. The value of wood and wood products closely reflects variability in national economic conditions and, as expected, the demand for forest products has decreased during two recessions in the past decade. The forests of Western North Carolina are now maturing, leading to an increase in the available volume of high-value sawtimber and veneer logs in the future.

Finally, population has increased steadily since 1960, with the highest populations residing in Buncombe, Henderson, Wilkes, and Haywood Counties. Newcomers appear to have different values and lifestyles than their predecessors, especially regarding the use and preservation of natural resources. Long-time residents depended on natural resources to make a living and to provide a setting for traditional events and activities, and hence generally favor use and conservation of natural resources. New residents, often relocating from large cities outside the region, are more inclined to see natural resources set aside and preserved for the ecological and aesthetic services they provide. This dichotomy of views continues to challenge the region to plan for and achieve sustainable outcomes.

Economic Overview
Social, Cultural, and Economic Factors

> More jobs are now related to recreation and tourism than in previous decades.

Economic trends in Western North Carolina

Although experiencing the effects of a contracting national economy from 2008 to 2010, regional economic activity in Western North Carolina has been steadily growing since 1970. Economic conditions vary considerably between the region and the State, but also within the region. The 2001 recession was especially difficult for Western North Carolina, but the subsequent recovery has been even more challenging. The regional economy continues to lag behind the rest of the State, and trends suggest the divide between the region and the State will continue to grow.

Jobs

There was a general increase in the number of jobs in all counties until the start of the 2000s. A slowdown occurred in the majority of counties, with some, like Buncombe, experiencing negative growth for two years (2001–2002) but recovering thereafter. In terms of distribution, the majority of jobs were located in Buncombe County, with Henderson and Wilkes a distant second and third. More jobs are now related to recreation and tourism than in previous decades. In the AdvantageWest region, which

encompasses all 18 counties plus Burke, Caldwell, and McDowell, the industries that have a demonstrated competitive advantage relative to North Carolina and the Nation are recreation and tourism, retirement and second homes, arts and crafts, vehicle parts assembly, metalworking, and chemicals and plastics.

Average wage and income

There was also a general increase in wages for nearly all counties until the start of the current decade. A slowdown occurred in some of the more affluent counties (Wilkes, Transylvania) at the start of the 2000s, but reversed itself thereafter. In terms of distribution, Buncombe County currently has the highest average wage, but Transylvania County had the highest wages for most of the period. It is also interesting to note that Haywood County had equal or higher wages than Buncombe during the 1970s and 1980s.

Wage rates quadrupled from 1975 to 2005; but when inflation is factored in, the real wage rate increased by only 9.1 percent. Real wages expressed in 1975 dollars actually declined slightly from the 1970s to 1980s, then increased 6.2 percent from the 1980s to the 1990s, and increased again 2.8 percent from 2000 to 2005. In the 1970s, the counties with the highest wages were Transylvania, Haywood, and Buncombe Counties. Most recently Buncombe, Wilkes, and Henderson Counties have the highest wages.

In spite of this, in 2007 the region's average income ($31,556) still lags behind national ($44,470) and State ($39,184) average income. All counties in the region fell behind North Carolina's $39,184 median household income level. Transylvania, Henderson, and Buncombe are closest to the State average, ranging from $36,000 to $38,000. Ashe, Swain, Cherokee, and Graham Counties have the lowest median household income, ranging from $26,645 to $28,800, respectively.

Average Number of Total Jobs Per Decade by Regional Council of Government

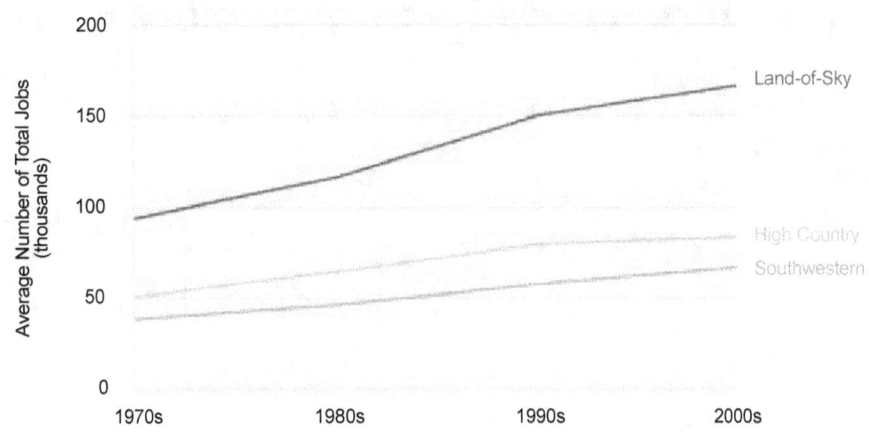

Average Wage Per Decade by Regional Council of Government

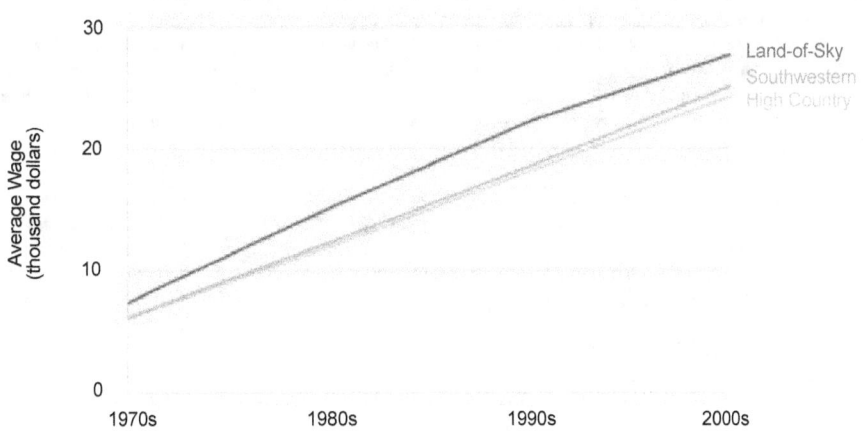

Economic Overview
Social, Cultural, and Economic Factors

> Population in the region has steadily increased since the 1970s. This increase is projected to continue into year 2020 for all counties.

Poverty

The regional poverty rate (13.2 percent) is higher than the national (12.6 percent) and State (12.3 percent) average rates, and the number of students going to college also lags behind: 16.1 percent in Western North Carolina compared to 22.5 percent across the State and 39.0 percent nationally. Twelve of the 18 counties have higher county-level poverty rates than the State and national average. Graham and Swain counties have the highest poverty rates, at 19.5 percent and 18.3 percent, respectively.

Unemployment

In July 2009, the average unemployment rate for the region was 10.6 percent, up 3.8 percent from 6.8 percent unemployment rate in July 2008. Moreover, 10 of the 18 counties had unemployment rates exceeding 10 percent. The city of Asheville, the largest metropolitan area in the region, had an unemployment rate of 8.7 percent in July 2009, compared to 5.0 percent the previous year. North Carolina overall had an unemployment rate of 11.0 percent in 2009, and 6.3 percent in 2008, an increase of 4.7 percent.

Arts, entertainment, and recreation jobs

From 2001 to 2007, there was a general increase in the number of arts, entertainment, and recreation jobs, mainly in Buncombe, Jackson, and Wilkes Counties. All other counties were stable in terms of job numbers for the duration of the period, with exceptions such as Haywood and Henderson, which lost jobs. In terms of distribution, Buncombe County, with the highest population, has the highest number of arts, entertainment, and recreation jobs, while Watauga, Henderson, and Jackson Counties represent the other major art centers. Buncombe County's considerable prominence in this field is highly attributable to the greater Asheville area's expanding arts and craft scene, as well as tourism hubs like the Biltmore Estate and the Grove Park Inn.

Forestry-related jobs

Reporting employment statistics for forestry-related sectors is difficult at this scale. In several counties in which mills are located, they are so few in number that publication of employment statistics violates their right of privacy.

Therefore, contribution of forest-related jobs cannot accurately be reported for the 18-county region. However, revenue to the region from total roundwood products indicates the number of forest-related jobs is significant. From 1995 to 2007, the average annual value of total roundwood output delivered to mills in the region ranged from $110 million to $155.4 million.

Population

Population in the region has steadily increased since the 1970s. This increase is projected to continue into year 2020 for all counties. In 1970, the region's population was 480,640 people. In 2010, the population grew to 744,630, an increase of 55 percent. The counties with the highest populations include Buncombe, Henderson, Wilkes, and Haywood. The total population is expected to grow at a rate of 9.8 percent over the next 10 years; however, this projection may not materialize due to current economic conditions.

Arts, Entertainment, and Recreation Employment by Regional Council of Government

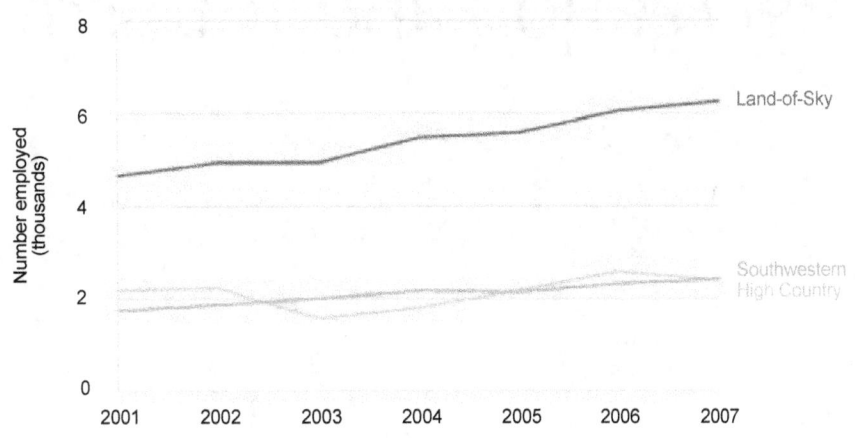

Population by Regional Council of Government

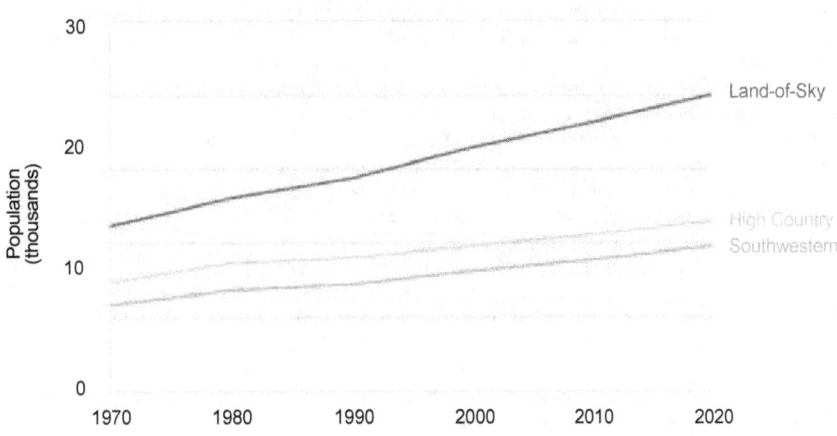

Recreation Areas
Forest Recreation and Tourism

Western North Carolina, a place of natural beauty marked by areas of ruggedness and isolation, is recognized as a revitalizing health destination, a highly ranked destination for outdoor enthusiasts, and a zone of ecological importance. As a result, forest recreation and tourism have long been important contributors to the regional economy.

At the beginning of the 20th century, little was known of the hydrology of mountain watersheds—specifically how water moves through soil to sustain mountain streams and prevent flooding. The recognition of the importance of forests in watershed protection and wildfire control were the primary justifications for acquisition of the region's national forests almost a century ago. The additional designations of the Great Smoky Mountains National Park (1940), the Blue Ridge Parkway (begun in 1935), and other significant sites secured the region's place as one of the most significant natural areas in Eastern North America.

Recreation areas
The region includes the North Carolina section of the Blue Ridge Parkway, the most visited national park unit; the Great Smoky Mountains National Park (located in Western North Carolina and Tennessee), the most visited national park; and the Pisgah and Nantahala National Forests, two of the most visited national forests in the United States. The Parkway winds through popular destination points such as Mount Mitchell, the highest mountain east of the Mississippi River, and Mount Pisgah, known for its panoramic mountain views. Many visitors enjoy abundant rivers and waterfalls, including the highest waterfall in the eastern United States—Whitewater Falls, in Transylvania County. The Nantahala National Forest includes the Joyce Kilmer Wilderness, which contains one of the largest stands of old-growth trees in the Eastern United States The Pisgah National Forest is the site of the Biltmore Forest School, the first forestry school in America, now open to the public as an educational and interpretive center. The North Carolina Arboretum near Asheville, NC, is one of the finest public gardens in the Southern Appalachians. Grandfather Mountain, elevation 5,946 feet above sea level, is a globally recognized nature preserve featuring beautiful mountain scenery, a mile-high swinging bridge, and a nature museum, as well as trails, picnic areas, and naturalist programs.

The Biltmore Estate, also located in Asheville, is known worldwide as "America's Largest Home." This private attraction includes a mansion with 250 rooms, 65 fireplaces, one indoor pool, a bowling alley, vineyards, an historic farm, crafts, and music performances. The estate annually draws approximately one million visitors to the Asheville area.

Outdoor recreation activities include innumerable hiking trails, including a 200-mile section of the famed Appalachian Trail. Top-ranked mountain biking, hunting, fishing, rafting, kayaking, canoeing, birding, rock climbing, camping, skiing, and even ziplining bring outdoor enthusiasts to the area. The ski slopes of Cataloochee, Sugar, and Beech Mountains and others summon winter sports travelers. Rivers such as the Nantahala, French Broad, Green, and Cheoah are among the region's waterways with world-class whitewater rafting, kayaking, canoeing, tubing, swimming, and other water fun. Asheville is repeatedly cited as one of the best travel destinations in the world, offering arts and crafts, outdoor adventures, eclectic cuisine, spas and resorts, public gardens, and more.

The Great Smoky Mountains National Park is the most visited national park.

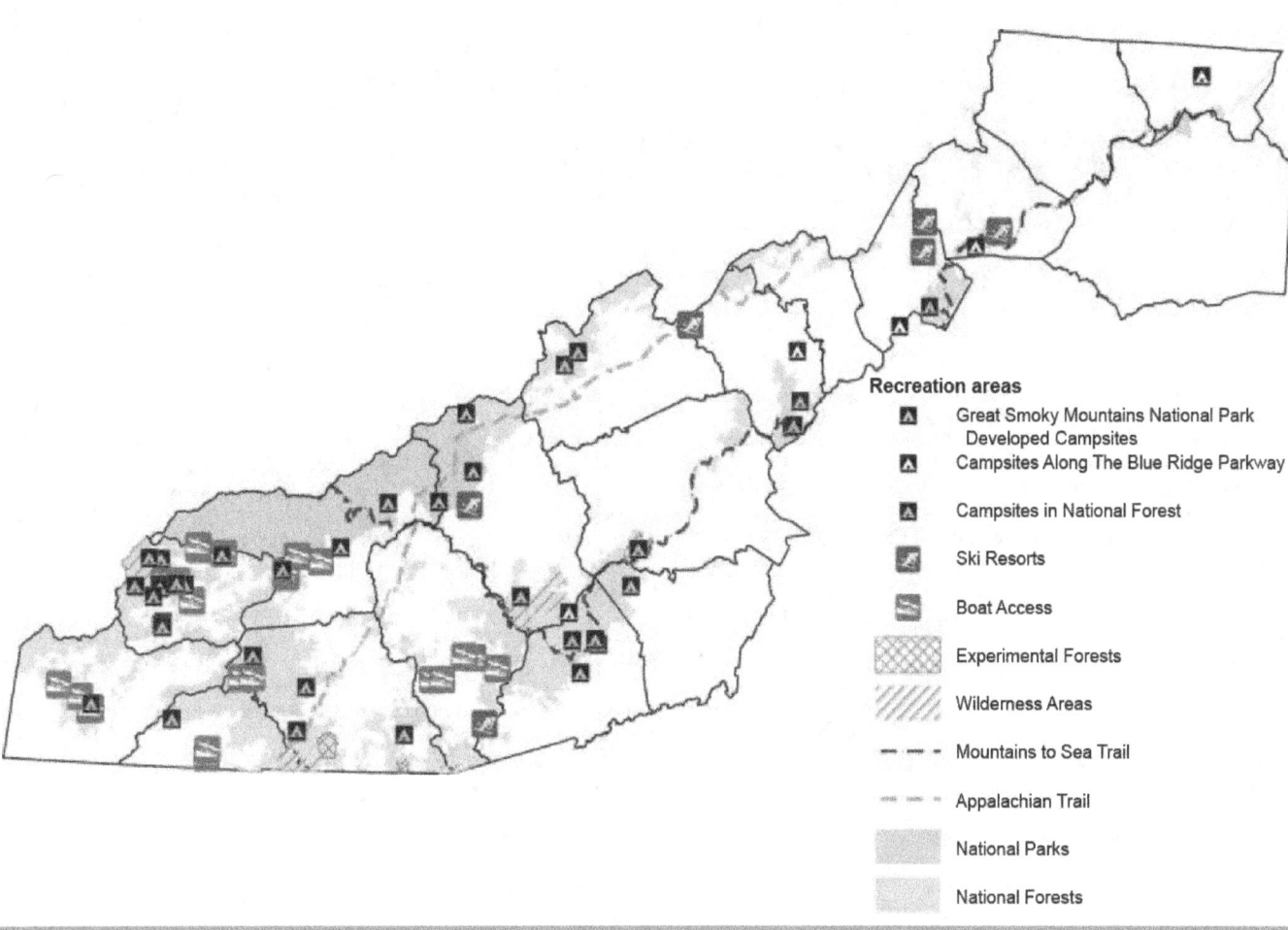

Recreation areas

⛰ Great Smoky Mountains National Park
  Developed Campsites

⛰ Campsites Along The Blue Ridge Parkway

⛰ Campsites in National Forest

🎿 Ski Resorts

S Boat Access

▨ Experimental Forests

▨ Wilderness Areas

– – – Mountains to Sea Trail

— — — Appalachian Trail

  National Parks

  National Forests

Recreation Use
Forest Recreation and Tourism

> The total number of recreation visits in the region's national forests increased from 2.9 million in 1985 to 6.8 million in 2009.

Blue Ridge National Heritage Area

In 2003, again recognizing the region's natural beauty, unique character, and cultural history, the U.S. Congress designated the mountains of Western North Carolina as the Blue Ridge National Heritage Area (BRNHA). The BRNHA includes the 18 counties in this Report Card, plus the Qualla Boundary and Burke, Caldwell, McDowell, Polk, Rutherford, Surry, and Yadkin Counties. The Federal Government cited "a distinctive landscape arising from patterns of human activity shaped by geography." The mission of BRNHA is to protect, preserve, interpret, and develop the region for the benefit of present and future generations and strive to stimulate improved economic opportunity in the area.

Who recreates here and why?

A 2008 study completed in the BRNHA counties found preferences of visitors differ with demographic and socioeconomic factors. It was discovered that a large portion of the visitors to the region come from those living nearby in North Carolina or from surrounding Southeastern States. Of the 4,125 respondents, 23 percent identified themselves as day trippers, and 77 percent as overnight visitors. The average age of day trippers is 50 years old, and for overnight, 53 years old. Most respondents, day or overnight, fell between the ages of 46 to 65. This is slightly higher than that of travelers to the State as a whole, which had a mean age, in 2006, of 45.

Almost half of all visitors to the region have a college degree or a graduate degree, making the BRNHA group more highly educated when compared to the U.S. population, of which 27 percent has a college degree. Well over half of the visitors have higher household incomes than the national median household income. A majority of visitors travel in parties of two, as the median party size for both overnight guests and day trippers was 2.7.

The results indicate the highest preference is for outdoor recreation, followed by festivals and events, gardens or trails, crafts, Cherokee sites, music activities, and farms and orchards. Preferences also appear to differ among men and women. For example, the top activities for women were craft activities, while men rated outdoor recreation or ecotourism at the top of their lists. This data has proved useful in targeting tourism marketing efforts.

The study also gives hints for development of tourism attractions that will appeal to particular visitor sectors.

Number of visitors

From 1985 to 2009, the total number of recreation visits in the region's national forests increased from 2.9 million to 6.8 million, an increase of 136 percent. From 1993–2002, the number of average annual visitors to the North Carolina section of the Blue Ridge Parkway was 11.6 million. The number of visitors to the Great Smoky Mountains National Park in North Carolina and Tennessee has varied slightly, but has remained around 9 million per year. The national forests in Western North Carolina, which offer a much broader range of recreational activities, are some of the most visited in the national forest system.

Tourist Activity Preferences in the Blue Ridge Natural Heritage Area

Total Visitation to Federal Parks and Forests

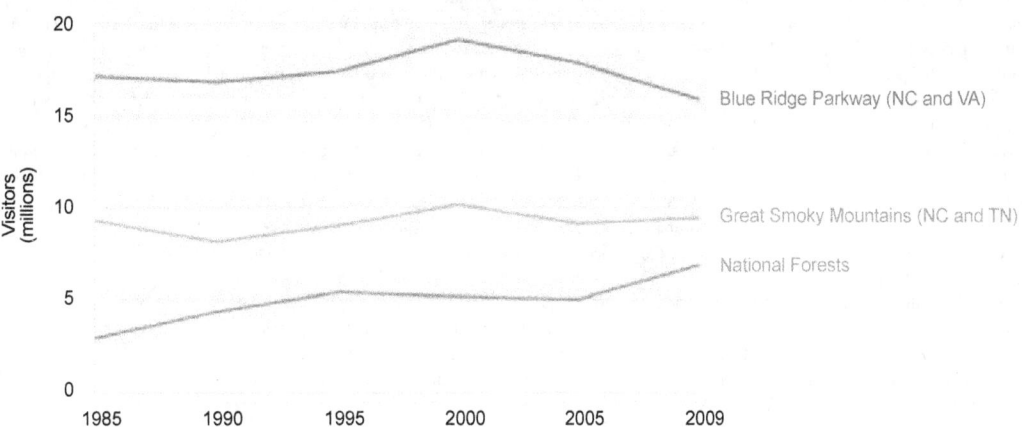

Paying for Recreation
Forest Recreation and Tourism

The region's public and private resources and attractions are a significant driver of the economy and have a strong influence on local employment and wages. In 2008, the annual budget for the entire Blue Ridge Parkway was $16.1 million. Between 1980 and 2006, the Parkway budget increased 0.5 percent after adjusted for inflation; thus, Federal allocations have not kept pace with operating and maintenance costs. Due to flat budget levels, staffing has decreased, many facilities close earlier in the fall and open later in spring, law enforcement officers are stretched beyond capacity, and vistas have become overgrown or non-existent. Preserving and protecting the Parkway and its millions of visitors each year is important. The Parkway is a sound economic engine for tourism, as it generates an estimated $2.3 billion annually in North Carolina and Virginia.

In the Great Smoky Mountains National Park, located in North Carolina and Tennessee, there are similar signs of budget shortfalls. With no entrance fee, the park suffers from overuse. Each year, 9 million people visit only 520,000 acres. In comparison, Yellowstone National Park, which encompasses 2.2 million acres, averages only 3 million visitors annually. The Great Smoky Mountains National Park is estimated to have a maintenance backlog approaching $170 million, and is operating under a shortfall of around $11 million annually.

From 2000 to 2010, total national forest recreation budgets have been steadily increasing. In the Pisgah and Nantahala National Forests, recreation operations and management funds have increased from $1.0 million to $1.8 million, an 80 percent nominal increase (42 percent increase when adjusted for inflation), while trail construction and maintenance has increased from $332,084 to $387,309 (16 percent nominal increase, but an 8 percent decline when adjusted for inflation). From 2000 to 2010, recreation fee receipts to the national forests in Western North Carolina increased from $1,028,477 to $1,338,532 (30 percent nominal increase, but only a 3 percent increase when adjusted for inflation). With passage of the 2005 Recreation Enhancement Act, special recreation uses, such as those that require extra measures to protect natural or cultural resources, saw almost a fourfold increase from $120,928 to $429,036 (but still more than a threefold increase when adjusted for inflation.)

The national forests in Western North Carolina are also dealing with a substantial recreation management and maintenance backlog. The forests have a large number of developed and dispersed recreation sites that are aging and showing signs of overuse.

In addition to the natural attractions, the region includes the city of Asheville, which receives over 2.9 million visitors per year. From 2000 to 2007, the economic contribution of tourism from the greater Asheville area, including direct and indirect revenue, almost doubled from $1.0 billion to $1.9 billion.

The national forests in Western North Carolina have a large number of developed and dispersed recreation sites that are aging and showing signs of overuse.

Couple fishing from picnic site, Nantahala River

Foggy View at Wayah Bald

Mountain Biking

Canoeing on Balsam Lake, Nantahala National Forest

Recreation Fees
Forest Recreation and Tourism

> Neither the Blue Ridge Parkway nor the Great Smoky Mountains National Park charge entrance or user fees.

With operating costs continually increasing and owners/operators rarely able to keep pace, many organizations, both public and private, have had to implement or increase a fee program to meet operating and maintenance costs.

Some national parks collect no entrance or users fees (Great Smoky Mountains and Blue Ridge Parkway), while others (Yellowstone, Yosemite, and Grand Canyon) individually generate more than $4 million a year in entrance fees. The reason the Great Smoky Mountains National Park does not charge an entrance fee dates back to the 1930s, when the land was privately owned. In 1936, the State of Tennessee transferred ownership of Newfound Gap Road to the Federal Government with a stipulation that to travel on the road, "no toll or license fee shall ever be imposed." At the time, the road was a major route crossing the Southern Appalachians, and the State wanted to continue free interstate transportation for its citizens. In order to charge a fee, the Tennessee legislature would be required to lift this deed restriction. Whether or not activity fees will be introduced or increased is still under debate.

With a more encompassing mission of multiple use, the national forests have had somewhat more flexibility in fees and revenue generation. In 2010, the Forest Service proposed modest fee increases for some recreation activities. The fee programs seek to defray the cost of providing services and facilities; however, most recreation is dispersed and the fee program does little to provide management funds for trails and management of backcountry recreation. The great majority of the recreation budget goes to support developed facilities.

User fees are continuing to raise awareness in all national forests and parks. Fee programs commonly referred to as "pay to play" may be the future of hiking and other recreation. Fees are beginning to show up at popular trailheads in some parts of the country where they can be used for trail management and restoration, as well as facility maintenance. Fees may also be implemented to encourage use of less popular areas and curtail use in overused areas. This could in turn lead recreationists to flock to more pristine, lightly used areas of land, which could cause environmental damage in its own regard.

Sample of Camping Fees in Pisgah and Nantahala National Forests

Camping Area	National Forest	1996	2009
Cheoah Point	Nantahala	$ 5	$ 15-35
Tsali	Nantahala	$ 15	$ 16
Jack Rabbit	Nantahala	$ 8	$ 15
Cable Cove	Nantahala	$ 5	$ 10
Hanging Dog	Nantahala	$ 4	$ 8
Lake Powhatan	Pisgah	$ 10	$ 20
Davidson River	Pisgah	$ 11	$ 20
Black Mountain	Pisgah	$ 8	$ 17
Carolina Hemlocks	Pisgah	$ 8	$ 17
Sunburst	Pisgah	$ 4	$ 13
North Mills River	Pisgah	$ 5	$ 13
Rocky Bluff	Pisgah	$ 5	$ 13
Mortimer	Pisgah	$ 4	$ 10

Group Camping Area	National Forest	1996	2009
Rattler Ford	Nantahala	1-50: $15	1-25: $50
Briar Bottom	Pisgah	1-50: $25	1-50: $50-$100
Cove Creek	Pisgah	1-50: $25, 51-100: $45	1-100: $95
Kuykendall	Pisgah	1-50: $50	1-100: $95
White Pines	Pisgah	1-25: $15	1-25: $50
Silvermine	Pisgah	1-25: $25, 26-50: $40	1-25: $25, 26-50: $40

Roadless Areas
Forest Recreation and Tourism

> Private land in the vicinity of public land carries a higher demand for development and may stimulate road construction.

Roadless areas are a limited resource in the Southern Appalachians and in the Eastern United States These areas, almost exclusively in public lands, have regained or are regaining a natural appearance, meaning that any signs of prior human activity are vanishing due to natural forces.

For an area to be identified as a roadless area, it must include no more than one-half mile of improved road for each 1,000 acres. Roadless areas contain the last remaining large tracts of the least disturbed land in the region, other than wilderness. Public land agencies are the primary owners of these areas.

Although the region as a whole is well roaded, there is an exceptionally high number of roadless areas. The largest roadless area in the region and the Southern Appalachian Mountains is in the Great Smoky Mountains National Park, an area containing some 464,544 acres. In addition to areas in the Great Smoky Mountains National Park, the Pisgah and Nantahala National Forests contain around 151,000 roadless acres, or 14.6 percent of total national forest acres.

Forest fragmentation refers to the breaking up of uninterrupted forested areas into smaller zones, and is viewed as harmful to the habitat of many birds, mammals, and plants, as well as entire ecosystems. Animals with large range and breeding requirements are most affected. Open roads can also diminish use for primitive recreation experiences as well as birdwatching, fishing, hiking, and hunting.

Roads also lead to increased erosion and air and water pollution. When new road construction occurs in roadless areas, the area is eliminated from the possibility of future wilderness designation. After construction, roads rarely return to their original state and, therefore, permanently transform the landscape.

New home builders commonly look for natural appearing viewsheds and the desire to share in the immediate benefits of living next to protected land. In Western North Carolina, 43 percent of land is publicly owned or located within 0.5 miles of public lands. An additional 9 percent is within 0.5 to 1 mile of public land. Private land in the vicinity of public land carries a higher demand for development and may stimulate road construction.

The "Road to Nowhere"
In the 1960s, the National Park Service built only 7 miles of a replacement road for Swain County along the north shore of Fontana Lake near Bryson City, NC. They abandoned the project due in part to severe erosion and acidic runoff that harmed fisheries in several streams. The road became known as the "Road to Nowhere."

In a settlement concluded in February of 2009, the U.S. National Park Service agreed to pay Swain County $52 million, which covers the present-day cost of rebuilding the country road that was flooded in the 1940s to create Fontana Lake. The settlement will bring resources to Swain County to create jobs, invest in schools, and improve the county's infrastructure, and the area will stay in a natural state for future generations.

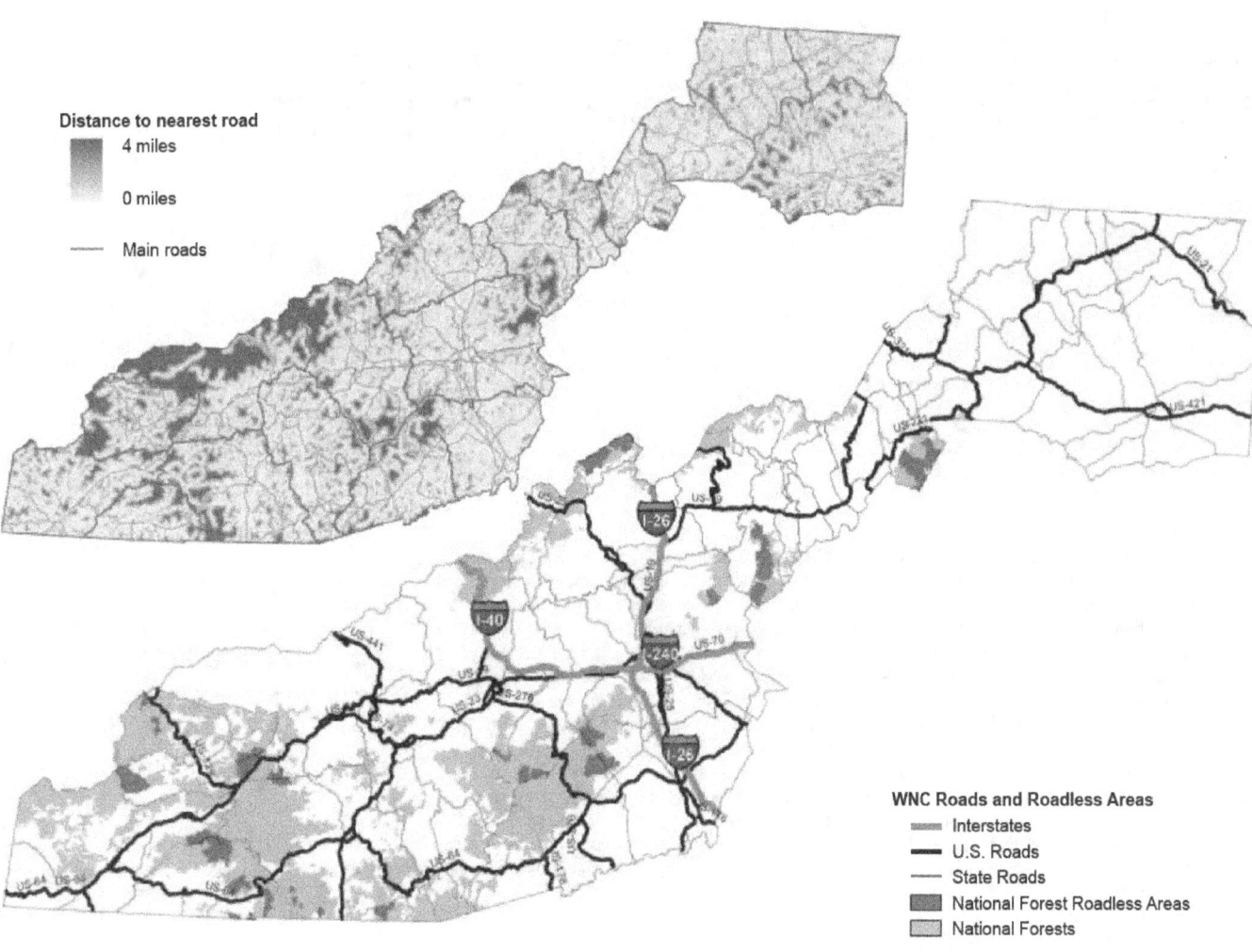

Distance to nearest road

4 miles

0 miles

—— Main roads

WNC Roads and Roadless Areas

▓▓▓ Interstates

■■■ U.S. Roads

—— State Roads

■ National Forest Roadless Areas

▢ National Forests

Development and Conservation
Forest Recreation and Tourism

Western North Carolinians are currently negotiating a balance between the development and conservation of our unique natural resources. If development increases, there will be less open space and more fragmented natural environments. The region needs more and better paying jobs and faces significant challenges in meeting the costs of growth. An important expanding growth sector is tourism and outdoor recreation.

Scenarios which portray conservation versus development are not always the best option. The challenge to our mountain communities is to manage growth and foster mixed-use development while balancing green (natural) and gray (concrete or man-made) infrastructure.

Communities around the country are using resourceful policies to develop in ways that conserve natural lands and critical environmental areas, protect natural resources, restore previously developed land, and create jobs in the process. In Western North Carolina, the Linking Lands Project of the Land-of-Sky Regional Council is an example of a project that is using a sustainable development planning approach to identify a possible green infrastructure in Buncombe, Henderson, Transylvania, and Madison Counties. The plan identifies a physical network of the region's most valuable elements, including recreation lands, wildlife habitat, forest lands, water resources, farmlands, and cultural resources. This plan can serve as a planning resource for local governments, land trusts, landowners, and developers.

Smart growth is a related component of sustainable development that helps to reduce urban sprawl. The features that distinguish smart growth in a community vary, but, in general, smart growth development is town-centered, public-transit and pedestrian oriented, and has a greater mix of housing, commercial, and retail uses than traditional sprawl development. It also preserves open space and critical environmental areas and takes advantage of compact building designs that will minimize impervious surfaces.

The Linking Lands Project of the Land-of-Sky Regional Council is an example of a project that is using a sustainable development planning approach.

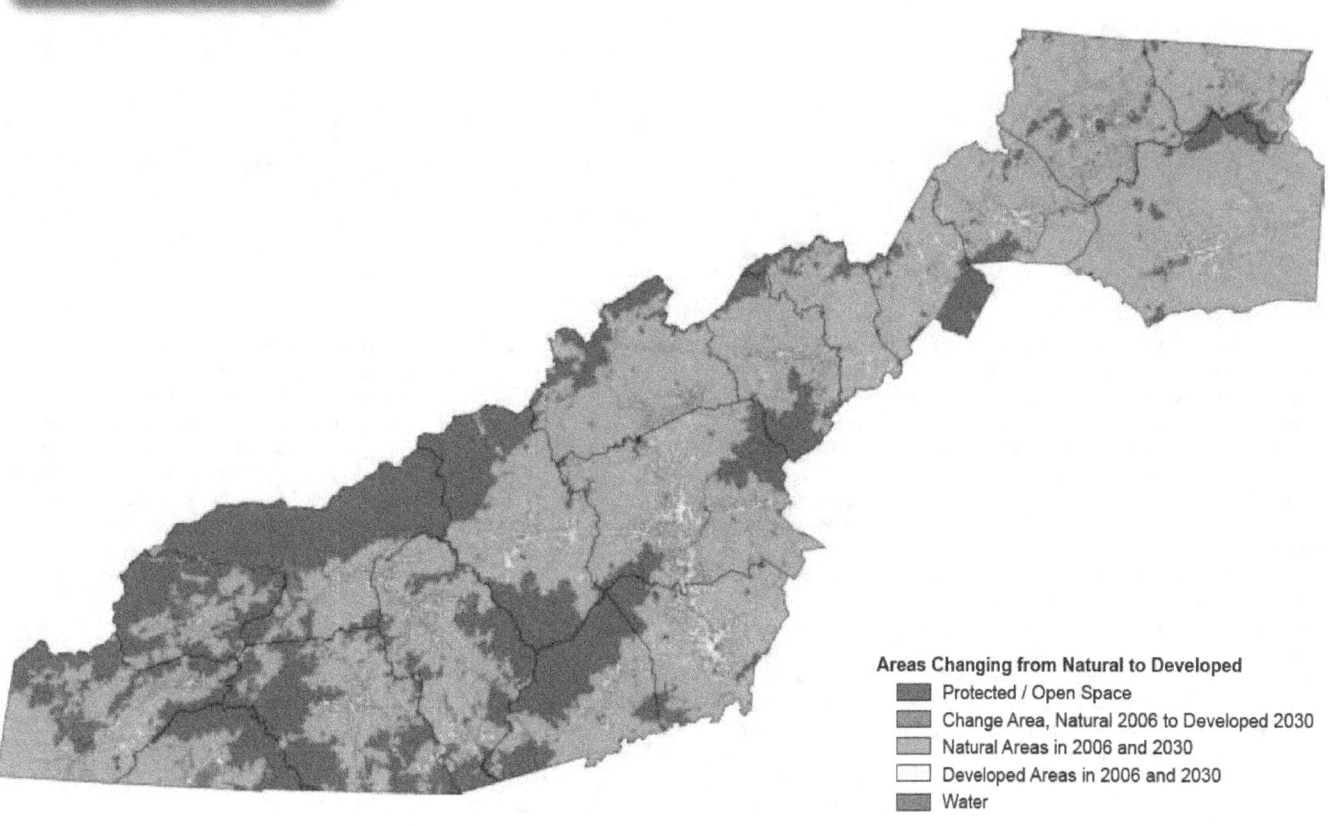

Areas Changing from Natural to Developed

- Protected / Open Space
- Change Area, Natural 2006 to Developed 2030
- Natural Areas in 2006 and 2030
- Developed Areas in 2006 and 2030
- Water

Roundwood Product Output and Distribution
Forest Products and Manufacturing

Western North Carolina has 3.2 million acres of timberland. The mountain region, an area of rugged terrain and limited access, has relatively few large cities compared to the rest of the State. Upland hardwoods cover the majority of the forested landscape, and white pine is the most common softwood type. Ownership of the region's timber is dominated by the private sector.

Sawlogs and veneer
Roundwood refers to logs, bolts, or other round sections cut from trees for industrial manufacture or consumer use. Saw logs are at least 8 feet in length and can be processed into a variety of sawn products, such as lumber, cants, pallets, railroad ties, and timbers. Veneer logs are roundwood products that are either rotary cut, sliced, stamped, or sawn into a variety of veneer products, such as plywood, finished panels, veneer sheets, or sheathing.

Pulpwood
Pulpwood is wood that is reduced to individual fibers by chemical or mechanical means. The fibers are used to make a broad generic group of pulp products that includes paper products as well as fiberboard, insulating board, and paperboard.

Fuelwood
Fuelwood is roundwood harvested for residential use. Fuelwood consumption is falling because it is labor intensive and considered less safe than alternative energy sources. Domestic fuelwood does, however, account for a fairly significant portion of hardwood product output (22 percent) in the region.

Other products
Other industrial wood products include composite panels manufactured into chips, wafers, strands, flakes, shavings, or sawdust and then reconstituted into a variety of panel and engineered lumber products.

Posts, poles, and pilings are milled or cut and peeled into standard sizes (lengths and circumferences) to be put in the ground to provide vertical and lateral support in buildings, foundations, utility lines, and fences. This category may also include nonindustrial unmilled products.

Product distribution
Saw logs dominate the market in both softwood and hardwood product distribution in the region. From 1995 to 2007, of the total average distribution of softwood products, 13.2 million cubic feet (71 percent) was saw logs. From 1995 to 2007, of the total average distribution of hardwood products, 26.1 million cubic feet (50 percent) was saw logs. Saw logs, the most valuable roundwood product, are cut from the largest and most mature trees. The volume of sawtimber is increasing in the region as the forest reaches maturity.

From 1995 to 2007, of the total average distribution of softwood products, 4.2 million cubic feet (22 percent) was pulpwood. From 1995 to 2007, of the total average distribution of hardwood products, 11.4 million cubic feet (22 percent) was pulpwood.

Ownership of the Western North Carolina region's timber is dominated by the private sector.

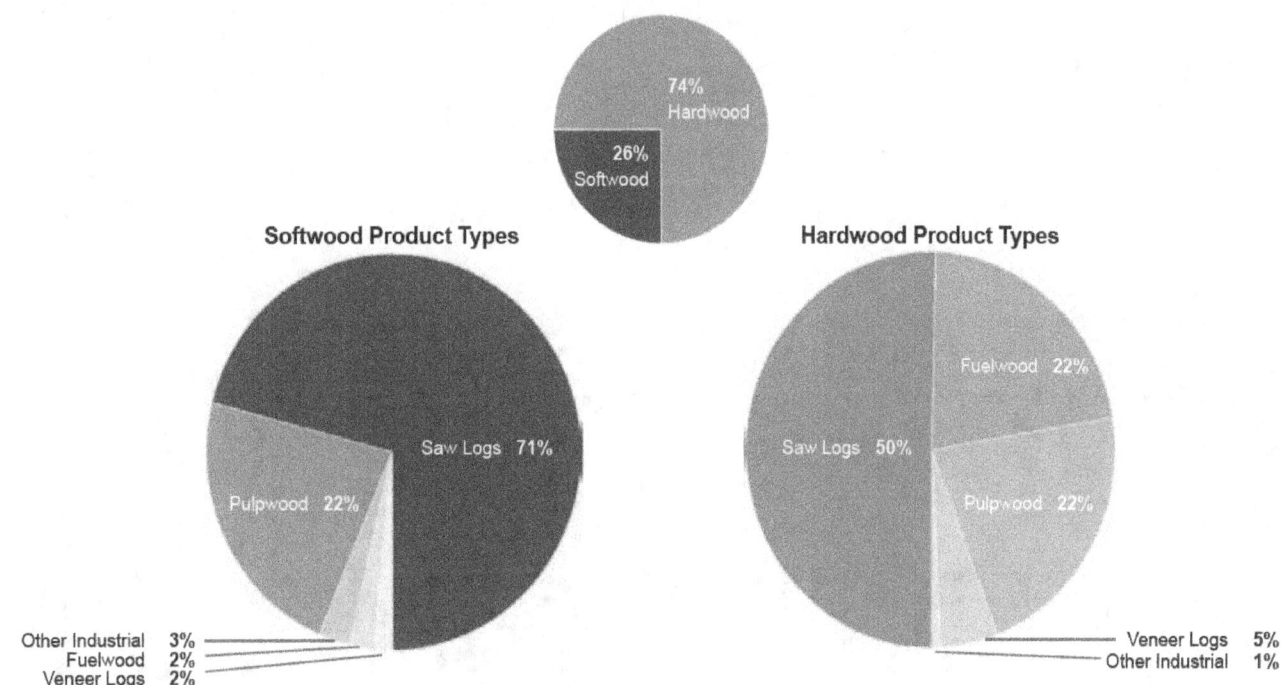

Average Wood Product Output 1995–2007

74% Hardwood

26% Softwood

Softwood Product Types

Saw Logs 71%

Pulpwood 22%

Other Industrial 3%
Fuelwood 2%
Veneer Logs 2%

Hardwood Product Types

Fuelwood 22%

Saw Logs 50%

Pulpwood 22%

Veneer Logs 5%
Other Industrial 1%

Contribution of Timberland to Economy
Forest Products and Manufacturing

Roundwood product output

Roundwood is cut from softwood and hardwood trees. Softwoods, such as pine, spruce, and fir, are evergreen trees with needle or scale-like leaves. Hardwoods, such as oak, maple, poplar, and hickory, have broad leaves with a large surface area that are shed annually. Hardwood product removal represents 74 percent of annual roundwood output in the region, while softwood output comprises the remaining 26 percent. In Western North Carolina during the period 1995–2007, the total average roundwood output was 70.6 million cubic feet per year.

Annual variation in roundwood production closely mirrors national economic trends. From 1995 to 1999, roundwood output declined by 8 percent. The following 3 years (2000–2003), however, roundwood output increased by 8 percent. From 2005 to 2007, outputs declined by 19.3 percent due to changing economic conditions, a trend that continues into the present. In addition, from 2005 to 2007, four sawtimber mills closed—one each in Yancey and Watauga Counties, and two in Alleghany County. In 2007, 37 manufacturing mills were operating in the region.

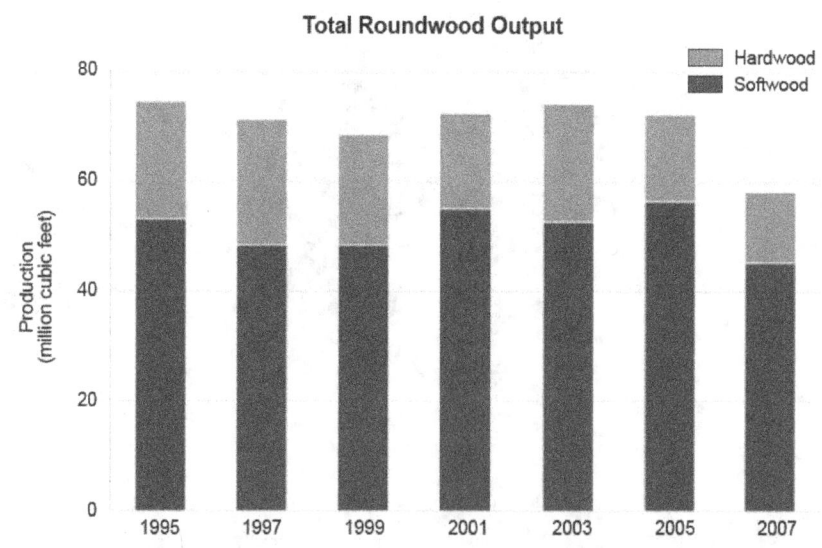

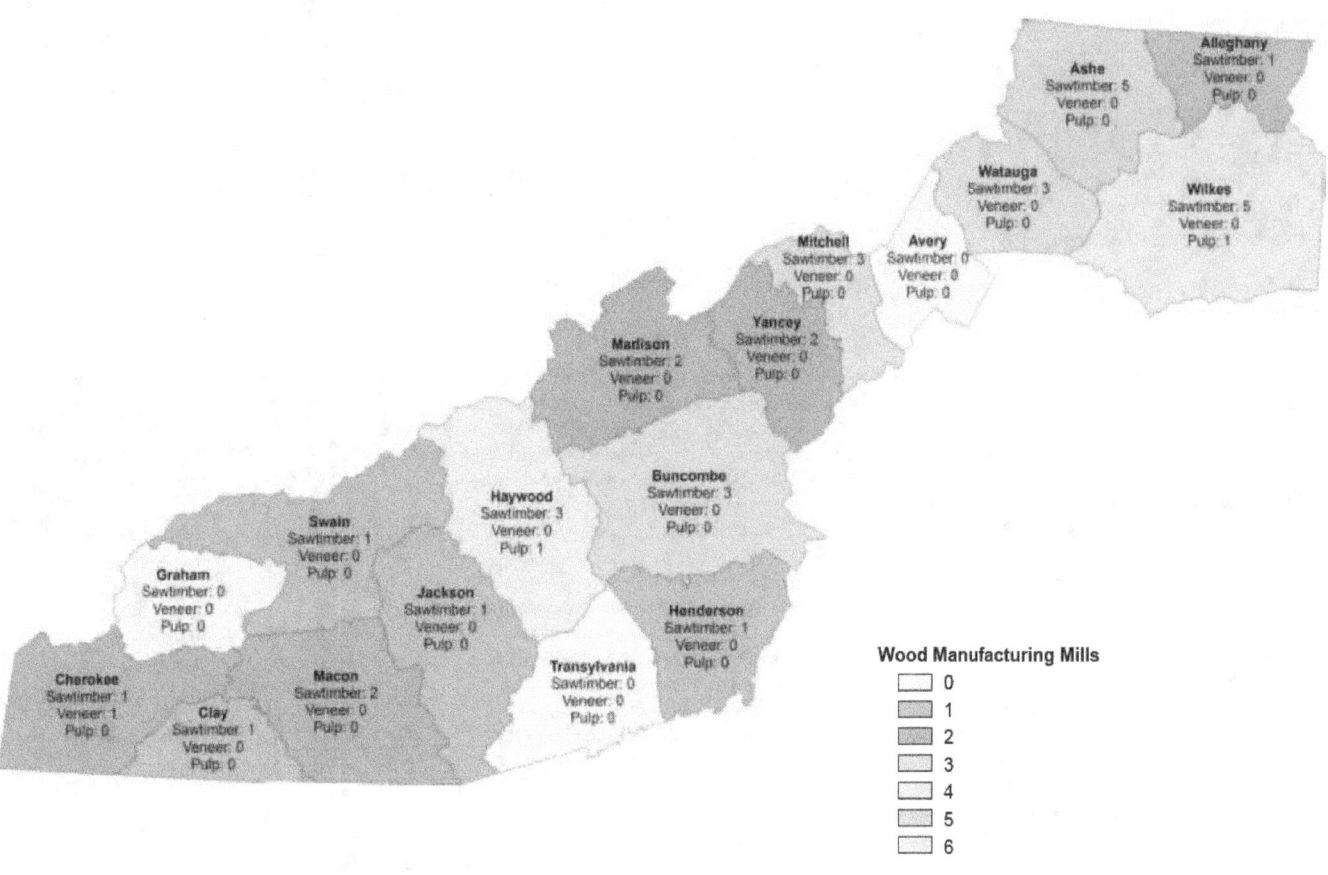

Ashe
Sawtimber: 5
Veneer: 0
Pulp: 0

Alleghany
Sawtimber: 1
Veneer: 0
Pulp: 0

Watauga
Sawtimber: 3
Veneer: 0
Pulp: 0

Wilkes
Sawtimber: 5
Veneer: 0
Pulp: 1

Mitchell
Sawtimber: 3
Veneer: 0
Pulp: 0

Avery
Sawtimber: 0
Veneer: 0
Pulp: 0

Madison
Sawtimber: 2
Veneer: 0
Pulp: 0

Yancey
Sawtimber: 2
Veneer: 0
Pulp: 0

Buncombe
Sawtimber: 3
Veneer: 0
Pulp: 0

Haywood
Sawtimber: 3
Veneer: 0
Pulp: 1

Swain
Sawtimber: 1
Veneer: 0
Pulp: 0

Graham
Sawtimber: 0
Veneer: 0
Pulp: 0

Jackson
Sawtimber: 1
Veneer: 0
Pulp: 0

Henderson
Sawtimber: 1
Veneer: 0
Pulp: 0

Cherokee
Sawtimber: 1
Veneer: 1
Pulp: 0

Macon
Sawtimber: 2
Veneer: 0
Pulp: 0

Transylvania
Sawtimber: 0
Veneer: 0
Pulp: 0

Clay
Sawtimber: 1
Veneer: 0
Pulp: 0

Wood Manufacturing Mills
- 0
- 1
- 2
- 3
- 4
- 5
- 6

Value of Forest Products
Forest Products and Manufacturing

> Recently, the U.S. Congress approximately doubled payments to Western North Carolina counties in lieu of taxes.

Stumpage value is the monetary value of standing timber, or the price a landowner typically receives for harvested trees. Delivered value is the price of stumpage plus logging, transportation, and site stabilization costs, also known as the price to the logger.

From 1995 to 2003, stumpage values of total roundwood output increased from $50.2 million to $71.3 million (42 percent). In 2005, stumpage values decreased to $57.7 million, and by 2007 had reached a low of $38.9 million, a 22 percent drop since 1995. Stumpage price is an important factor in determining when timberland owners will offer their trees for sale.

From 1995 to 1999, delivered average annual values decreased from $155.4 million to $134.2 million (down 14 percent). From 1999 to 2003, delivered average annual values increased from $134.2 to $165.2 million (up 23 percent). With a shrinking regional forest-based economy and closing of four mills, both the delivered and stumpage values continued to decline after 2003. From 2003 to 2007, delivered average annual values dropped from $165.2 million to $110 million.

According to North Carolina Agricultural Statistics, the total forest products income for years 2005 and 2006 for all 18 counties was $93.9 million and $86.2 million, respectively (totals vary due to data-collection differences). In these 2 years, the counties with the highest revenues were Wilkes, Haywood, Yancey, Ashe, and Madison.

Payments in lieu of taxes

Payments in lieu of taxes are Federal payments to local governments that help offset losses in property taxes due to nontaxable Federal lands within their boundaries, such as national forests. The funds are reserved for local governments (usually counties) that provide services related to public safety, environment, housing, social assistance, and transportation. From 2001 to 2007, counties with land in the Pisgah and Nantahala National Forests received on average $1.35 an acre, or $2.2 million annually. Recently, the U.S. Congress increased the allocation to $2.35 per acre, and in 2009 the counties received twice that of the previous yearly average, or $4.4 million.

Loading Roundwood

Value of Timber Products

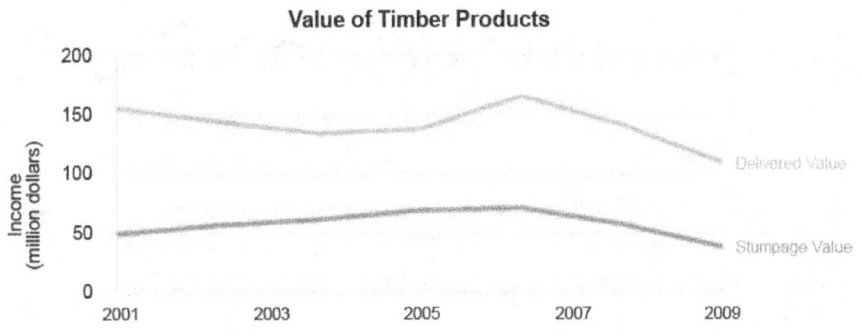

Total Forest Products Income by Regional Council of Government

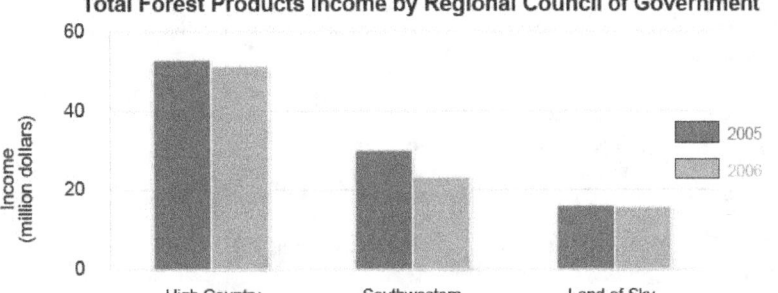

Payment in Lieu of Taxes and Total National Forest Acres

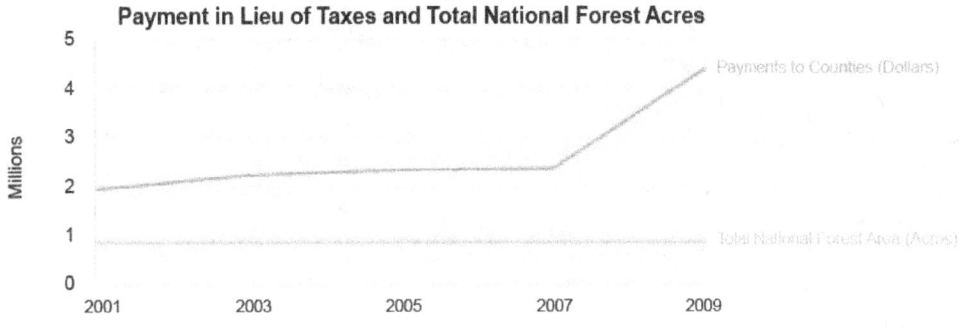

Recycling
Forest Manufacturing and Products

In fiscal year 2008–2009, Buncombe County ranked fourth out of North Carolina's 100 counties in residential recycling.

Paper, plastic, metal, and glass recovery

In fiscal year 2008–2009, Buncombe County ranked fourth out of North Carolina's 100 counties in residential recycling. Three counties outside the region—Pitt, Catawba, and Dare—were the only counties in North Carolina that ranked above Buncombe in per county recycling. Buncombe has a per capita recovery rate of around 443 pounds, which is almost three times the State average. The success of Buncombe County's program can be credited to recycling infrastructure (curbside recycling and drop-off centers), educational efforts, and community leadership.

Nearly half of the top 20 per capita recycling counties are located in Western North Carolina. Rural counties like Swain County ranked sixth, with a per capita recovery of 270 pounds and a population of around 14,000. Swain has stationed recycling trailers, mostly at schools, throughout the county, and also works with businesses to facilitate the recycling of cardboard and plastics. State grants to Swain County have helped improve recycling efforts by allowing the county to purchase trucks and other equipment. Macon, Haywood, and Watauga Counties also performed well in the ranking. The amount of materials recycled statewide in fiscal year 2008–2009 increased by 3.2 percent.

Paper and wood recovery

Buncombe County is also the leader in the region for wood product recovery, reporting around 43,000 tons of cardboard and paper recovery in 2008–2009. Haywood County recycles over 4,000 tons of wood products, followed by Watauga (3,500 tons), Macon (2,300 tons), and Henderson (2,000 tons) Counties.

Local recycling programs are important to economic development, as companies in the State rely on the flow of materials from recycling programs to sustain and create new jobs. By 2012, the State hopes to recycle 2 million tons annually from local programs and to successfully implement upcoming disposal bans on plastic bottles, wooden pallets, and motor vehicle oil filters.

Average Recycling Rates by Regional Council of Government, 2009

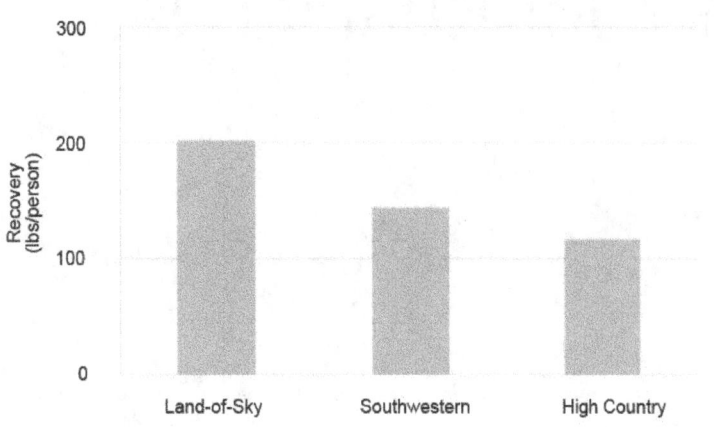

Paper and Wood Recovery, July 2008 – June 2009

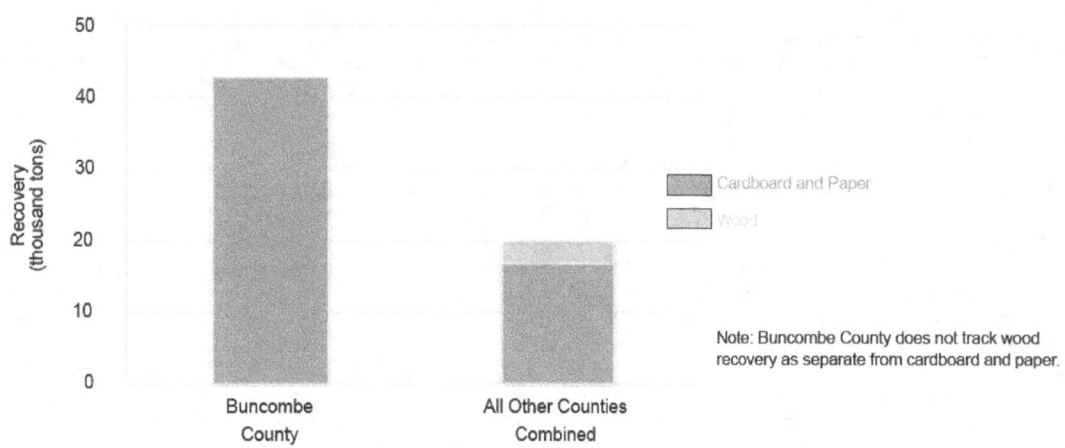

Note: Buncombe County does not track wood recovery as separate from cardboard and paper.

Arts and Craft
Cultural and Spiritual Values

From indigenous tribes that populated the region long ago to the present day, people have taken advantage of the natural materials around them to create, either out of need or desire.

Arts and craft

The people of Western North Carolina continue to maintain long-held traditions of craft making and artistic achievement. From indigenous tribes that populated the region long ago to the present day, people have taken advantage of the natural materials around them to create, either out of need or desire. In this way, they have helped shape the culture around them.

Over the last two centuries, wood and other indigenous plants harvested from forests and open areas were used to produce furniture, tools, utensils, crates, frames, mantles, bowls, vessels, sculpture, musical instruments, and looms. Woodcarving, which was mostly done with a pocket knife, was an important source of income, and successful carving centers developed in Cherokee, Asheville, Tryon, and Brasstown.

Basketry, often made with river cane, once an abundant plant in the Southeast but now less so, was a highly profitable craft in Western North Carolina. Mostly attributed to Cherokee origins, this art form has remained a popular craft in the region. While white oak (or "basket oak") and hickory are the materials generally used in baskets, other usable native materials include ash, broom sedge, corn husks, corn stalks, wheat and rye straw, willow branches and twigs, rushes, honeysuckle vine, hickory bark, and peeled willow bark. Metalwork, pottery, glasswork, and textiles are also important crafts in the region.

During the Great Depression (1930s), many Western North Carolinians remained financially solvent by meeting continued demand for their work from outside the region. In Asheville and closely surrounding areas, in particular, the Vanderbilt family supported local artisans by either purchasing their hand-made products to furnish the lavish Biltmore Estate or through Biltmore Industries, an innovative venture that provided education, guidance, and support to local craftspeople.

Inspired expression

Many past and present musicians, photographers, painters, and other artists have found inspiration in the region's geographic and cultural diversity. Brought to the region by early immigrants of mostly Scotch, Irish, and English descent, mountain music has always held center stage in community life. Ballads of homelands left behind, songs of the Civil War, and religious songs were exchanged and combined to form a particular sound, pitch, and feeling of connectedness. From the 1870s through the 1940s, small medicine shows traveled throughout the region selling their homemade remedies and drawing a crowd with music. Music retains a firm place in the ear of the region's culture.

George Masa, a Japanese immigrant, settled in Asheville in 1915 and spent the rest of his life photographing the mountains in and around the Blue Ridge Parkway, the Appalachian Trail, and what would become, with his untiring support, the Great Smoky Mountains National Park. His work is the largest and most complete collection of photographs of the region during the early 20th century.

Painter Robert Scott Duncanson (1821–1872), an African-American artist, came to Asheville in 1850. He frequented the area thereafter and made numerous paintings, capturing the face of the region, not only in rural areas, but also in the city of Asheville.

Art and crafts have been prominent in Western North Carolina for over two centuries, and these trades remain an ever growing and flourishing sector today. Several schools, such as The Penland School of Craft in Yancey County and the John C. Campbell Folk School in Cherokee County, as well as numerous guilds, galleries, and festivals, support and grow this sector of the region's economy. In 2007, a study done by HandMade in America covering the 18 counties as well as Burke, Caldwell, McDowell, Polk, Rutherford, Surry, and Yadkin Counties, found that the professional craft industry had an economic impact of $206 million, an increase from $122 million in 1995.

George Masa, 1933

Total Economic Impact of the Professional Craft Industry, 2007

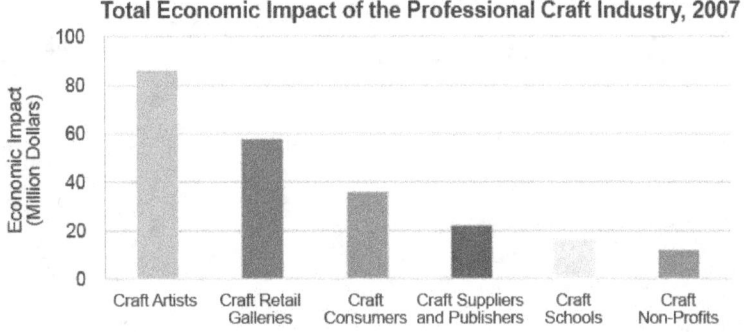

Musicians Jim Proffitt
and Grace Newman, circa 1930,
Great Smoky Mountains National Park

Mack McCarter family working
on baskets on front porch, 1930–1936,
Great Smoky Mountains National Park

Non-Consumptive Values
Cultural and Spiritual Values

> Western North Carolina is home to over 100 spiritual retreats, many located in forested areas.

Experiencing nature

The beauty of Western North Carolina affects all who come here, and its landscapes inspire a deep psychological reaction in most individuals. The Cherokee Indians, early inhabitants of the region, sought to protect and nurture their land, not only through personal and communal activities, but also by the way they applied the beliefs they hold about the land. Perhaps one of their most pervasive concepts is the belief that land is alive.

Cherokee land is traditionally held in common by the tribe, allowing individual family groups to occupy it as needed. The tribe's connection with the land drives their responsibility for its conservation and protection. They depend on the land for food and herbs, materials for shelter, clothing and utensils, visual pleasure, and artistic inspiration. Decisions are based on the concept of reciprocity—the knowledge that life is cyclical and actions have both short- and long-term consequences.

Another examination of human response to the natural environment was documented in a 1999 study, which confirmed that spending time in natural areas, specifically wilderness, provides people with a rich array of visual, auditory, olfactory, and other cues that make them feel that the place has come "alive," and hence spiritually inspirational.

The beneficial aspects of wilderness recreation include not only the potential for physical and emotional growth, but moreover, the opportunity to grow spiritually. What's more, once people are faced with questions about one's own spirituality, and begin to contemplate and define their own conceptualization of "that which is spiritual," they may find unique opportunities in their everyday lives of ways to enhance their spiritual growth.

Additionally, Western North Carolina is home to over 100 spiritual retreats, many located in forested areas. The mountains offer a respite from busy lives and an opportunity to experience the mysteries of the natural world.

Photo by George Masa

A contemplative moment

Spiritual Retreats by Theology or Denomination, 2010

Theology	Total
Catholic	21
Christian-Ecumenical	16
Methodist	14
Non-Denominational	12
Episcopal	9
Presbyterian	7
Yoga	6
Baptist	6
Trappist	3
Meditation	3
Lutheran	3
Inter-Denominational	3
Adrian Dominican Sisters	2
Zen Buddhist	1
Sisters of the Holy Cross	1
Seventh-Day Adventist	1
Redemptorist	1
Jewish	1
Jesuit	1
Greek Orthodox	1
Disciples of Christ	1
Community of St. Mary	1
Church of Brethren	1

Policy
Planning and Monitoring, Laws, and Public Participation

Residents of Western North Carolina desire a sustainable stream of products and services from the region's forests, including healthy ecosystems, economic opportunities, attractive communities, scenic vistas, and wild places for recreation, to name only a few.

Scattered development, eroding hillsides, air pollution, nonnative species invasion, altered surface hydrology, forest pests and diseases, and changes in climate pose risks to the region's ecosystems.

Western North Carolina policy makers have the opportunity to combine management, conservation, and preservation of the region's natural resources to reach desired future conditions. Setting land use and resource conservation goals are essential for effective long-term environmental protection. Moreover, if we want to continue to build capacity to rapidly respond to a changing landscape, we need good information from which to base actions.

The sustainability of our forests, therefore, is largely dependent on the region's institutional ability to comprehensively evaluate trends and conditions. Western North Carolina has a long history of cooperation between resource professionals and interested parties to define issues of concern and to provide decision makers with alternatives.

Private and Public Lands
PlanningandMonitoring

Federal, State, and local planning and monitoring programs are enabling the region to assess information and prepare for change. Programs are in place for land conservation and protection, aquatic and terrestrial wildlife, water quality and quantity, and air quality.

A forest plan identifies short- and long-term management objectives such as thinning, harvesting, and regeneration, nontimber product management, soil and water protection, wildlife habitat creation and protection, natural beauty, and other important resource activities.

Resource specialists with the North Carolina Division of Forest Resources, as well as professional consulting foresters, provide land management planning services to nonindustrial forest landowners. The American Tree Farm System, a national program begun in North Carolina in 1944, also provides planning expertise. Tree farmers are recognized by the Tree Farm sign, which is received when a significant portion of a management plan is implemented and certified. The property is monitored every 5 years to verify plan implementation.

The USDA Forest Service has several ongoing programs that monitor forest resources in Western North Carolina. The Forest Inventory and Analysis (FIA) Program has been tracking wildlife habitat, forest health, plant diversity, insect outbreaks, wood supply, timber resources, and other forest characteristics since the 1930s.

FIA tracks the movement of logs from forest to mill and surveys the location, size, and type of mill in the region. Additionally, information is periodically collected on forest-land ownership, the reasons for owning forest land, and possible futures of these lands.

The USDA Forest Service Eastern Forest Environmental Threat Assessment Center, located in Asheville, monitors the effects and consequences of complex stresses on forest health and provides land managers with credible predictions of potentially severe disturbances with sufficient warning to take preventative actions.

The USDA Forest Service Forest Health Monitoring (FHM) program tracks changes and trends in forest condition on an annual basis. FHM uses data from ground plots and surveys, aerial surveys, and other biotic and abiotic sources to evaluate forest health conditions affecting the sustainability of forest ecosystems.

Many communities have developed management plans for their urban forests. These include urban forest master plans or strategic plans, street tree planting and maintenance plans, city parks vegetation management plans, and hazard tree reduction and replanting plans.

Local municipalities in Western North Carolina monitor trees along city streets, parks, and natural areas by periodically collecting data on tree condition, size, damage, and defects. The larger municipalities in the region have annual budgets to track the vitality of watersheds and urban forests, including the removal of damaged or dead trees and the maintenance of healthy trees as necessary.

Forest Stewardship Plans (1990–2007)

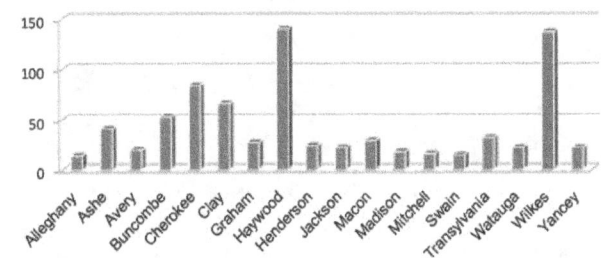

Forest Stewardship Plans (1990–2007)

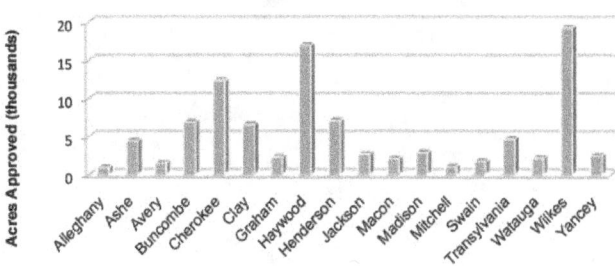

National forest plans are prepared in accordance with detailed planning regulations authorized by the U.S. Congress. The major themes of a national forest plan are identified with input from resource planners, the public, and in collaboration with those interested in the future of the forest.

The current Nantahala and Pisgah National Forest Plan was published in 1994 and is scheduled for revision in 2011. It guides activities on 1,041,451 acres in 15 counties in Western North Carolina and specifically addresses resource development, management, and conservation. The plan also established desired future conditions and overall objectives for recreation areas, trails, visual resources, forest roads, minerals, wildlife and fish, cultural resources, timber production, nontimber forest production, vegetative management, wild and prescribed fire, forest pests and disease, and rehabilitation and stabilization of eroding areas.

Several new issues have arisen or have become significant since the 1994 plan was written and will be addressed in the upcoming revision. These include invasive nonnative plants, forest fragmentation, loss of the Carolina and eastern hemlock, and maintenance and restoration of Southern Appalachian bogs.

On a periodic basis, specialists monitor a number of resource conditions in the Pisgah and Nantahala National Forests. They monitor trends in biodiversity (rare, threatened, and endangered plant and animal communities), timber growth and removals (softwood and hardwood products), forest botanical products (Galax, vines, ginseng, bloodroot, and black cohosh), and mineral extraction (limestone, dimension and aggregate stone), road construction, closure, and maintenance, and wildfires (number, acreage, and intensity).

They also monitor forest health concerns, such as damage from insects and disease (southern pine beetle, gypsy moth, hemlock and balsam woolly adelgid, oak decline, and dogwood anthracnose) and the spread of invasive species such as princess tree, Japanese honeysuckle, multiflora rose, kudzu, and oriental bittersweet.

Additional monitoring efforts include air quality (sulfate particles and low-level ozone), soil and water resources (riparian areas, floodplains, wetlands, water quality, soil erosion, and stream sedimentation), and maintenance and protection of vistas, recreation sites, and cultural resources.

Some monitoring programs are not sufficiently funded to accomplish necessary site visits and management treatments. Of particular concern are trends in biodiversity and the spread of invasive plants.

Land Conservation and Protection
Planning and Monitoring

North Carolina's Department of Environment and Natural Resources (DENR), through the initiative One North Carolina Naturally, has created a planning tool to help prioritize land and resources of exceptional value. Other planning efforts include the Natural Heritage Program, which inventories, catalogues, and supports conservation of the rarest and the most outstanding elements of natural diversity, the Conservation Tax Credit Program, which offers a tax credit to promote conservation of ecosystem functions, and the Stewardship Program, which provides guidance and funding for conservation easements held by the State of North Carolina.

Blue Ridge Forever is a long-term campaign led by 13 land conservation organizations located throughout Western North Carolina. The goal is to identify and safeguard land and water in the southern Blue Ridge mountains. Their landscape level plan guides the protection of nationally or State designated ecological areas of significance, including wildlife habitat, high water quality, areas of cultural and economic significance and scenic value, and working farms and forests.

The Land-of-Sky Regional Council, serving Buncombe, Henderson, Madison, and Transylvania Counties, is currently designing a regional conservation framework called Linking Lands and Communities, which will help guide future growth in those counties.

In 2005, the High Country Council of Governments, serving Alleghany, Ashe, Avery, Mitchell, Watauga, Wilkes, and Yancey Counties, created a description and synthesis of conservation activities and plans in their region. The new oversight plan reports on priority sites for future protection as identified by various organizations, local governments, and public agencies. In 2008, the High Country Regional Trail plan was created, identifying general trail locations and connections as well as 389 miles of proposed local and regional trails.

The Mountain Landscapes Initiative, a partnership project between The Community Foundation of Western North Carolina and the Southwestern Commission Council of Government serving Cherokee, Clay, Graham, Haywood, Jackson, Macon, and Swain Counties, identifies sound practices for clearing home sites and grading roads on a slope as well as guiding farmland preservation, affordable housing, and green building techniques.

Currently, specialists at the University of North Carolina at Charlotte are collaborating to forecast the impacts of urban growth on natural and rural lands in Western North Carolina. The project evaluates the expansion of urban development since 1976 and predicts the loss of natural and agricultural areas in 2030. Results of the study will heighten community awareness of the consequences of unmanaged development and provide important information to guide planners in management decisions.

Several initiatives are in place to identify and safeguard land and water in Western North Carolina.

The Southern Appalachian Man and the Biosphere Program (SAMAB) is a public/private partnership whose mission is to promote the environmental health and stewardship of natural, economic, and cultural resources in the Southern Appalachians. SAMAB partners include Federal, State, and regional resource management agencies, universities, and the private sector. Established in 1988, SAMAB has supported numerous projects and conferences that have improved communication and cooperation within the region. Among these is an assessment, completed in July 1996, that created a framework for future management of the region. The Southern Appalachian Assessment was completed by resource agencies with input from a large segment of the natural resources community and the public. The report assessed atmospheric, social/cultural/economic, terrestrial, and aquatic resources. The assessment revealed no major crises but did identify several issues of concern, including outbreaks of forest pests, water pollution and water acidification, and forest fragmentation. The report also shed light on the types of changes expected across the landscape as the region's forests reach maturity.

The Appalachian Trail is a unique corridor traversing the highest ridge tops between Maine and Georgia. It is considered a "barometer" for the air, water, and biological diversity of the Appalachian Mountains. The National Park Service and Appalachian Trail Conservancy, in cooperation with other organizations, have created a monitoring program on the 2,170-mile trail. The Appalachian Trail Environmental Monitoring Program assesses and monitors natural resource trends across the trail's 270,000-acre land base.

In 2002, the U.S. Fire Learning Network (FLN) was created through a multi-agency cooperative agreement. Since 2007, the Southern Blue Ridge division of the FLN has taken charge of 2.7 million acres across Georgia, North Carolina, and Tennessee. The FLN identifies specific plant communities, such as oak-hickory and pine-oak forests, in need of fire restoration, chooses and monitors fire demonstration sites, and educates the public on the benefits of prescribed burning. The FLN approach encourages the practitioner community to share experience and learning across geographies and to improve integrated fire management practices over time.

GeoBook is a monitoring tool designed by the U.S. Environmental Protection Agency primarily for county planners, watershed managers, or local land trusts and conservation groups needing a wide range of information on an area the size of a few counties or a watershed. It is intended for people who need geographical data but do not have access to the technical expertise or software to use such information. GeoBook provides a simple way to visualize local land uses and natural resources such as urban, agriculture, and forest land use, water resources, and demographic trends within a defined geographical area.

Aquatic and Terrestrial Wildlife
Planning and Monitoring

The North Carolina Wildlife Resources Commission Wildlife Action Plan (WAP) guides the management of the region's fish and wildlife. The plan was developed to improve the understanding of species diversity, make informed decisions for all species, conserve and enhance habitats and the communities they support, foster cooperation with other regional resource managers, support educational efforts, and improve existing regulations and programs.

The plan targets imperiled animals and their required habitats early, preventing them from becoming extinct. Along the Little Tennessee River, biologists are stabilizing banks, reintroducing species, and improving flow management to restore habitat for threatened fish and mussels.

The continued availability of natural lands and wildlife populations will allow those engaged in wildlife-oriented recreation, be it consumptive or non-consumptive, to continue to enjoy their pursuit.

The North Carolina Wildlife Resources Commission (NCWRC) is responsible for monitoring fish and wildlife in Western North Carolina. The agency monitors hunter harvest of big game animals (deer, bear, turkey, and boar) through the Big Game Harvest Reporting System. Population estimates are derived for deer and bear using collected data including age, gender, and non-harvest mortality. Annual hard and soft mast (acorns, hickory nuts, berries, and tree fruit) surveys determine food availability for many species of wildlife, such as bear, deer, turkey, squirrels, and songbirds. Bait-station surveys are conducted to monitor black bear abundance.

Small game animal surveys include the Furbearer Trapper Harvest Survey, which annually monitors beaver, muskrat, otter, fox, mink, raccoon, and other animals. Fur prices and fur sales are tracked by surveying fur dealers and buyers. Results of raccoon field trials are used as an index to raccoon abundance. Game birds are monitored through annual surveys including a summer turkey brood count, call counts of breeding populations of mourning doves, quail call counts, a grouse drumming survey, as

well as wood duck banding. Hunter harvest surveys are conducted every 3 years to estimate hunter harvest levels of selected wildlife species.

NCWRC also conducts disease surveillance in wild animals, such as chronic wasting disease in deer (not yet present in North Carolina) and investigates and responds to various individual disease incidents. A less rigorous monitoring program is the Wildlife Observation Survey. In their professional capacity, NCWRC biologists observe and report sightings of species seen outside of their normal range (e.g., fox squirrels, spotted skunk, and river otter) as well as sightings of non-harvest mortality.

NCWRC monitors non-game wildlife including mammals, reptiles, birds, amphibians, fish, freshwater mussels, snails, and crayfish. Through the Wildlife Diversity Program, the Commission strives to prevent species from becoming endangered by maintaining viable, self-sustaining populations of all native wildlife, with an emphasis on priority species and habitats.

Blue Grouse

Wood Duck

Red Fox

Raccoons

River Otter

White-tailed Deer

Black Bear

NCWRC aquatic biologists monitor fresh water mussels, snails, crayfish, and fish throughout the region. Biologists also conduct population assessments of rare bog turtles and salamanders and work to conserve yellow-bellied sapsuckers, painted buntings, golden-winged warblers, and cerulean warblers, among many others.

Since 1966, the North American Breeding Bird Survey (BBS) has monitored the status and trends of avifauna in the southern Blue Ridge Mountains. BBS data provide an index of population abundance that can be used to estimate population trends and relative abundances at various geographic scales. Declining population trends can act as an early warning system to galvanize research and management action to determine causes of avian declines and reverse them before populations reach critically low levels.

Water Quality and Quantity
Planning and Monitoring

The State of North Carolina develops a Water Supply Plan for Western North Carolina to assure the availability of adequate supplies of good quality water to protect public health and support economic growth. The State also provides assistance in the development of Local Water Supply Plans, which project present and future water supplies and water use.

The North Carolina Division of Water Quality (DWQ) develops a basin-wide water quality plan that is a non-regulatory, watershed-based approach to restoring and protecting the quality of Western North Carolina's surface waters. The goals of basin-wide planning are to identify water quality problems and restore full use to impaired waters, identify and protect high-value resource waters, and protect unimpaired waters while allowing for reasonable economic growth.

Basin-wide water quantity and quality plans are in place and updated every 5 years for each of the major river basins in the region: the Hiawassee, the Little Tennessee, the French Broad, the Watauga, the Broad, and the Catawba.

The most imperative water quality concerns in Western North Carolina include unacceptable rates of sedimentation (resulting from land clearing activities, loss of riparian vegetation, rural roads, and livestock grazing on stream banks), straight pipes and failing septic systems, and mining activities.

The U.S. Environmental Protection Agency (EPA), the U.S. Geological Survey (USGS), and many other Federal and State agencies conduct extensive chemical monitoring at fixed locations on large rivers and streams around the region. A regional focus is applied to study status and trends in water, sediment, and biota. Private entities such as universities, watershed associations, environmental groups, and permitted dischargers also conduct water quality monitoring, as do the Eastern Band of Cherokee Indians and local governments, such as city and county environmental offices.

The Volunteer Water Information Network was initiated at the University of North Carolina at Asheville in January 1990 to provide monitoring of the French Broad River watershed. Data is collected monthly at most sites and includes pH, alkalinity, turbidity, suspended solids, conductivity, nutrients, and heavy metals. The program has expanded from 27 sites in Buncombe County to over 250 sites on streams, rivers, and lakes in Western North Carolina and beyond.

Straightpiping sewage into streams

Sedimentation from muddy runoff

Grazing on streambanks

Failing septic systems

Mining activities

Air Quality
Planning and Monitoring

Air quality affects the health and well-being of humans, wildlife, and vegetation. Forests are negatively impacted by gaseous waste products, such as sulfur and nitrogen dioxide, as well as ozone. Common sources of these pollutants are coal-fired power plants, industrial manufacturing sources, and on-road and off-road vehicles.

Air pollution can lead to foliar injury, decreased nutrient availability, reduced carbohydrate production, lower vigor, and decreased growth in trees. The main ecosystems at risk in the mountains due to air pollution, however, are aquatic ecosystems. Reduction of ozone and fine particulate matter will help to reduce deposition of acids and mercury.

Our region is fortunate in that it has been chosen as one of three areas across the United States (North Carolina, New York, Illinois-St. Louis, MO) to pilot the concept of integrating Federal, State, and tribal air quality management requirements into a comprehensive Air Quality Management Plan (AQMP).

The North Carolina Department of Air Quality (NCDAQ) is developing a process to complete plans that address the control of multiple pollutants and air-related considerations, such as land use, transportation, energy, and climate change. NCDAQ is working with other State, Federal, and local agencies, the energy and manufacturing community, interest groups, and the general public. Fifty-six mitigation measures have been developed for controlling and reducing greenhouse gas emissions.

The NCDAQ Air Monitoring Program tracks pollutant levels and airborne toxics. The ambient Air Quality Index compares local pollutant levels including ozone, particulate matter, carbon monoxide, sulfur dioxide, nitrogen dioxide, and lead.

The regional office in Asheville compiles and makes available data for Western North Carolina. The Air Toxics Analytical Support Team evaluates the concentrations of pollutants in a community or area in addition to providing rapid response to accidental chemical releases and their potential impacts on a community.

Spruce-Fir Forest Response to
Balsam Woolly Adelgid and Air Pollution

Coal-Fired Power Plants

Automobile Exhaust

Laws, Regulations, and Guidelines
Legal Framework

National

In 1900, approximately 75 percent of the Southern Appalachian region was forested. By 1920, however, much of our forests had been heavily cut, burned, and abandoned. A conservation community organized and began to influence legislators on the need to assess, actively manage, and protect our natural resources. Their efforts resulted in the designation of parks and national forests around the region.

Fifty years later, in the early 1970s, the concepts of "sustained yield," "resource conservation," and "environmental science" again resonated with American citizens. During this period, the U.S. Congress passed a suite of legislation underscoring the importance of sustainable management of our Nation's natural resources.

Laws enacted include the National Environmental Policy Act (1969), the Clean Water Act (1972), the Endangered Species Act (1973), the Resources Planning Act (1974), and the National Forest Management Act (1976). This series of legislation followed two additional mandates handed down in the 1960s: the Multiple-Use Sustained-Yield Act of 1960 and the Wilderness Act of 1964.

Together, this legislation laid the groundwork for the regulatory standards applied today. Federal and State Governments along with myriad citizen groups ensure that the Nation's streams, rivers, and lakes retain high water quality, plant and animal species remain viable, timber harvest is in balance with growth, impacts of activities on the environment are identified and mitigated, and wilderness, defined as an area where "man himself is a visitor who does not remain," is preserved.

> Current statutes help limit environmental degradation and provide guidance on best management practices; however, erosion on steep slopes, septic system failures, and air and water quality remain issues of concern.

State and local

The North Carolina Forest Practices Guidelines set forth performance standards to assure that forestry activities are conducted in a manner that protects water quality. These regulations are administered as part of the North Carolina Sedimentation Pollution Control Act of 1973. The Guidelines require sediment, waste, and debris to be kept out of streams, the number of stream crossings to be kept to a minimum, limited use of pesticides and fertilizer, mitigation of adverse stream temperature fluctuations, and rehabilitation of the project site.

The North Carolina Prescribed Burning Act recognizes that controlled burning of forest land is a management tool that is beneficial to North Carolina's public safety, forest and wildlife resources, environment, and economy. The Act requires a certified person to properly assess vegetative fuels under safe weather and safe environmental conditions and follow precautionary measures that will confine the fire to a predetermined area and accomplish the intended management objectives.

Various sections of river basins in the region are required to maintain riparian buffers, i.e., sections of the Catawba River. The buffers filter runoff, protect banks from erosion, remove excess nutrients such as phosphorus and nitrogen from fertilizers and animal waste, and provide shade and improve habitat.

The State also regulates the use of pesticides – how they are sold, stored, transported, applied, and disposed of. Best management practices are provided for chemical application of fertilizer and pesticide.

North Carolina also classifies surface waters and wetlands, identifying their best use and associated guidelines for protection of that use. Classifications include water supply source, swimming and recreation, trout waters, waters of exceptional State or national recreational or ecological significance, and waters that are rated as excellent based on biological and physical/chemical characteristics.

Counties and local municipalities develop a variety of regulations to protect citizens and natural resources. These statutes often regulate such activities as mountain ridge development, farmland preservation, high-impact land uses, property rights protections, flood damage prevention, zoning, and erosion and sediment control. The success of local land use regulations ultimately depends on public support for laws and regulations that prevent environmental degradation, e.g., steep slope and storm water management ordinances.

Cooperators and Concerns
Public Participation

Public interest in the conservation of Western North Carolina's natural resources spans more than a century. We surveyed approximately 40 interest groups with a relatively small response rate. However, we can still present the issues those groups identified independently of the survey, as well as list the types of groups (forest industry, land trusts, Federal and State agencies, institutions of higher education, conservation and preservation) that are active in Western North Carolina.

_____

* These entities are not included in the graph on the facing page.

Cooperators
Non-Profit Organizations
American Forests
American Tree Farm System *
Appalachian Voices
Dogwood Alliance
Southern Appalachian Forest Coalition
Western North Carolina Alliance
Wild South

Federal/State/Other Agencies
USDA Forest Service, Southern Research Station
U.S. Department of the Interior
USDI National Park Service *
USDI Fish and Wildlife Service *
U.S. Geological Survey, Division of Water Quality
USDA National Forest Systems *
Eastern Forest Environmental Threat Assessment Center
Southeastern Forest Experiment Station *
Office of U.S. Congressman Heath Shuler
Office of U.S. Senator Richard Burr
Tennessee Valley Authority Economic Development Administration *
U.S. Department of Energy *
Appalachian Regional Commission *
N.C. Department of Environment and Natural Resources, Division of Forest Resources
N.C. Forestry Association
N.C. Natural Heritage Program
N.C. Wildlife Resources Commission
National Forests in North Carolina
Eastern Band of Cherokee Indians in North Carolina

Councils
Fish & Wildlife Conservation Council
Land of Sky Regional Council
Southwest Commission *
High Country Council of Governments *
Southern Appalachian Multiple-Use Council

Higher Education Institutions
Clemson University
Haywood Community College
Mars Hill College
N.C. State University
University of North Carolina, Asheville
University of Tennessee
Warren Wilson College
Western Carolina University

Land Trusts, Conservancy
BlueRidge Forever *
Conservation Trust for North Carolina
Land Trust Alliance
Land Trust for the Little Tennessee River
Foothills Conservancy
The Nature Conservancy
The Wilderness Society

Public Education Centers
Cradle of Forestry Interpretive Association

Hunting/Recreation Organizations
WNC Sportsman's Federation
Trout Unlimited
Ruffed Grouse Society
National Wild Turkey Federation
Nantahala Outdoor Center

Forest Products
Appalachian Hardwood Manufacturers
Columbia Forest Products
N.C. Tree Farmers
T & S Hardwoods
Southern Forestry Foundation
WNC Pallet

Offices, Businesses
Equinox Environmental
Southern Environmental Law Center

Issues

Count of groups focusing on issue

Category	Issue	
Biodiversity	Conservation	
	Old-Growth Forests	
	Fire-Dependent Areas	
	Development	
	Restoration	
	Species Loss	
Production	Forest Management	
	Sustainable Harvest	
Ecosystem Health	Invasive Species	
Soil, Water, and Air	Reducing Sedimentation	
	Flood Planning	
	Air Pollution	
Socioeconomic Benefits	Resource Economies	
Policy	Cooperative Decision Making	
	Public Education	

◻ One group

Public interest in the conservation of Western North Carolina's natural resources spans more than a century. Currently, over 40 such interest groups are active in Western North Carolina.

Appendix
Montreal Process Criteria and Indicators

Criterion 1: Conservation of biological diversity

1.1   Ecosystem Diversity
1.1.a Area and percent of forest by forest ecosystem type, successional stage, age class, and forest ownership or tenure
       Community and Species Inventory
       Land Use Change
1.1.b Area and percent of forest in protected areas by forest ecosystem type, and by age class or successional stage
       Lands Managed for Conservation
       Significant Natural Heritage Areas
       Land Use Change
1.1.c Fragmentation of forests
       Land Use Change
       Forest Fragmentation

1.2   Species Diversity
1.2.a Number of native forest-associated species
       Community and Species Inventory
1.2.b Number and status of native forest-associated species at risk, as determined by legislation or scientific assessment
       Community and Species Inventory
1.2.c Status of on site and off site efforts focused on conservation of species diversity
       Lands Managed for Conservation
       Significant Natural Heritage Areas

1.3   Genetic Diversity
1.3.a Number and geographic distribution of forest-associated species at risk of losing genetic variation and locally adapted genotypes
1.3.b Population levels of selected representative forest-associated species to describe genetic diversity
1.3.c Status of on site and off-site efforts focused on conservation of genetic diversity

Criterion 2: Maintenance of productive capacity of forest ecosystems

2.a   Area and percent of forest land and net area of forest land available for wood production
       Timberland Ownership
       Biomass Production Potential
       Timber Composition and Age
2.b   Total growing stock and annual increment of both merchantable and non-merchantable tree species in forests available for wood production
       Volume of Timber
       Timber Composition and Age
2.c   Area, percent, and growing stock of plantations of native and exotic species
       Timberland Ownership
2.d   Annual harvest of wood products by volume and as a percentage of net growth or sustained yield
       Volume of Timber
2.e   Annual harvest of non-wood forest products
       Non-Timber Forest Products

Criterion 3: Maintenance of forest ecosystem health and vitality

3.a   Area and percent of forest affected by biotic processes and agents (e.g., disease, insects, invasive alien species) beyond reference conditions
       Insects and Disease
       Invasive Species

3.b   Area and percent of forest affected by abiotic agents (e.g., fire, storm, land clearance) beyond reference conditions
       Forest Fire
       Severe Weather
       Climate Change

Criterion 4: Conservation and maintenance of soil and water resources

4.1   Protective Function
4.1.a   Area and percent of forest whose designation or land management focus is the protection of soil or water resources
       Lands Managed for Conservation

4.2   Soil
4.2.a   Proportion of forest management activities that meet best management practices or other relevant legislation to protect soil resources
       Planning and Monitoring
       Legal Framework
4.2.b   Area and percent of forest land with significant soil degradation
       Soil Resources
       Soil Loss and Degradation

4.3   Water
4.3.a   Proportion of forest management activities that meet best management practices, or other relevant legislation, to protect water related resources
       Planning and Monitoring
       Legal Framework
4.3.b   Area and percent of water bodies, or stream length, in forest areas with significant change in physical, chemical or biological properties from reference conditions
       Water Resources
       Aquatic Ecosystems

Criterion 5: Maintenance of forest contribution to global carbon cycles

5.a   Total forest ecosystem carbon pools and fluxes
       Carbon Cycles
5.b   Total forest product carbon pools and fluxes
       Carbon Cycles
5.c   Avoided fossil fuel carbon emissions by using forest biomass for energy
       Biomass Production Potential
       Carbon Cycles

Criterion 6: Maintenance and enhancement of long-term multiple socio-economic benefits to meet the needs of societies

6.1   Production and consumption
6.1.a Value and volume of wood and wood products production, including primary and secondary processing
       Forest Products and Manufacturing
6.1.b Value of non-wood forest products produced or collected
       Forest Products and Manufacturing
6.1.c Revenue from forest based environmental services
       Forest Products and Manufacturing
6.1.d Total and per capita consumption of wood and wood products in round wood equivalents
6.1.e Total and per capita consumption of non-wood products
6.1.f Value and volume in round wood equivalents of exports and imports of wood products
6.1.g Value of exports and imports of non-wood products

6.1.h Exports as a share of wood and wood products production and imports as a share of wood and wood products consumption
6.1.i Recovery or recycling of forest products as a percent of total forest products consumption
       Forest Products and Manufacturing

6.2   Investment in the forest sector

6.3.a Employment in the forest sector
       Social, Cultural, Economic Factors
6.3.b Average wage rates, annual average income and annual injury rates in major forest employment categories
       Social, Cultural, Economic Factors
6.3.c Resilience of forest-dependent communities
6.3.d Area and percent of forests used for subsistence purposes
6.3.e Distribution of revenues derived from forest management
       Forest Products and Manufacturing

Criterion 6: Maintenance and enhancement of long-term multiple socio-economic benefits to meet the needs of societies (continued)

6.4   Recreation and tourism
6.4.a   Area and percent of forests available and/or managed for public recreation and tourism
        Forest Recreation and Tourism
6.4.b   Number, type, and geographic distribution of visits attributed to recreation and tourism and related to facilities available
        Forest Recreation and Tourism

6.5   Cultural, social and spiritual needs and values
6.5.a   Area and percent of forests managed primarily to protect the range of cultural, social and spiritual needs and values
        Cultural and Spiritual Values
6.5.b   The importance of forests to people
        Cultural and Spiritual Values

Criterion 7: Legal, institutional and economic framework for forest conservation and sustainable management

7.1.a Legislation and policies supporting the sustainable management of forests
 Planning and Monitoring
 Land and Resource Planning
7.1.b Cross sectoral policy and programme coordination

7.2.a Taxation and other economic strategies that affect sustainable management of forests

7.3.a Clarity and security of land and resource tenure and property rights
7.3.b Enforcement of laws related to forests
 Legal Framework

7.4.a Programmes, services and other resources supporting the sustainable management of forests
 Planning and Monitoring
 Land and Resource Planning
7.4.b Development and application of research and technologies for the sustainable management of forests

7.5.a Partnerships to promote the sustainable management of forests
 Planning and Monitoring
 Land and Resource Planning
7.5.b Public participation and conflict resolution in forest-related decision making
 Public Participation
7.5.c Monitoring, assessment and reporting on progress towards sustainable management of forests
 Planning and Monitoring
 Land and Resource Planning

Glossary

Abiotic processes: interactions of non-biological factors (sunlight), materials (sulfur dioxide), or process (hydrolysis) that can affect living or non-living constituents of an ecosystem.

Airborne particulates: total suspended particulate matter found in the atmosphere as solid particles or liquid droplets, including windblown dust, emissions from industrial processes, smoke from wood/coal burning, and engine exhaust.

Air Quality Index: compares local pollutant levels, including ozone, particulate matter, carbon monoxide, sulfur dioxide, nitrogen dioxide, and lead.

American chestnut blight: a fungal disease that destroys bark tissue and kills chestnut trees. No longer a viable component of Western North Carolina's forest ecosystem, chestnut was the dominant tree in the canopy over a century ago. Presently, hybridized chestnut trees resistant to the fungus are being reintroduced into the forest.

Anaerobic: without air, where air is generally used to mean oxygen, as opposed to aerobic, which means with air.

Appalachian Trail: a 2,170 mile corridor traversing the highest ridge tops between Maine and Georgia. Conditions on the Trail are considered a barometer for the air, water, and biological diversity of the Appalachian Mountains.

Apparently secure: a species uncommon but not rare (although it might be rare in parts of its range, particularly on the periphery) and usually widespread.

Aspect: in physical geography, aspect generally refers to the horizontal direction to which a mountain slope faces.

Atmospheric deposition: the transfer of acidic or acidifying substances from the atmosphere to the surface of the earth or to objects on its surface.

Balsam woolly adelgid: a tiny sucking insect that first appeared in North Carolina in the 1950s. The insect robs a Fraser fir tree of nutrients, leading to its decline and eventual death.

Beech bark disease: a disease that occurs when the bark of the beech tree is attacked by and altered by an insect, the beech scale, and then invaded and killed by fungi.

Bioenergy: renewable energy made available from materials derived from biological sources.

Biomass: any organic material that has stored sunlight in the form of chemical energy. As a fuel, it may include wood, wood waste, straw, manure, sugar cane, and many other by-products from a variety of agricultural processes.

Biological diversity (biodiversity): describes the variety and abundance of all life forms in a given place – plants, animals, fungi, lichens, and mosses. It also describes the processes, functions, and structures that sustain that variety and allow it to adapt to changing circumstances. Moreover, it encompasses the complexity of gene pools, species, communities, and ecosystems at spatial scales from local to regional to global.

Biotic processes: an interaction or series of interactions produced or caused by living organisms.

Bog: a wetland with acidic substrate mainly composed of moss and peat and having a characteristic flora.

Bole: the main stem of a tree, usually covered with bark. The bole is usually the part that is used commercially for lumber.

Boreal forest: occurring between 50 and 60 degrees north latitudes. Seasons are divided into short, moist, and moderately warm summers and long, cold, and dry winters. The average length of the growing season in boreal forests is 130 days.

Cardinal directions: the four directions of north, south, east, and west. North and south point toward the geographical poles defined by the axis of the earth's rotation.

Clean Air Act of 1970: law which defines the U.S. Environmental Protection Agency's responsibilities for protecting and improving the Nation's air quality and stratospheric ozone layer; Title 42, Chapter 85.

Climate: the average weather in a location over a long period of time. Climate is not only the measure of average conditions, but also the characteristic range of variability from those conditions.

Climate change: shifts in the average state of climate and in its variability.

Climate projection models: mathematical tools for projecting future climate. Climate model projections are not predictions, but rather scenarios of how the climate might change based on observed patterns.

Composite panels: roundwood products that are manufactured into chips, wafers, strands, flakes, shavings, or sawdust and then reconstituted into a variety of panel and engineered lumber products.

Conservation easement: a legally binding restriction placed on a piece of property to protect its associated resources. An easement selectively targets only those rights necessary to protect specific conservation values, such as water quality or migration routes, and is individually tailored to meet a landowner's needs.

Contiguous: connected; abutting; adjacent; neighboring; connecting without a break.

Continuous gradient: an uninterrupted change in the value of a quantity (e.g., temperature, pressure, or concentration) of a given variable, and especially per unit distance in a specified direction.

Critically Imperiled: a species critically at risk globally because of extreme rarity or because of some factor(s) making it especially vulnerable to extinction.

Dogwood anthracnose: a fungus introduced into Western North Carolina in the 1980s. Dogwood anthracnose is expected to intensify in the future, with flowering dogwood mortality heaviest at higher elevations and on shaded, north-facing slopes.

Developed land: land that has large amounts of paved (impervious) surfaces, such as major roads, subdivisions, towns, and shopping areas.

Decomposition: the process by which tissues of a dead organism break down into simpler forms of matter. The process is essential for new growth and development of living organisms because it recycles the finite matter that occupies physical space in the biome.

Degradation: in geology, the wearing down of the land by the erosive action of water, wind, or ice. In chemistry, the breakdown of an organic compound. In the environment, the deterioration and depletion of resources such as air, water and soil; the destruction of ecosystems and the extinction of wildlife.

Delivered value: the price of wood, transportation, and site restoration necessary to get wood to the mill; the price to the logger.

Disturbance: a relatively discreet event in time that disrupts ecosystem, community, or population structure and changes resources, substrate availability, or the physical environment; for example, a wildfire.

Dry deposition: settling out of fine to coarse particles, gases, and aerosols from the atmosphere to the surface of the earth.

Ecological niche: the role an organism plays within the structure and functions of an ecosystem, and the way it interacts with other living things and with its physical environment.

Ecoregion: large areas of land and water that are broadly mapped using specific climate, vegetation, and physical characteristics, e.g., the southern Blue Ridge Mountains.

Ecosystem: a specific unit of organisms occupying a given area that interact with the physical environment.

Elevation: the altitude of a place above sea level or ground level.

Evapotranspiration: the process of water passing through the leaves of trees and evaporating into air.

Forest fragmentation: the breaking up of uninterrupted forested areas into smaller zones; harmful to the habitat of many birds, mammals, and plants, as well as entire ecosystems.

Forest productivity: a measurement of timber stocking levels, forest health, and species mix. Forest productivity depends on many factors, including climate, soils, elevation, aspect, latitude, and timber management.

Forest structure: the distribution of trees by species and size. Forest structure is the result of the growth habit of tree species, especially the degree of shade tolerance; ecological conditions; and the history of disturbance and management.

Fuelwood: roundwood harvested to produce some form of energy, as in heat or steam, in residential, industrial, or institutional settings.

Galax: a tufted evergreen perennial herb having spikes of tiny white flowers and glossy green round to heart-shaped leaves that become coppery to maroon or purplish in fall; collected for commercial floral use.

Geobook: a monitoring tool designed by the U.S. Environmental Protection Agency primarily for county planners, watershed managers, or local land trusts and conservation groups needing a wide range of information on an area the size of a few counties or a watershed.

Ginseng: any of several plants of the genus Panax, having forked roots; collected for its medicinal properties.

Gneiss: metamorphic rock that forms when sedimentary or igneous rock is subjected to high temperatures and pressures. Granite often becomes gneiss rock.

Green infrastructure: conserves ecosystem values and functions and provides associated benefits to human populations by developing strategically planned and managed networks of natural lands, working landscapes, and other open spaces.

Ground-level ozone: ozone emitted at ground level by a chemical reaction between oxides of nitrogen and volatile organic compounds in the presence of sunlight.

Groundwater: the water beneath the surface of the ground, consisting largely of surface water that has seeped down: the source of water in springs and wells.

Growing stock: a common term used to describe timber volume. The volume of growing stock trees is a subset of all live trees in a forest or stand. Growing stock includes sawtimber, pole timber, saplings, and seedlings, but excludes rough, rotten, and cull trees. It is a fundamental element in determining the productive capacity of an area identified as forest available for timber production.

Gypsy moth: a pest introduced into the United States in the mid-1800s and now permanently established in 17 States, but not yet permanently established in Western North Carolina counties even though there have been instances of human-mediated introductions. The insect defoliates trees, making them more vulnerable to other killing agents. Gypsy moths feed on a wide variety of trees, shrubs, and vines, but prefer all oak species, apple, beech, birch, basswood, and willow.

Hardwoods: trees that have broad leaves with a large surface area which are shed annually, such as oak, maple, poplar, and hickory.

Harvest residue: wood left in the forest after a timber harvest; the residue can be broken down to a composite of lignin and cellulose and burned to generate energy.

Headwaters: the source and the initial part of a stream.

Hemlock woolly adelgid: a tiny insect that feeds in fall, winter, and spring, depleting eastern and Carolina hemlocks of nutrients and leading to mortality in less than 5 years.

Horticulture: the cultivation of plants.

Hydrologic cycle: a continuous process by which water is transported from the oceans to the atmosphere by a process of evaporation, then to the land by clouds and precipitation (rain), and back to the sea again through rivers and underground waters.

Igneous: rocks formed from melting in the Earth's crust (e.g., granite).

Imperiled: a species at global risk because of rarity or because of some factor(s), making it very vulnerable to extinction.

Inflation: a general upward price movement of goods and services that is representative of the economy as a whole.

Invasive plants: plants introduced accidently into a natural system or brought into an area for ornamental use, food, or medicinal use, living fences, or livestock forage. They multiply rapidly because they are not kept in check by insects and diseases that evolved with them in their native setting.

Invasive vertebrate and invertebrate animals: any species that has been introduced to an environment where it is not native, and that has since become a nuisance through rapid spread and increase in numbers, often to the detriment of native species.

Land conveyances: a transfer system usually designed to ensure that a buyer of land secures title to the land together with all the rights that run with the land, and is notified of any restrictions in advance of purchase.

Lithology: the physical characteristics of rock, including color, composition, and texture.

Loam: a rich soil consisting of a mixture of sand, clay, and decaying organic materials.

Microclimate: a small, local region having a unique pattern of weather or weather effects.

Microcosm: a representation of something on a much smaller scale, e.g., artificial, simplified ecosystems that are used to simulate and predict the behavior of natural ecosystems under controlled conditions.

National Ambient Air Quality Standards: as required by the Clean Air Act, the U.S. Environmental Protection Agency has set standards for wide-spread pollutants from numerous and diverse sources considered harmful to the public health and the environment. The two main types of standards are primary, which set limits to protect public health, and secondary, which set limits to protect public welfare (protection against visibility impairment, damage to animals, crops and buildings).

National Forests: under the authority of the U.S. Department of Agriculture, the agency manages 191 million acres of forest and range land to provide Americans with a wide variety of ecological services and commodities.

National Heritage Area: an area specifically designated by the U.S. Congress recognizing natural, cultural, and historic resources that form a cohesive, nationally distinctive landscape.

National Parks: under the authority of the Department of the Interior, these lands are managed to emphasize preservation of pristine areas, protection of natural and historic features, plus light-on-the-land recreation. The ultimate goal is to preserve resources "unimpaired for future generations."

Native species: a species that was not introduced and historically, or currently, occurs in a given ecosystem.

Net growth: total growth minus mortality.

Nitrate deposition: deposition of nitrate, a compound containing nitrogen that can exist in the atmosphere or as a dissolved gas in water and that can have harmful effects on humans and animals.

Nitrogen oxide emissions: a product of combustion from transportation and stationary sources; a major contributor to the formation of ozone in the troposphere and to acid deposition.

Nonpoint source pollution: the deposition of natural and human-made pollutants, from rainfall or snowmelt, moving over and through the ground, and into lakes, rivers, wetlands, coastal waters, and underground sources of drinking water.

Non-timber forest products: any commodity obtained from the forest that does not necessitate harvesting trees. It includes plants, parts of plants, and other biological material, as well as fungi, mosses, lichens, herbs, vines, shrubs, and trees.

Open space: land that is valued for natural processes and wildlife, agricultural and forest production, aesthetic beauty, active and passive recreation, and other public benefits. Such lands include working and natural forests, rangelands and grasslands, farms, ranches, parks, stream and river corridors, and other natural lands within rural, suburban, and urban areas.

Orographic effect: rainfall that results from or is enhanced by mechanical lifting of an air mass over mountains.

Overstory: upper portion of a forest made up of tree branches and leaves; tree canopy.

Palmer Hydrological Drought Index: a measure of long-term (cumulative) meteorological drought and wet conditions.

Particulates: fine liquid or solid particles such as dust, smoke, mist, fumes, or smog found in air or emissions. Also very small solids suspended in water that can vary in size, shape, density, and electrical charge.

Pathogen: any disease-producing agent (especially a virus or bacterium or other microorganism).

Pesticide: chemicals designed to kill, control, or repel insects, plant diseases, weeds, rodents, and germs.

Population dynamics: how a given population grows and shrinks over time; as controlled by birth, death, and emigration or immigration.

Posts, poles, and pilings: wood products milled or cut and peeled into standard sizes that provide vertical and lateral support in buildings, foundation, utility lines, and fences. This category may also include nonindustrial (unmilled) products.

Precipitation: any form of water; rain, snow, or hail, that falls from the atmosphere and reaches the ground.

Protected land: land owned or managed by entities that strive to limit the amount of land use conversion, such as national and State forests and parks and land conservancies.

Pulpwood: wood reduced to individual fibers by chemical or mechanical means. The fibers are used to make a broad generic group of pulp products that includes paper products as well as fiberboard, insulating board, and paperboard.

Rain shadow: a dry area on a mountainside facing away from the direction of the wind. The mountains block the passage of rain-producing weather systems, casting a "shadow" of dryness behind them.

Ramps: an early spring vegetable with a strong garlic-like odor and a pronounced onion flavor.

Regional haze rule: a 1999 Federal regulation mandating improved visibility in 156 Class I areas across the country by the year 2064.

Reservoir: an artificial lake used to store water; often created by building a reinforced dam, usually out of concrete, earth, rock, or a mixture across a river or stream.

Riparian buffer: a transition zone between water and upland environments to protect the aquatic environment from pollution and sedimentation. It is measured from the top of the bank of the stream or the wetland boundary.

River basin: the entire geographical area drained by a river and its tributaries.

Roadless areas: designated areas that have regained or are regaining a natural appearance because signs of prior human activity are diminishing due to natural forces; the area must include no more than one-half mile of improved road for each 1,000 acres.

Roundwood: logs, bolts, or other round sections cut from trees for industrial manufacture or consumer use.

Runoff: surface water flow that occurs when soil is infiltrated to full capacity and excess water from rain, meltwater, or other sources flows over the land.

Saw logs: logs usually 8 feet in length or longer that can be processed into a variety of sawn products such as lumber, cants, pallets, railroad ties, and timbers.

Sawtimber: the diameter of softwood trees 9.0 inches and larger measured at 4.5 feet above ground; the diameter of hardwood trees 11.0 inches measured at 4.5 feet above ground.

Schist: fine-grained rock, altered after formation by heat or pressure or both, so that mineral content is in roughly parallel layers. It can therefore be split into thin plates.

Secure: a species which is considered common, widespread, and abundant (although it may be rare in parts of its range, particularly on the periphery). Not vulnerable in most of its range.

Sedimentary rock: a form of rock made by the deposition and compression of small particles.

Sedimentation: mineral or organic matter deposited by water, air, or ice.

Shade tolerance: in forest ecology, a tree's ability to tolerate differing light levels, e.g., if a tree does not thrive in full sunlight, it will usually be found in the understory, receiving filtered light through the upper canopy.

Silviculture: the art and science of controlling the establishment, growth, composition, health, and quality of forests to meet diverse needs and values of landowners, societies, and cultures.

Size class distribution: variation in the amount of stand density or number of trees per size class.

Smart growth: a development strategy that helps reduce urban sprawl, featuring town-centered, pedestrian oriented development, public transit, and a greater mix of housing, commercial, and retail uses. It also preserves open space and critical environmental areas and takes advantage of compact building designs that will minimize impervious surfaces.

Softwoods: evergreen trees with needle or scale-like leaves, such as pine, fir, and spruce.

Soil aeration: the replacement of air in soil with air from the surface of the earth.

Soil erosion: the displacement of soil by wind, water, or other moving currents; sometimes leading to landscape degradation, ecosystem damage, or waterway pollution.

Soil exhaustion: soil which has lost its natural level of nutrients; infertile.

Soil moisture: the amount of water in a soil type; important for biological processes and forest health. Soil moisture levels are determined both by temperature and precipitation.

Soil structure: the arrangement of soil particles into larger aggregates; influences aeration, water movement, erosion resistance, and root penetration.

Southern pine beetle: an insect native to U.S. southeastern forests that attacks loblolly, shortleaf, Virginia, pitch, and table mountain pine.

Speciation: the evolutionary process by which new biological species arise.

Species: a taxonomic division that generally refers to a group of plants or animals that are similar in structure and descent and are able to breed among themselves.

Stressor: any kind of event or action that, at certain levels, causes stress to organisms; for example, a period of drought.

Strip mining: a mining technique in which the land and vegetation covering the mineral being sought are stripped away by large machines; without proper mitigation strategies, this technique can damage land and water, limiting subsequent uses.

Stumpage value: the monetary value of standing timber, or the price a landowner typically receives for harvested trees.

Succession: the natural replacement of plant or plant communities in an area over time.

Sustainability: the maintenance and restoration of natural conditions, whereby humans and nature coexist into perpetuity fulfilling social, economic, and other requirements of present and future generations.

Temperate forests: forests occurring in Eastern North America, Northeastern Asia, and Western and Central Europe and characterized by four seasons with a distinct winter, moderate climate, and a growing season of 140–200 days during 4–6 frost-free months.

Temperature zone: an area characterized by a particular set of organisms, whose presence is determined by environmental conditions, as an altitudinal belt on a mountain.

Terrain: the physical features of a tract of land.

Terrestrial: animals that live predominantly or entirely on land, as compared with aquatic animals, which live predominantly in or around water.

Threshold: the point that must be exceeded to begin producing a given effect or result or to elicit a response.

Timberland: forest land capable of producing 20 cubic feet of industrial wood per acre per year and not withdrawn from timber utilization.

Topographical feature: the spatial representation of a particular place or region indicating their relative positions and elevations.

Typhoid: a potentially life-threatening disease caused by *Salmonella typhi* bacteria. It is usually carried via water or by food contaminated with sewage.

Understory: the lower layer of plants and shrubs in a forest ecosystem.

Undeveloped land: includes forests and farms with minor roads and farm buildings.

Vascular plants: (also known as tracheophytes or higher plants) have lignified tissues for conducting water, minerals, and photosynthetic products through the plant; includes ferns, clubmosses, flowering plants, conifers, hardwoods, and other gymnosperms.

Veneer log: roundwood product that is either rotary cut, sliced, stamped, or sawn into a variety of products, such as plywood, finished panels, sheets, or sheathing.

Vertebrate: an animal with a backbone, or spinal column, made of interlocking units called vertebrae.

Volcanic rock: rock formed from the cooling of lava (hot liquid rock) on or near the earth's surface.

Vulnerable: a species at risk globally either because it is very rare throughout its range, found only in a restricted range (even if abundant at some locations), or because of other factors making it vulnerable to extinction.

Water stress: stress defined by the availability of water; it impacts forests primarily by its affect on soil moisture.

Wet deposition: precipitation, in the form of rain, snow, or hail; "acid rain" is a type of wet deposition referring to the delivery of strong acid ions (sulfate and nitrate) and acid-forming ions (ammonia) from the atmosphere to the earth's surface.

Wetlands: an area of land where soil is saturated with moisture either permanently or seasonally.

Wholesale prices: measures the changes in price paid by retailers for finished goods. Inflationary pressures typically show up here earlier than the headline retail price.

References and Credits

Introduction

Data Sources
Ecoregion
  USDA Forest Service ECOMAP Team, 2005 Northern Region Geospatial Library.
  Ecological Subregions: Sections and subsections of the conterminous United States, Cleland et al., 2007.

Text Sources
Time Line
  USDA Forest Service, Southern Research Station, Gen. Tech. Rep. SRS–18, The Southern Appalachians: A history of the landscape, Yarnell, S.L., 1998.

Photo and Illustration Sources
  Bundled corn, American Indian settlement, ceramic vessels, European settlers on porch, standing chestnut bole, harvested spruce forest in Pisgah National Forest, File Photos, USDA Forest Service, Asheville, NC.

Biodiversity

Data Sources
Ecological Communities
  NatureServe, Classification of the natural communities of North Carolina, 3rd approximation, Schafale and Weakley, 1990.
Lands Managed for Conservation
  Southern Forest Land Assessment: A cooperative project of the Southern Group of State Foresters, Jacobs, J.R., Srinivasan, R., and Barber, B., Texas Forest Service, College Station, TX, 83 p., 2008.
Significant Natural Heritage Areas
  North Carolina Department of Environment and Natural Resources, Natural heritage program, http://www.ncnhp.org/.
Land Use
  RENCI Engagement Site at University of North Carolina – Charlotte, NC, May 2010.
Forest Fragmentation
  USDA Forest Service, Research Triangle Park, NC, Kurt Riitters, Ecologist, June 2008.

Text Sources
  USDA Forest Service, Southern Research Station–GTR–64, Human influences on forest ecosystems, 2003.
  USDA Forest Service, Pacific Northwest Research Station, GTR–728, National forests on the edge, 2007.
  The Institute for the Economy and the Future at Western Carolina University, Western North Carolina population growth, Figure 1, Population changes 2010–2030, 2008. For uses of this study, population projection for Western North Carolina is based on five additional counties: Burke, Caldwell, McDowell, Polk, and Rutherford. http://www.wncpulse.com/index.php?option=com_content&view=article&id=109:western-north-carolina-population-growth-rates&catid=30:demographics&Itemid=119.

Photo Sources
Biodiversity Intro
  Swamp pink: Katie Hicks

Biodiversity

Photo Sources

Community Examples
> Small whorled pogonia, shortia, Fraser's loosestrife, pale yellow trillium, Gray's lily, Virginia spirea, spruce-
> fir forest, montane alluvial forest, acidic cove forest: Gary Kauffman
> Santeetlah dusky salamander: Michael Graziano
> Indiana bat: Traci Hemberger
> Rich cove forest: Bill Lea
> Carolina northern flying squirrel: John Mays
> Grassy bald: Ed Burress

Land Use
> Water: Bridget O'Hara, NEMAC
> Agriculture, developed: Larry Korhnak, Interface South
> Natural: David Cappaert, Michigan State

Lands Managed for Conservation
> Federal: Katie Hicks
> State and local: David Brown, North Carolina Department of Environment and Natural Resources
> Other conservation lands, other forest land: Larry Korhnak, Interface South

Production

Data Sources

Timberland Ownership
> USDA Forest Service, National Forest Inventory Data Online (FIDO), custom retrieval for 18 counties, private
> and public timberland ownership (acres), 1984–2006.

Volume of Timber
> USDA Forest Service, National Forest Inventory Data Online (FIDO), custom retrieval for 18 counties, volume
> of growing stock on timberland (billion cubic feet); average annual net growth and removals of hardwood and
> softwood growing stock on timberland (million cubic feet), 1984–2006.

Timber Composition and Age
> USDA Forest Service, National Forest Inventory Data Online (FIDO), custom retrieval for 18 counties, volume
> of growing stock by diameter class (million cubic feet), 1984–2006.

Non-Timber Forest Products
> USDA, Forest Service, National Forests of North Carolina, Total value of nontimber products sold in the Pisgah
> and Nantahala National Forests, Remington, D., Asheville, NC, 2005–2009.
> USDA Forest Service, Science update SRS-006, Special forest products: a southern strategy for research and
> technology transfer, February, 2004.

Biomass Production Potential
> USDA Forest Service, National Forest Inventory Data Online (FIDO), custom retrieval for 18 counties, Forest
> biomass (dry tons per acre) and USDA, Forest Service, Forest Inventory and Analysis, Remote Sensing
> Applications Center.

Continued...

Production

Text Sources

Timberland Ownership

Southern Appalachian Man and the Biosphere Program, The southern Appalachian assessment, summary report, July 1996.

North Carolina Department of Environment and Natural Resources, Managing your forest, http://www.dfr.state.nc.us/Managing_your forest/consulting_foresters.htm, November 2009.

USDA Forest Service, Forest Inventory and Analysis, National Woodland Owner Survey, 2004. Preliminary results for North Carolina, Butler, B. J. and Leatherberry, E. C., September 2005.

Timber Composition and Age

Forest Watch, *Ecological Forestry*, Early successional forest: too much or not enough? Lapin, M., September 2002.

USDA Forest Service Resource Bulletin, SRS-87, Forest statistics of the mountains of NC, Brown, M., 2002.

Non-Timber Forest Products

USDA Forest Service, National strategy for special forest products, FM-713, Washington, DC, 2001.

USDA Forest Service, Science update SRS-006, Special forest products: a southern strategy for research and technology transfer, February 2004.

Biomass Production Potential

Institute for Agriculture and Trade Policy, Harvesting fuel: cutting costs and reducing forest fire hazard through biomass harvest, Arnosti, D. et al., June 2008.

USDA FS-899, USDA Woody biomass utilization strategy. Marcia Patton-Mallory, editor, 2008.

USDA FS SRS, Compass, What are we going to do with all that wood?, ed. Thinning the forest, boosting local economies, R. Rummer, Winter 2006, Vol. 1, Number 1.

USDA-FIA Recommended methodology for assessing forestry biomass for bio-energy utilization, Prepared for Services, Utilization, and Marketing Task Force, Southern Group of State Foresters, prepared by: Nathan McClure http://www.southernforests.org/documents/Methodology%20for%20Assessing%20Forest%20Biomass.pdf.

Photo Sources

Tree Farm Sign, Anonymous Tree Farm owner, Grandin Tree Farm: Michael E. Cheek, NC Division of Forest Resources

National forest sign, sawn lumber, green fork lift, man in mill, rolling logs, log pile: File Photo, USDA Forest Service, Asheville, NC

Data Sources

<u>Insects and Diseases</u>

USDA Forest Service, National Forest Inventory Data Online (FIDO) custom retrieval for 18 counties, total volume of live trees by species for 18 counties: southern yellow pines, eastern hemlock, flowering dogwood, 1984–2006.

USDA Forest Service, Southern Research Station, Asheville, NC, custom retrieval for 18 counties, outbreak years for southern pine beetle (1960 to 2006), hemlock woolly adelgid (1992 to 2006), beech bark disease (1993 to 2006), gypsy moth (1993 to 2007) Yockey, E., October, 2007.

<u>Forest Fire</u>

North Carolina Division of Forest Resources, Michael Creek, custom retrieval for 18 counties, location of fires, 1997–2002.

<u>Severe Weather</u>

Historical Tropical Cyclone Tracks 1851–2004, U.S. National Atlas, www.nationalatlas.gov.

<u>Elevation</u>

LIDAR, NC One Map, www.nconemap.com.

<u>Temperature and Precipitation</u>

Oregon State University, PRISM Group.

<u>Historical Temperature and Precipitation</u>

USDA Forest Service, Southern Research Station, Average derived from yearly average observations in Avery, Henderson, Macon, Madison, and Haywood counties (1893 to 2006), Moore Myers, J., Raleigh, NC, June 2007.

<u>Precipitation Pattern</u>

Oregon State University, Spatial Climate Analysis Service, NOAA Cooperative Station.

PHDI Graphs, Mera, R., North Carolina State University, Raleigh, NC, January 2008.

<u>Climate Scenarios</u>

USDA Forest Service, Southern Research Station, Southern Global Change Program, Scenarios and water stress (HAD & CGC1): Ge Sun et al., Impacts of multiple stresses on water demand and supply across the Southeastern United States, 44(6), 1441-1457, 2008.

State Climate Office of North Carolina, Climate Division Data. http://www.nc-climate.ncsu.edu/climate/climdiv.php#thumb.

Continued...

Text sources

Insects and Diseases

USDA Forest Service, Southern Region, Forest Health Protection, Southern Forest Health Atlas of Insects and Diseases, September 2009.

Journal of Forestry, The southern pine beetle prevention initiative: working for healthier forests, Nowak, J. et al., July/August 2008.

USDA Forest Service, Forest Health Protection, Asheville, NC, Slowing the Spread of the Gypsy Moth, http://www.datcp.state.wi.us/arm/environment/insects/gypsy-moth/pdf/sts_facts.pdf.

Invasive Species

North Carolina State University, Fletcher, NC, Invasive plants and the nursery industry, Proceedings of the international plants propagators society, Bir, R.E., February 2000.

USDA Forest Service and University of Georgia, Center for invasive species and ecosystem health, Non-native invasive species in southern forest and grassland ecosystems, http://www.invasive.org/.

North Carolina Natural Plant Society, invasive exotic species list, compiled by Misty Franklin, 2006, http://www.ncwildflower.org/invasives/list.htm.

USDA Forest Service, Southern Research Station, *Compass* 1(2), Silent invaders of our southern forests, Spring 2005.

Forest Fire

University of Georgia, School of Forest Resources Extension Pub. FOR 99-010, Drought damage to trees, Coder, K. D., April 1999.

Severe Weather

One North Carolina Naturally, partnerships in conservation, quarterly electronic newsletter, Western North Carolina hurricanes reveal opportunities in floodplain areas, Gibson, P., Fall 2004.

Atlantic Tropical Cyclones layer at http://www.nationalatlas.gov/mld/huralll.html.

Climate Change

U.S. National Atlas, Raw data download, http://www.nationalatlas.gov/atlasftp.html.

Climate Change and Forest Disturbances, Dale et al., 2001, 51(9), 723-734.

U.S. Environmental Protection Agency, Office of Policy (2111), 236-F-98-007q, Climate change and North Carolina, September 1998.

USDA, Forest Service, In brief: climate change and water- perspectives from the forest service. FS-908. Washington, DC, 2008.

Photo Sources

Damaged tree: Norbert Frank, University of West Hungary, Bugwood.org

Mimosa: James H. Miller, USDA Forest Service, Bugwood.org

Multiflora rose: Leslie J. Mehrhoff, University of Connecticut, Bugwood.org

Oriental bittersweet: James H. Miller, USDA Forest Service, Bugwood.org

Crimson fountaingrass: John M. Randall, The Nature Conservancy, Bugwood.org

Soil, Water and Air

Data Sources

Soil Formation
North Carolina State University, Department of Soil Science, Soil systems map of Western North Carolina, Daniels, R.B. et al., Tech. Bull. 314, 1999. Data transfer by Robert Austin, North Carolina State University.

Soil Loss and Degradation (Acidic deposition)
USDA Forest Service, Asheville, NC, and E&S Environmental Chemistry, Inc., Corvallis, OR, Model-based assessment of the effects of acidic deposition on sensitive watershed resources in the national forests of NC, TN, and SC, final report, Sullivan, T.J., B.J. Cosby, K.U. Snyder, A.T. Herlihy, B. Jackson, 2007, http://webcam.srs.fs.fed.us/pollutants/acid/index.shtml.

River Basins in Western North Carolina
NC Wildlife Resources Commission, NC Wildlife Action Plan, NC river basins, 2005, http://www.ncwildlife.org/plan/WSC_WAP_Basins.htm.

Atmospheric Deposition Impacts to Streams
USDA Forest Service, Asheville, NC, and E&S Environmental Chemistry, Inc., Corvallis, OR, Model-based assessment of the effects of acidic deposition on sensitive watershed resources in the national forests of NC, TN, and SC, final report, Sullivan, T.J., B.J. Cosby, K.U. Snyder, A.T. Herlihy, B. Jackson, 2007, http://webcam.srs.fs.fed.us/pollutants/acid/index.shtml.

Aquatic Species at Risk
USDA Forest Service, National Forests in North Carolina, Federally listed aquatic threatened, endangered, and species of concern, Pers. Comm., Kauffman, G., 2010.

Water Quantity
USDI Geological Survey, Surface-Water Data for the Nation, Estimated Water Use Summary, 1990, http://waterdata.usgs.gov/nwis/sw.
USDI Geological Survey, Surface-Water Data for the Nation, Estimated Water Use Summary, 2005, http://waterdata.usgs.gov/nwis/sw.

Introduction
USDA Forest Service, Asheville, NC, and E&S Environmental Chemistry, Inc., Corvallis, OR, Model-based assessment of the effects of acidic deposition on sensitive watershed resources in the national forests of NC, TN, and SC, final report, Sullivan, T.J., B.J. Cosby, K.U. Snyder, A.T. Herlihy, B. Jackson, 2007, http://webcam.srs.fs.fed.us/pollutants/acid/index.shtml.

Visibility
North Carolina Department of Environment and Natural Resources, Division of Air Quality, NC Division of Air Quality, Regional Haze State Implementation Plan, http://daq.state.nc.us/planning/RH_SIP_Imp_Plan_12-17-2007.pdf.
Jackson, W., Pers. Comm., 2010.

Ambient Air Quality (Particulates, Ozone, Growth of Trees)
Colorado State University, Visibility Information Exchange Web System, Fine particle speciation, http://views.cira.colostate.edu/web/.
U.S. Environmental Protection Agency, Air Explorer, Particulate Matter 2.5, http://www.epa.gov/airexplorer/.
USDA Forest Service, Region 8, Air Resource Management, http://svinetfc6.fs.fed.us/wqmsbeta/frameview.phtml?winwidth=800&winheight=600&language=0 Ozone calculator, http://webcam.srs.fs.fed.us/tools/calculator/index.shtml)

Continued...

Soil, Water, and Air

Data Sources

Ambient Air Quality (Particulates, Ozone, Growth of Trees) - Continued

USDA Forest Service, Final report: Southern Appalachian Mountains Initiative, 2002.

U.S. Environmental Protection Agency, Emissions monitoring, Clean air markets, http://www.epa.gov/airmarkets/emissions/index.html.

Sources of Air Pollution

U.S. Environmental Protection Agency, Emissions monitoring, Clean air markets, http://www.epa.gov/airmarkets/emissions/index.html.

Text Sources

Geologic History

USDA Forest Service, Southern Research Station, Gen. Tech. Rep. SRS-18, The southern Appalachians: A history of the landscape, Yarnell, S.L., 1998.

Soil Formation

North Carolina State University, Department of Soil Science, Soil Systems of North Carolina, Daniels, R.B. et al., Tech. Bull. 314, 1999.

Virginia Department of Conservation and Recreation, Natural Heritage, 2006, http://www.dcr.virginia.gov/natural_heritage/ncTIf.shtml.

Western Carolina University, Dept. of Biology, University of North Carolina, Asheville, Dept. of Environmental Studies, Vascular flora of a southern Appalachian fen and floodplain complex, Warren, R.J. et al., *Castanea* 69(2), 2004.

A nature guide to northwest NC, Skeate, S., Parkway Publishers, Boone, NC, 2004.

Soil Loss and Degradation (Erosion and Sedimentation)

North Carolina Department of Environment, The Division of Land Resources, Sedimentation Pollution Control Act of 1973, http://www.dlr.enr.state.nc.us/pages/sedimentpollutioncontrol.html.

North Carolina Division of Forest Resources, North Carolina Forest Practice Guidelines Related to Water Quality, Leaflet WQ-1 December, 2007, http://www.dfr.state.nc.us/publications/Forestry%20Leaflets/WQ01.pdf.

North Carolina Forest Service, Best management practices: quick reference field guide. http://dfr.nc.gov/publications/WQ0407/01%2002%20Chapters%20Field%20Guide%20WEB.pdf.

North Carolina State University, Department of Soil Science, http://www.soil.ncsu.edu/about/publications.php.

North Carolina Department of Environment, Health, and Natural Resources, Land Quality Section, Soil Facts, North Carolina Erosion and Sedimentation Control Program, http://www.soil.ncsu.edu/publications/Soilfacts/AG-439-32/#BasicMandatoryRequirements.

Soil Loss and Degradation (Roads, Steep Slopes, Landslides, Acidic Deposition)

USDA Forest Service, Southern Research Station, Determining the Range of Acceptable Forest Road Erosion, Grace, J.M., American Society of Agricultural and Biological Engineers, Meeting Presentation, Paper Number: 083984, 2008. http://www.srs.fs.usda.gov/pubs/ja/ja_grace034.pdf.

Canadian Geotechnical Society, 1st North American landslide conference, Vail, CO, Landslide hazards and landslide hazard mapping in North Carolina, Wooten, R.M. et al., AEG special publication 23, 2007. http://www.cgs.ca/cgssociety/Boards%20and%20Committees/Committees/lanslides-committee/meeting-report-by-akturner-aug-2007.pdf/view.

North Carolina Geological Survey, Geologic Hazards in North Carolina – Landslides, http://www.geology.enr.
state.nc.us/Landslide_Info/Landslides_main.htm.

USDA Forest Service, Asheville, NC, and E&S Environmental Chemistry, Inc., Corvallis, OR, Model-based
assessment of the effects of acidic deposition on sensitive watershed resources in the national forests of NC,
TN, and SC, final report, Sullivan, T.J., B.J. Cosby, K.U. Snyder, A.T. Herlihy, B. Jackson, 2007, http://
webcam.srs.fs.fed.us/pollutants/acid/index.shtml.

Soil Conservation

U.S. Environmental Protection Agency, Model ordinances to protect local resources, 2007, http://www.epa.gov/
nps/ordinance/mol1.htm#sec3.

River Basins and Health of River Basins in Western North Carolina

NC Wildlife Resources Commission, NC Wildlife Action Plan, NC river basins, 2005, http://www.ncwildlife.
org/plan/WSC_WAP_Basins.htm.

NC Wildlife Resources Commission, Basinwide Planning Program: 2002 Little Tennessee River, Basinwide
Water Quality Plan, Water quality issues related to the entire Little Tennessee river Basin, http://www.
wildlifeactionplans.org/pdfs/action_plan_summaries/north_carolina.pdf.

North Carolina Department of Environment and Natural Resources, Office of Environmental Education,
Savannah River Basin, 2007, http://www.ee.enr.state.nc.us/public/ecoaddress/riverbasins/savannah.150dpi.
pdf.

North Carolina Department of Environment and Natural Resources, Office of Environmental Education, New
River Basin, 2007, http://www.ee.enr.state.nc.us/public/ecoaddress/riverbasins/new.150dpi.pdf.

Clean Water for North Carolina, A River in Jeopardy: The Yadkin and Pee Dee Rivers of North Carolina,
Carpenter, B. et al., October 2002, http://www.cwfnc.org/Yadkinreport.pdf.

Atmospheric Deposition Impacts to Streams

USDA Forest Service, Asheville, NC, and E&S Environmental Chemistry, Inc., Corvallis, OR, Model-based
assessment of the effects of acidic deposition on sensitive watershed resources in the national forests of NC,
TN, and SC, final report, Sullivan, T.J., B.J. Cosby, K.U. Snyder, A.T. Herlihy, B. Jackson, 2007, http://
webcam.srs.fs.fed.us/pollutants/acid/index.shtml.

Aquatic Species at Risk

USDA Forest Service, National Forests in North Carolina, List of threatened, endangered, and species of
concern, Pers. Comm., Kauffman, G., 2010.

Crayfish, Crandall, K.A., Fetzner, J.W., Crayfish conservation, http://crayfish.byu.edu/conservation.htm,
updated, 2006.

NC Wildlife Resources Commission, wildlife species & conservation, North Carolina freshwater mussels,
2010, http://www.ncwildlife.org/wildlife_species_con/wsc_fwmussels_endfish_mussels.htm.

Davidson College, Salamanders of North Carolina, Wilson, J. et al., http://www.bio.davidson.edu/projects/
herpcons/herps_of_nc/salamanders/salamanders.html.

Water Quantity

U.S. Geological Survey Open-File Report 2008-1104, Inventory of Well Yields in Avery and Watauga Counties,
North Carolina, Huffman, B.A. et al., http://pubs.usgs.gov/of/2008/1104/.

Continued...

Soil, Water and Air

Text Sources

Introduction

USDA Forest Service, Asheville, NC, and E&S Environmental Chemistry, Inc., Corvallis, OR, Model-based assessment of the effects of acidic deposition on sensitive watershed resources in the national forests of NC, TN, and SC, final report, Sullivan, T.J., B.J. Cosby, K.U. Snyder, A.T. Herlihy, B. Jackson, 2007, http://webcam.srs.fs.fed.us/pollutants/acid/index.shtml.

Visibility

North Carolina Department of Environment and Natural Resources, Division of Air Quality, NC Division of Air Quality, Regional Haze State Implementation Plan for North Carolina Class I Areas, http://daq.state.nc.us/planning/RH_SIP_Imp_Plan_12-17-2007.pdf.

USDA Forest Service, National Forests in North Carolina, Jackson, W., Pers. Comm., 2010.

Ambient Air Quality (Particulates, Ozone, Growth of Trees)

Colorado State University, Visibility Information Exchange Web System, Fine particle speciation, http://views.cira.colostate.edu/web/.

U.S. Environmental Protection Agency, Air Explorer, Particulate Matter 2.5, http://www.epa.gov/airexplorer/.

USDA Forest Service, Region 8, Air Resource Management, http://svinetfc6.fs.fed.us/wqmsbeta/frameview.phtml?winwidth=800&winheight=600&language=0 Ozone calculator, http://webcam.srs.fs.fed.us/tools/calculator/index.shtml).

USDA Forest Service, Final report: Southern Appalachian Mountains Initiative, 2002.

U.S. Environmental Protection Agency, Emissions monitoring, Clean air markets, http://www.epa.gov/airmarkets/emissions/index.html.

USDA Forest Service, National Forests in North Carolina, Jackson, W., Pers. Comm., 2010.

Sources of Air Pollution

Final report of the Southern Appalachian Mountains Initiative, 2002.

USDA Forest Service, National Forests in North Carolina, Air quality trends in Western North Carolina, Jackson, W., Pers. Comm., 2010.

Photo and Illustration Sources

Introduction

Waters of Coweeta: USDA Forest Service, Southern Research Station file photo

Soil Formation

Western North Carolina soil systems map: NEMAC

Soil Loss and Degradation

Steep Slope Development: Patrick Parton, Haywood County

Case Camp Ridge Road: Dick Jones

Steep Slope Development: North Carolina Geological Survey, North Carolina Department of Environment and Natural Resources

Map of Landslides: NEMAC

Landslide, Debris pile: North Carolina Geological Survey, North Carolina Department of Environment and Natural Resources

Map of lithology: NEMAC

Soil, Water and Air

Photo and Illustration Sources

<u>Water Basins in Western North Carolina</u>
Map of river basins: NEMAC
Total land in Western North Carolina river basins: NEMAC

<u>Atmospheric Deposition Impacts to Streams</u>
Buffering capacity for brook trout survival: Sullivan et al., 2007
Acid Neutralizing Capacity: Sullivan et al., 2007

<u>Aquatic Species at Risk</u>
Blotched Chub: Brett Albanese, Georgia Department of Natural Resources
Appalachian elktoe mussel, littlewing pearly mussel, noonday globe: U.S. Fish and Wildlife Service, Asheville Field Office, NC
Pygmy Salamander: Matthew Niemiller, http://www.herpetology.us/field_trips/2009/cherokee_national_forest_mo.html
Smoky dace, Betty Creek: Katie Owers
Wounded darter: Bud Freeman, Georgia Museum of Natural History, 2008

<u>Water Quantity</u>
Average Water Withdrawals in WNC (million gallons per day), 1990: NEMAC
Average Water Withdrawals in WNC (million gallons per day), 2005: NEMAC

<u>Visibility</u>
Simulated visibility conditions in Joyce Kilmer-Slickrock Wilderness Area (1860, 2000–2004, 2018, 2064), Winhaze model (http://www.air-resource.com/resources/downloads.html)
Visibility Conditions at Shining Rock Wilderness: http://www.fsvisimages.com/image-library-start.aspx

<u>Ambient Air Quality (Airborne Particulates, Ground-level ozone, Nitrous Oxides)</u>
Fine particulates: http://views.cira.colostate.edu/web/
Visibility, Shining Rock Wilderness Area: http://www.fsvisimages.com/image-library-start.aspx
Sensitivity of Tree Species to Ozone Exposure: Southern Appalachian Mountains Initiative, 2002
Hourly Average Ozone Exposures: U.S. Environmental Protection Agency, 2002
Ozone Monitor Elevations: Southern Appalachian Mountains Initiative, 2002

<u>Sources of Air Pollution</u>
Sulfur dioxide/Nitrogen oxide emission maps: U.S. Environmental Protection Agency, 2002
Wet sulfate deposition, 1993, Jackson, W., USDA Forest Service, National Forests in North Carolina, 2010
Wet sulfate deposition, 2008, Jackson, W., USDA Forest Service, National Forests in North Carolina, 2010

Data Sources

Carbon Storage in Western North Carolina, USDA Forest Service, Southern Research Station, Forest Inventory Data Online (FIDO), EVALIDator 4.01 tool, http://fiatools.fs.fed.us/fido/index.html.

Text Sources

Introduction

U.S. Global Change Research Program. National Climate Change, "Global Climate Change Impacts in the United States," 27, 2009, http://www.globalchange.gov/images/cir/pdf/National.pdf.

National Geographic, "It starts at home," Miller, P., March 2009, http://ngm.nationalgeographic.com/2009/03/energy-conservation/miller-text.

Carbon Storage and Release

U.S. Environmental Protection Agency, Climate change-greenhouse gas emissions, Carbon dioxide, March 2010, http://www.epa.gov/climatechange/emissions/co2.html.

National Aeronautics and Space Administration, Goddard Space Flight Center, EOS project science office, Earth observatory, The ocean's carbon balance, Riebeek, H., June 2008, http://earthobservatory.nasa.gov/Features/OceanCarbon/.

U.S. Department of Energy, Fossil energy office of communications, How fossil fuels were formed, October 2008, http://www.fe.doe.gov/education/energylessons/coal/gen_howformed.html.

Carbon Storage in Western North Carolina Forests

Biotic and abiotic factors regulating forest floor CO_2 flux across a range of forest age classes in the southern Appalachians, Vose, J.M., and Bolstad, P.V., Pedobiologia, 50:577-587, 2007.

Haida climate forest, general information on trees, carbon and climate, 2007, http://www.haidaclimate.com/content/view/28/34/.

Carbon Market in Western North Carolina

Exploring the feasibility of a local carbon offset market in western North Carolina, Chipley, S., Proceedings of the national conference on undergraduate research, University of Montana, April 2010.

USDA Forest Service, Rocky Mountain Research Station, A description and comparison of selected forest carbon registries: a guide for States considering the development of a forest carbon registry, SRS-107, 2007.

The economic effects of climate change, Tol, R.S., *Journal of Economic Perspectives* 23(2), Spring 2009.

Market-based policy options to control U.S. greenhouse gas emissions, Metcalf, G.E., *Journal of Economic Perspectives* 23(2), Spring 2009.

Paying for avoided deforestation - Should we do it?, Sohngen, B., *Choices: The magazine of food, farm, and resource issues* 23(1), 28 (2008).

Photo and Illustration Sources

The Greenhouse Effect, U.S. National Assessment of the Potential Consequences of Climate Variability and Change: A Detailed Overview of the Consequences of Climate Change and Mechanisms for Adaptation, http://www.usgrcp.gov/usgcrp/nacc/default.htm.

Global Average Temperature and Carbon Dioxide Concentrations, 1880–2004, Data source temperature: ftp://ftp.ncdc.noaa.gov/pub/data/anomalies/annual_land.and.ocean.ts; data source CO_2 (Siple Ice Cores): http://cdiac.esd.ornl.gov/ftp/trends/co2/siple2.013; data source CO2 (Mauna Loa): http://cdiac.esd.ornl.gov/ftp/trends/co2/maunaloa.co2; graphic design by Michael Ernst, The Woods Hole Research Center.

Carbon Storage in Western North Carolina: NEMAC.

Carbon Cycling and Sustainable Forestry illustration: Forest Foundation, 2006. http://www.forestboundation.org.

Avoided deforestation carbon offset market, USDA Forest Service file photo.

Socioeconomic Benefits

Data Sources

Economic Trends in Western North Carolina

U.S. Department of Commerce, Bureau of Economic Analysis, 1970–2000s, Average number of total jobs and wage rate per decade, Mera, R.

North Carolina State University, The Western North Carolina Economy: Overview and Challenges, The Harold and Mazie Jones Levenson Program on Growth and Change in Western North Carolina: Are We Ready for Change? Cherry, T.L., 2008.

Appalachian State University, Center for Economic Research & Policy Analysis, WNC economic index, county unemployment rankings, Cherry, T.L. et al., July 2009.

U.S. Department of Commerce, Bureau of Economic Analysis, Arts, Entertainment, Recreation Employment, 2001–2007.

U.S. Department of Commerce, Bureau of Economic Analysis, CA30, Regional Economic profiles, NC, 1998–2007.

Recreation Areas

USDA Forest Service, National Forests in North Carolina, Internal annual visitation and receipt report, 2000–2009.

Recreation Use

Cornell Hospitality Quarterly, Sustainable tourism: the case of the blue ridge national heritage area, Stoddard, J.E., Evans, M.R., Dinesh, D.S., August 2008.

Total Visitation for the Pisgah and Nantahala National Forests, Blue Ridge Parkway, and Great Smoky Mountains National Park, 1985–2009, http://usparks.about.com/gi/dynamic/offsite.htm?zi=1/XJ&sdn=usparks&cdn=travel&tm=30&gps=423_406_1276_818&f=00&su=p531.50.336.ip_&tt=2&bt=1&bts=1&zu=http%3A//www.nature.nps.gov/stats/park.cfm.

Development and Conservation

University of North Carolina, Charlotte, RENCI, Trends in land use and development in the Western North Carolina (2006–2030), 2010.

Roundwood Product Output and Distribution

USDA Forest Service, Southern Research Station, Forest Inventory and Analysis, Average volume of roundwood products by product and years, 1995–2007.

USDA Forest Service, Southern Research Station, Forest Inventory and Analysis, Number of mill operations in the region, Pers. Comm., Johnson, T., 2010.

Arts and Craft

Billy Graham Training Center at the Cove, Spiritual Retreats, Spiritual Retreats, Pers. Comm., 2010.

Find the Divine - Directory of Spiritual Retreats, Religious Retreats and Conference Centers, Retreat centers by State and region, 2010, http://www.findthedivine.com.

Socioeconomic Benefits

Data and Text Sources

Paying for Forest-Based Recreation

US Department of the InteriorI, National Park Service in cooperation with the Blue Ridge Parkway foundation, Blue Ridge Parkway Facts, October, 2008, http://www.brpfoundation.org/parkway_facts.php#Facts1.

National Park Service, http://www.nps.gov/grsm/planyourvisit/whyfree.htm.

BlueRidgeNow.com, Congress seeks $75 million for Blue Ridge Parkway land purchase, staff report, January 2010 http://www.blueridgenow.com/article/20100127/NEWS/100129811?p=all&tc=pgall&tc=ar.

UNC Asheville, *The Blue Banner*, Officials Aim to get $75 million for Blue Ridge Parkway, Brooks, K., 2010, http://www.thebluebanner.net/.

National Parks Conservation Association, State of the Parks, Great Smoky Mountains National Park, 2004, http://www.npca.org/stateoftheparks/smokies/smokies.pdf.

Asheville: Anyway you like it, Asheville Area Tourism Research, January, 2010,www.exploreasheville.com.

Coloradoan.com, Public Lands Fees Creating a Dispute, Magill, B., May, 2010, http://www.coloradoan.com/article/20100524/NEWS01/100524001/Public-lands-fees-creating-a-dispute.

USDA Forest Service, National Forests in North Carolina, Designated Fee Areas, 1996.

USDA Forest Service, National Forests in North Carolina, Carolina connections, 2009.

Roadless Areas

The Southern Appalachian Forest Coalition, A Forest Link Report, Our Green is Our Gold, Economic Benefits of National Forests for Southern Appalachian Communities.

The Southern Appalachian Assessment, Social Cultural, Economic Technical Report 4 of 5. Prepared by Federal and State agencies, July 1996.

Southern Appalachia Forest Coalition, Roadless Facts, Updated June 2009, http://www.safc.org/campaigns/roadless/roadless_facts.php.

Mountain Express, North Shore Road settlement brings $52 million to Swain County, Williams, M., February 2010.

Value of Forest Products

USDA Forest Service, Southern Research Station, Forest Inventory and Analysis, Average volume of roundwood products by product and years, 1995–2007.

North Carolina Agricultural Statistics, Forest, fish, and seafood income, 2007.

USDA Forest Service, Southern Research Station, Research Triangle Park, TimberMartSouth, June 2010.

USDA Forest Service, National Forests in North Carolina, Fact sheets, Payment in lieu of taxes, 2001–2009.

Recycling

Asheville Citizen-Times, Morrison, C., Buncombe rates 4th in State for recycling; resident's attitudes, county programs get credit, 2010.

North Carolina Department of Environment and Natural Resources, North Carolina recycling data sends mixed signals, May, 2009, nc_county_recycling_rates.pdf.

Paper and wood recovery by WNC counties, 2009: Pers. Comm., Mour, S., 2010.

Socioeconomic Benefits

Text Sources

<u>Economic Trends in Western North Carolina</u>

U.S. Department of Commerce, Bureau of Economic Analysis, 1970–2000s, Average number of total jobs and wage rate per decade, Mera. R., 2009.

North Carolina State University, The Western North Carolina Economy: Overview and Challenges, The Harold and Mazie Jones Levenson Program on Growth and Change in Western North Carolina: Are We Ready for Change? Cherry, T.L., 2008.

Average wage rates, 1970s–2000s adjusted for inflation using consumer price index, 1975–2005, http://crisistimes.com/calculator.php.

Appalachian State University, Center for Economic Research & Policy Analysis, The 2001 recession and WNC: Illustrating the urban-rural divide, Policy brief #1, Cherry, T.L. et al., January 2009.

Appalachian State University, Center for Economic Research & Policy Analysis, WNC economic index, county unemployment rankings, Cherry, T.L. et al., July 2009.

<u>Recreation Areas</u>

USDA Forest Service, WO History Unit, Research in the USDA Forest Service: a historians view: The Weeks act and eastern forests, West, Terry, 1991.

Asheville: Anyway you like it, www.exploreasheville.com.

USDI National Park Service, Blue Ridge Natural Heritage Area, Heritage and history, attractions and destinations, www.blueridgeheritage.com.

<u>Development and Conservation</u>

U.S. Environmental Protection Agency, Smart Growth, http://www.epa.gov/smartgrowth/about_sg.htm.

The Conservation Fund, What is Green Infrastructure?, greeninfrastructure.net/content/definition-green-infrastructure.

Land-of-Sky Regional Council, Linking lands and communities in the land of sky region, http://www.linkinglands.org/.

<u>Roundwood Product Output and Distribution</u>

USDA Forest Service, Southern Research Station, North Carolina's forest, 2002, Brown, M.J., New, B.D., Oswalt, S.N., Johnson, T.G., Rudis , V.A., Resource Bulletin SRS–113, 2002.

North Carolina's Timber Industry; An assessment of Timber Product Output and Use, 1995–2007, Resource Bulletins SRS–18,39, 73,94, 112,127,156.

Internal Auditor, Auditing timber assets, Straka, T.J., June 1995, http://www.allbusiness.com/accounting/methods-standards/509452-1.html.

<u>Arts and Craft</u>

May we all remember well, A journal of the history & cultures of Western North Carolina, Vol. 1, Brunk, S., editor, 1997.

Western Carolina University, Hunter Library, Craft revival: Shaping Western North Carolina past and present, The crafts, the people, the collection, 2010, http://www.wcu.edu/craftrevival/index.htm.

HandMade in America, Economic impact of the professional craft industry in Western North Carolina, 2010, http://s3.amazonaws.com/hia_user_files/files/12/original.pdf?1271338510.

Foxfire 40th anniversary book: faith, family, and the land, Cheek, A., Nix, H.L., 2006.

Asheville.com community news, Biltmore Industries Holds Distinguished Position in Asheville's History, 1999.

The roots of mountain music, Holt, D., 2002, http://www.davidholt.com/music/rootsmtnmsc.html.

Continued...

Text Sources
Arts and Craft - Continued
The heritage of western North Carolina: a collaborative database, Western North Carolina artists & illustrators to 1950, http://www.heritagewnc.org/WNC_artists/artists2.htm.
Journal of Environmental Psychology, A qualitative exploration of the wilderness experience as a source of spiritual inspiration, Fredrickson, L.M., Anderson, D.H., 1999, http://www.ncrs.fs.fed.us/pubs/jrnl/1999/nc_1999_Fredrickson_001.pdf.

Photo and Illustration Sources
Introduction
Historic Cabin Nantahala National Forest: USDA Forest Service file photo
Economic Trends in Western North Carolina
Average number of total jobs and wage rate: NEMAC
Arts, Entertainment, Recreation Employment, 2001–2007: U.S. Bureau of Economic Analysis
Western North Carolina Population by County, 1970–2020: NEMAC
Recreation Areas
Map of Recreation Areas in Western North Carolina: NEMAC, 2010.
Recreation Use
Tourist Activity Preferences in BRNHA: NEMAC
Total Visitation on National Forests, Great Smoky Mountains National Park, Blue Ridge Parkway: NEMAC
Paying for Forest-Based Recreation
Foggy View at Wayah Bald: Delce Dyer, National Forests in North Carolina
Mountain Biking: Doug Byerly
Couple Fishing from Picnic Site: Delce Dyer, National Forests in North Carolina
Canoeing on Balsam Lake, Nantahala National Forest: Delce Dyer, National Forests in North Carolina
Recreation Fees
Sample of camping fees in Pisgah and Nantahala National Forests: NEMAC
Development and Conservation
Distance to roads: NEMAC
WNC Roads and Roadless Areas: NEMAC
Map of areas changing from natural to developed, 2006–2030: NEMAC
Roundwood Product Output and Distribution
Distribution of Softwood and Hardwood Products, 1995–2007: NEMAC
Total roundwood output in WNC, 1995–2007: NEMAC
Number of wood manufacturing mills in WNC: NEMAC
Value of Forest Products
Loading Roundwood: Tony Johnson, SRS
Value of Timber Products in WNC, 1995–2007: NEMAC.
Total forest products income by county, 2005–6: NEMAC
Payment in Lieu of Taxes and Total National Forest acres, 2001–2009: NEMAC

Socioeconomic Benefits

Recycling
  Average Recycling Rates by Regional Council of Government, 2009: NEMAC
  Paper and wood recovery by WNC counties, 2009: NEMAC
Arts and Craft
  George Masa, 1933: NPS.gov
  Musicians, circa 1930: USDA Forest Service, National Forests in North Carolina file photo
  Economic impact of craft industry in WNC: Sarah Jackson
  McCarter family making baskets (1930–1936): USDA Forest Service, National Forests in North Carolina file photo
  Photograph by George Masa: http://ashevilleart.org
  Contemplative Moment: D. Hiden Ramsey Library, UNC Asheville
  Spiritual Retreats in WNC: Sarah Jackson

Policy

Data Sources

<u>Planning and Monitoring</u>

North Carolina Department of Environment and Natural Resources, Division of Forest Resources, Forest Stewardship Plans, custom retrieval for 18 counties (number and acres), Michael Creek (1970–2007).

<u>Public Participation: Cooperators and Concerns</u>

National Forests of North Carolina, Public Affairs Office, Asheville, NC, List of public and private cooperators and their concerns regarding issues of sustainability in Western NC.

USDA Forest Service, Southern Research Station, Questionnaire to Western North Carolina natural resource groups regarding issues of sustainability, Fox, S., January 2009.

Text Sources

<u>Planning and Monitoring</u>

<u>Private and Public Lands</u>

North Carolina Department of Environment and Natural Resources, Division of Forest Resources, Forest stewardship plan program, http://www.dfr.state.nc.us/Managing_your_forest/.

USDA Forest Service, Southern Research Station, FS-865 Forest inventory and analysis strategic plan, a history of success; a dynamic future, January, 2007.

USDA Forest Service, Southern Research Station, Eastern forest environmental threat assessment program, http://www.forestthreats.org/.

USDA Forest Service, Southern Research Station, National forest health monitoring program, http://fhm.fs.fed.us/.

North Carolina Department of Environment and Natural Resources, Division of Forest Resources, Urban and Community Forestry, http://www.dfr.state.nc.us/Urban/Urban_Forestry.htm.

City of Asheville, NC, Street Services, Urban Forestry, http://www.ashevillenc.gov/residents/public_services/streets/default.aspx?id=756&terms=urban+forest&searchtype=2&fragment=False.

USDA Forest Service, Southern Region, Land and Resource Management Plan, Amendment 5, Nantahala and Pisgah National Forests, North Carolina, March 1994.

http://www.ashevillenc.gov/residents/public_services/streets/default.aspx?id=756&terms=urban+forest&searchtype=2&fragment=False.

<u>Land Conservation and Protection</u>

North Carolina Department of Environment and Natural Resources, Natural Resources Planning and Conservation, One NC-naturally, http://www.onencnaturally.org/.

North Carolina Department of Environment and Natural Resources, Natural heritage program, http://www.ncnhp.org/.

Blue Ridge Forever, Conservation vision, http://www.appalachian.org/blueridgeforeverinfo/ConservationVisionES.pdf.

NC Land of Sky Regional Council of Government, Linking lands and communities, green infrastructure initiative, http://www.landofsky.org/planning/p_linking_lands.html.

NC High Country Council of Government, Regional trail plans, http://www.regiond.org/images/regionaltrailsmap2.pdf.

Policy

Text Sources

Land Conservation and Protection *(Continued)*

NC High Country Council of Government, Regional water resources assessment and plan, Personal communication, Kelly Coffey, October, 2009.

NC Southwestern Commission Council of Government, Mountain Landscapes Initiative, http://www.mountainlandscapesnc.org/.

UNC Charlotte Urban Institute, Forecasting urbanization in the Carolina piedmont region, http://www.gis.uncc.edu/ospc/.

Southern Appalachian Man and the Biosphere, Brevard, NC, http://www.samab.org/

National Park Service, Inventory & monitoring program, southern Appalachian, http://www.nbii.gov/portal/community/Communities/Geographic_Perspectives/Southern_Appalachian/SAIN_Special_Focus_Areas/Regional_Ecosystems/Appalachian_Trail_Environmental_Monitoring/.

Southern Blue Ridge Fire Learning Network, http://www.wiserearth.org/group/sbrfln, http://www.gafw.org/newsletters/2009summer_newsletter.pdf.

U.S., Environmental Protection Agency, geobook project, southeastern ecological framework, Decision support for ecosystem protection, http://geobook.sain.utk.edu/.

Aquatic and Terrestrial Wildlife

North Carolina Wildlife Resources Commission, Wildlife action plan,
http://www.wildlifeactionplan.org/pdfs/action_plan_summaries/north_carolina.pdf.

North Carolina Wildlife Resources Commission, Wildlife species & conservation, Wildlife diversity program, http://www.ncwildlife.org/give/WD_Projects.htm#volunteer.

USDI, U.S. Geological Survey, North American breeding bird survey, http://www.pwrc.usgs.gov/BBS/ .

Water Quality and Quantity

North Carolina Department of Environment and Natural Resources, Division of Water Resources, Water supply planning, http://www.ncwater.org/basins/.

North Carolina Department of Environment and Natural Resources, N.C. Division of Water Resources, Rules, policies and regulations, http://www.ncwater.org/Rules_Policies_and_Regulations/.

U.S. Environmental Protection Agency, Monitoring and assessing water quality, http://www.epa.gov/owow/monitoring/monintr.html.

University of North Carolina, Asheville, The Environmental Quality Institute,
Volunteer water information network, http://orgs.unca.edu/EQI/vwin.html.

Air Quality

North Carolina Department of Environment and Natural Resources, Division of Air Quality, AQMP workshop: update from North Carolina, Boothe, L., June, 2008,
http://www.ncair.org/planning/AQMP_Presentation_06082009.pdf.

North Carolina Department of Environment and Natural Resources, Division of Air Quality, Planning and Attainment, http://daq.state.nc.us/planning/.

North Carolina Department of Environment and Natural Resources, Division of Air Quality, Ambient monitoring program, http://daq.state.nc.us/monitor/.

North Carolina Department of Environment and Natural Resources, Division of Air Quality, Air toxics program, http://daq.state.nc.us/toxics/.

Policy

Text Sources

Laws, Regulations, and Guidelines

North Carolina Cooperative Extension, Trees and Local Regulations in North Carolina,
http://www.ces.ncsu.edu/forestry/ordinance/regulations.html#federal

Photo Sources

Policy introduction

Workshop: UNC Asheville's NEMAC

Aquatic and Terrestrial Wildlife

Red fox: Ronald Laubstein, U.S. Fish and Wildlife Service, Bugwood.org

Deer, black bear, river otter: Terry L. Spivey, Terry Spivey Photography, Bugwood.org

Wood duck, blue grouse: Alfred Viola, Northeastern University, Bugwood.org

Raccoons: Johnny N. Dell, Bugwood.org

Water Quality

Mountain stream: Gary Kaufman

Straight piping sewage into stream: Riverlink

Sedimentation from muddy runoff: NCDENR

Mining activity: Jim Fox

Grazing near stream: Keith Weller, USDA Agricultural Research Service, Bugwood.org

Failing septic system: U.S. Environmental Protection Agency, http://www.epa.gov/region09/tribal/success/04/
communities.html

Air Quality

Red spruce-Fraser fir forest: Manfred Mielke, USDA Forest Service, Bugwood.org

Mountains and sky: Chris Evans, River to River CWMA, Bugwood.org

Coal fired power plants: U.S. Environmental Protection Agency, http://www.epa.gov/ttn/naaqs/ozone/areas/
etscem.htm.

Automobile exhaust: U.S. Department of Transportation, Federal Highway Administration, Ramp Management
& Control: A Primer, Report No: FHWA-HOP-06-080, http://ops.fhwa.dot.gov/publications/ramp_mgmt_
handbook/primer/primer.htm

General Reference

County Boundaries: NC OneMap, http://www.nconemap.com/

County Seats: U.S. National Atlas, cities and towns layer, http://www.nationalatlas.gov/mld/citiesx.html.

Rivers: NC OneMap, http://www.nconemap.com/

Lakes: NC OneMap, http://www.nconemap.com/

Highways: U.S. National Atlas, roads layer at http://www.nationalatlas.gov/mld/roadtrl.html

Interstates: U.S. National Atlas, roads layer at http://www.nationalatlas.gov/mld/roadtrl.html

Corporate Limits: NC DOT, http://www.ncdot.org/

Council of Government: NC OneMap, http://www.nconemap.com/

Fox, Susan; Jackson, Bill; Jackson, Sarah [and others]. 2011. Western North Carolina report card on forest sustainability. Gen. Tech. Rep. SRS-142. Asheville, NC: U.S. Department of Agriculture Forest Service, Southern Research Station, 198 p.

Western North Carolina encompasses 4.8 million acres of highly valued temperate forests. To help address future management and conservation decisions surrounding these resources, the report card evaluates environmental, social, and economic conditions in recent decades across an 18 county area. The report card describes the status of indicators of forest sustainability as improving, worsening, uncertain, stable, stable/at risk, or dynamic. Results varied considerably among criteria measured. Conditions that show improvement include lands managed for conservation; timber volume, growth, and removals; water and air quality; forest economics; cultural/spiritual values; resource planning and monitoring; and public participation in policy formation. Conditions that are worsening include loss of natural communities and species, rate of land conversion, rate of forest fragmentation, spread of invasive species, developed recreation resources, and soil movement associated with development on steep slopes.

Keywords: biodiversity, carbon cycling, forest economy, forest health, forest policy, forest productivity, forest recreation, forest sustainability, resource conditions, Western North Carolina.

www.ingramcontent.com/pod-product-compliance
Lightning Source LLC
Chambersburg PA
CBHW081207280526
45787CB00006B/2367